The Hiker's Guide
to ALASKA

by

Evan and Margaret Swensen

FALCON PRESS

ACKNOWLEDGMENTS

This book would not have been possible without the assistance of State, Federal, and other government agencies. Everyone, from park rangers to secretaries, helped and encouraged. They demonstrated a sincere desire to serve the hiking public by giving us accurate and timely information as we prepared this guide. Without exception, they asked for a copy of the guide to aid them in their work. We trust they will be satisfied with our treatment of their contributions.

Cover Photo: Hiking near the Kejulik Mountains in Katmai National Park and Preserve. Linda Cauble photo.

CONTENTS

Introduction

THE HIKES

LOCATION OF HIKES

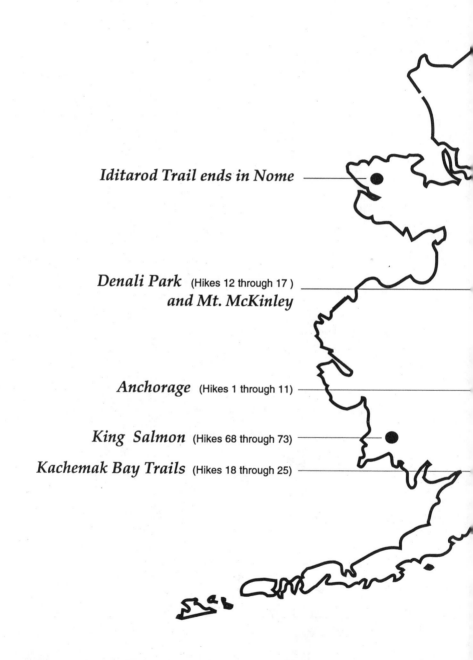

Iditarod Trail ends in Nome —————

Denali Park (Hikes 12 through 17) —————
and Mt. McKinley

Anchorage (Hikes 1 through 11) —————

King Salmon (Hikes 68 through 73) —————

Kachemak Bay Trails (Hikes 18 through 25) —————

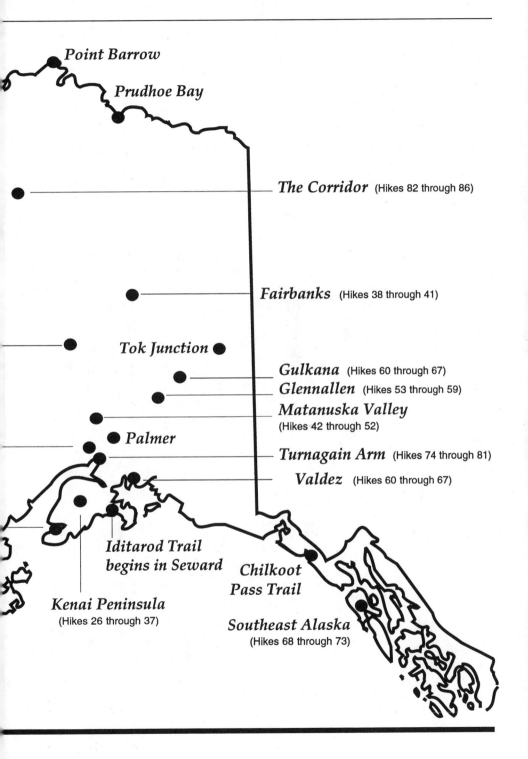

Point Barrow

Prudhoe Bay

The Corridor (Hikes 82 through 86)

Fairbanks (Hikes 38 through 41)

Tok Junction

Gulkana (Hikes 60 through 67)

Glennallen (Hikes 53 through 59)

Matanuska Valley
(Hikes 42 through 52)

Palmer

Turnagain Arm (Hikes 74 through 81)

Valdez (Hikes 60 through 67)

Iditarod Trail
begins in Seward

Chilkoot
Pass Trail

Kenai Peninsula
(Hikes 26 through 37)

Southeast Alaska
(Hikes 68 through 73)

Hiking in Denali National Park. Chris Cauble photo.

HIKING IN ALASKA, AN INTRODUCTION

The Trail of Ninety Eight

Readers of The Hiking Guide to Alaska will have difficulty comprehending the enormous size of the state and variety of hikes available. The guide can serve only as a primer for the newcomer to the last frontier. Included are hikes for all ages and abilities, from neophyte to experienced. The guide tells how to climb North America's highest mountain and describes the Iditarod Trail. Climbing Mt. McKinley takes the climber for a vertical rise of nearly 0.5 miles. The Iditarod follows the historic trail across 1,500 miles of Alaska. The Mckinley hike begins at the base of the mountain in ancient forest and Arctic tundra and finishes in timeless snow at 20,320 feet above sea level. Hiking the Iditarod takes adventurers from the saltwater port of Seward to the old gold fields of Nome: traverses three mountain ranges, crosses three major rivers and hundreds of small streams, and circumvents thousands of lakes.

The climb to the top of McKinley or walking to the shores of Nome on Norton Sound may be interesting to read about, but most of us will never make the trek. We list the Iditarod and McKinley more to show the extremes of hiking Alaska rather than as a practical guide for hikers.

The Hiking Guide to Alaska is a catalog of the modern Trail of Ninety Eigh,. not a trek to gold fields or riches, but an experience of discovery and recreation. The guide takes you to fields of flowers and places to enrich your spirit. It goes on new hikes and those of historic interest. Some hikes are only a half mile long, along a beach in or near a population center, others lead the treker 100 miles into the bush. Some terminate at a favorite fishing hole, ghost

It is important to pack out what you take into the wilderness.

town, mountain top, or alpine valley. All are interesting, enjoyable, unique, and worth the steps.

For the purposes of this guide, the state is divided into distinct areas, each with its own singular topography, weather, and interesting aspects. Trail systems are grouped together within the areas but not all hikes in the area are included. Nearly every area has hikes too numerous to mention. Many times a hike or a system of hikes in a particular area is shown just as a representation of what's available.

Alaska is huge. It is one fifth the size of the Continental United Sates. If Alaska was divided into two states it would make Texas the third largest state. Super-imposing a map of Alaska over a map of the United States of the same scale would show parts of Alaska touching both borders and both oceans. Kodiak Island is larger than the state of Vermont. Some glaciers are bigger than whole states. Prince William Sound has a longer coastline than the rest of the United States combined. The state is big. Too big to include all trails in one volume, or to hike in one lifetime. We trust you'll enjoy your Alaska hikes.

MAP LEGEND

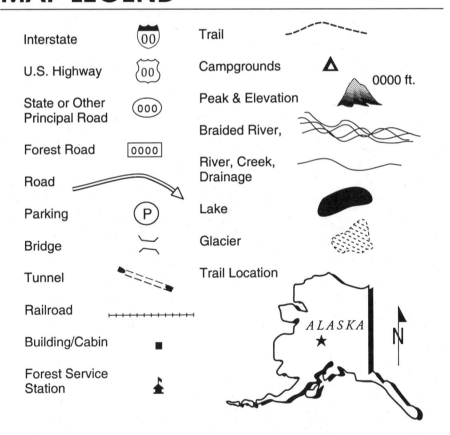

Interstate	(00)	Trail
U.S. Highway	(00)	Campgrounds △
State or Other Principal Road	(000)	Peak & Elevation 0000 ft.
Forest Road	[0000]	Braided River,
Road		River, Creek, Drainage
Parking	(P)	Lake
Bridge		Glacier
Tunnel		Trail Location
Railroad		
Building/Cabin	■	ALASKA ★ N
Forest Service Station		

GEARING UP

Welcome to Alaska's outdoor recreation. Hiking in Alaska can be a healthful and enjoyable experience if you are properly prepared and certain precautions are followed. Failure to prepare and observe certain rules of the trail could mean displeasure, distress, discomfort, possible sickness, injury, and even death. Alaska is a wonderful place to vacation and the following information will help hikers safely enjoy Alaska and provide the basic information for a memory building outing.

Access

Access to Alaska is accomplished by utilizing commercial airlines, riding the state ferry system, or driving the Alaska Highway. Once in the state the highway system in Alaska differs from most other states. Southeast Alaska, Southwest Alaska, the Far North, and many other areas are not connected by roads. Many Alaska communities claim there are two places to drive if leaving town: the end of the road, and the other end of the road.

Nearly all hikes contained herein are accessible by road. Although the extent of highways may be limited, the numbers and variety of available trails are not. In addition to many designated trails, hikers may stop and hike from almost any spot along the highway.

Many trails originally were access routes to mining areas, old villages, settlements or hunting or fishing areas. Because of the increasing number of hikers on many trails, it is important to have respect for the trails you hike. Switchbacks occur on many steep slopes. Although it may be quicker to cut

Nearly all the hikes in The Hikers Guide to Alaska *are accessible by road.*

across switchbacks, it is dangerous and causes soil erosion and rapid deterioration of trails.

It is helpful to know the system of numbering roads in Alaska.

- •Glenn Highway: Mileposts begin in Anchorage.
- •Parks Highway: Mileposts begin in Anchorage.
- •Richardson Highway: Mileposts begin in Valdez.
- •Seward Highway: Mileposts begin in Seward.
- •Sterling Highway: Mileposts begin in Seward.
- •Edgerton Highway: Mileposts begin at the Richardson Highway.

Animals

A large variety of wildlife may frequent trails. Some may be annoying, others may be dangerous, but most are friendly. Annoying animals are mosquitos, black flies, no-see-ums, black-socks, white-socks, and others. Alaska's insects are not known to transmit disease-causing agents such as bacteria or viruses. Mice, squirrels, martens, hoary marmots, beavers, and muskrats are friendly. Mammals, including bear, deer, goats, sheep, moose, and caribou are mostly friendly, but moose with young become very protective, and bears are unpredictable.

Three bears—black, brown, and polar—make Alaska special. Any hiker may be lucky enough to see a bear. Brown bears are found from the islands of Southeastern to the Arctic. Black bear inhabit most of Alaska's forests. Polar bear frequent the pack ice and tundra of extreme Northern and Western Alaska.

Most people who see a bear in the wild consider it the highlight of their trip. The presence of these majestic creatures is a reminder of how privileged we are to share some of the country's dwindling wilderness.

Bear Facts

Polar Bear
Length: 8 to 10 feet
Weight: Males 600 to 1200 pounds, females 400 to 700 pounds.
Color: All white
Alaska population estimate: 4,000 to 6,000

Black Bear
Length: 5 feet
Weight: Males 150 to 400 pounds, females 125 to 250 pounds
Color: Brown to black, white patch on front of chest
Alaska population estimate: more than 50,000

Brown Bear
Length: 7 to 9 feet
Weight: Males 400 to 1,100 pounds, females 200 to 600 pounds
Color: Dark brown to blonde
Alaska population estimate: 35,000 to 45,000

Hikers must be aware of bears in the back country.

Bears rarely attack humans but must be considered dangerous at all times. Hiking near streams during salmon spawning season requires care. Make noise when in bear country and plenty of noise near creeks and waterfalls when fish are running. The State of Alaska Department of Fish and Game publishes a brochure, *The Bears and You.* It is available from their offices and other state agencies and visitor and information centers. First-time Alaska hiker or those unfamiliar with bears should read a copy before entering bear country.

Many hikers are concerned about bears and may even have an occasional bear encounter. Grizzly and brown bear are an important part of exploring the wilderness. If precautions are taken the risk is greatly reduced. The following tips can help prevent problems.

- Plan a hike to minimize chances of trouble with bears Odors attract bear. Before beginning to hike thoroughly wash pack, clothing, and other gear in an unscented detergent to be sure it is free of odors. Clean fishing tackle. Don't carry smelly foods like bacon or smoked fish, and leave scented soaps, lotions, deodorants, toothpaste, and other toiletries at home. The idea is to smell human, not delicious. Dogs may attract bear. Leave them at home. Solo campers are more likely to be attacked than members of a group. Where possible, travel with others for safety sake.

- Do things that prevent meeting bears in close quarters. Food attracts bears. Store all foods in sealed plastic bags or airtight containers. Take plenty of extra bags, including enough to double wrap all garbage. Carry out all garbage that won't burn. Never bury it.

- The best bear protection is to prevent a close encounter. Make lots of noise. Bears will usually avoid humans if alerted. Most attacks occur when people surprise bears at close range. Sows with cubs are particularly dangerous because they tend to see any intruder as a threat to their offspring.

- Don't risk sneaking up on one. Talk, rattle pebbles in a can, or wear bells. Wind and running water muffle the noise. Entering thickets from upwind may let a bear smell danger and move away. Be especially careful and noisy if traveling through prime bear habitat, such as along salmon streams, through willow thickets, berry patches, and areas with a lot of trails, prints, and droppings.

- Watch for bear evidence. Droppings may look like a cow's, or like a pile of partially digested berries. Bear trails are common along streams, on ridgetops, and in berry patches. Watch for torn up patches of soil and vegetation. Bear dig up tundra hunting for rodents, roots, and bulbs. If decomposing meat is smelled or an animal carcass covered with leaves and branches is discovered, leave immediately. A bear food cache may have been found and a bear is probably nearby. Check around potential campsites carefully and if bear sign is found consider camping elsewhere.

- Don't invite bear into camp. Keep food odors to a minimum. Cook and eat several hundred yards downwind from camp or, better yet, cook, eat, and then move on a mile or so to camp. Don't cook more than can be eaten, and wash dishes immediately. Dump waste water far from camp. Store all food, soap, and any other smelly items well sealed and far from camp, high in a tree if possible. Keep food and food odors off clothes. Never sleep in the same clothes worn while cooking.

- If you catch a fish, clean it far from camp. Puncture the air bladder and throw the entrails far out into the water. Clean hands, clothing, and gear carefully before camping.

- Know what to do if a bear is encountered. If a bear is seen in the distance, alter the route to avoid it. Move out of its sight downwind if possible. If the bear sees something curious, it may stand up and sway its head from side to side. It is trying to figure out what it is seeing. Help it! Speak loudly, hold arms up, and back slowly away. If the bear approaches, keep talking. Climb a tree, if possible. If the bear turns sideways to, or if it pops its teeth together or makes a series of woofs, it is a warning. Retreat slowly. Never run; that could entice the bear to give chase. Never imitate the sounds or postures of a bear; that may challenge it to attack.

- If a bear charges, freeze, facing the bear. Most charges are bluffs. The bear will probably stop, turn, and run away. If it does not stop, drop to the ground and play dead. Lay on stomach or knees-to-chest, with hands linked across the back of neck. Leave pack on. Keep silent and still. The bear may lose interest and leave.

• It is legal to carry firearms in most National Parks in Alaska, except Sitka Natural History Park, Glacier Bay and Katmai National Parks, or in that part of Denali National Park formerly known as Mt. McKinley National Park. Don't carry a gun unless you are hiking in areas of high brown bear concentrations, and then only if you are comfortable with firearms and are trained in their use. A firearm adds weight to gear and can be more dangerous than a bear if proper training or practice has not been done. A suitable gun, properly used and kept handy, can be a little extra insurance. Rifles larger than 30-06 and twelve-gauge shotguns loaded with rifled slugs are adequate. It is legal to shoot a bear in defense of life or property if reasonable effort is made to avoid the problem in the first place. The hide of a black bear or the hide and skull of a grizzly must be turned over to state officials immediately.

Birds

It is the rare hike that does not produce opportunity for seeing birds up close. Alaska has many nesting and resting areas for birds, and many trails offer excellent opportunities for viewing them. Golden eagles, hawks, grouse, and numerous varieties of songbirds nest in Alaska. Bald eagles are common throughout much of the panhandle and around Southcentral Alaska, especially near salmon spawning streams and tidal areas. Ptarmigan, the state bird,

Alaska boasts unparalleled wildlife viewing opportunities.

may be seen in alpine areas. Crows and ravens are common and may be seen and heard on the trail. Waterfowl may be spotted near lake shores, sloughs, and ponds.

Fox and Wolves

Now and then fox and wolves may be attracted to campsites in remote areas. Only under unusual circumstances do these canine creatures attack humans. They are shy but if encountered and, they appear tame or unafraid they may be rabid. Do not attempt to handle them, they may bite. Rabies could be fatal; therefore, avoid exposure by avoiding sick animals.

Bugs

Mosquito repellents containing diethyl toluamide (DEET) are most effective when used in roughly 50% concentrations of the active ingredient. Repellents for white-sox and no-see-ums are less effective. Breeze and low relative humidity deter insect activity and should be considered when locating a campsite. A five-mile-per-hour breeze will ground most mosquitoes. Alaska has mosquitoes that winter as adults. They emerge from hibernation before snow has entirely disappeared. Insect population reaches its peak in June and declines thereafter. Mosquitoes are the most active at twilight and early morning.

Fires

Use extreme caution at all times with fire. Always thoroughly extinguish matches, cigarettes, cigars, or pipe ashes before discarding. Permits for campfires are not required in Alaska except in Denali National Park and Katmai National Monument. As a general rule, in areas where improved campsites exist, fires are restricted to established fire sites. Many of the soils in Alaska are rich in organic materials which may continue to burn unseen underground; therefore, extra care must be taken to extinguish campfires completely. Thorough soaking, stirring, and burying are best.

Some simple rules:

- Use only dead and down wood for fires.
- Keep fires small.
- Don't hack into trees or stumps.
- Disperse rocks from rock fire rings.
- Use camp stoves in wilderness areas.
- Be sure of the rules concerning campfires on each trail you hike.
- Fireworks are strictly prohibited in almost every area of Alaska particularly on public lands.

Help Others

Do not hesitate to stop and help others in need of emergency care. Alaska has a good samaritan statute. State laws protect persons from liability for civil damages for acts related to rendering emergency care, or treatment to injured persons.

Alaska has hikes for all ages, Thunderbird Falls. Photo by Curtis Hight.

Hiking with Children

Experienced hikers take children with them. Try easy hikes first, ones with views or small animals to see or photograph, and let children graduate to more difficult trips. Hiking with youngsters can be a real treat and should be done as often as possible. Practice and teach good trail manners as well as an appreciation for the outdoors. It will build a child's self confidence, help create trust in themselves, and assist in understanding the earth's environment.

Hygiene and Health

Wash dishes with soap and hot water away from streams or ponds. Waste water from washing should not be poured into a stream or directly onto the ground. It is best to pour waste water into a hole located away from water sources, so that it may disperse into the subsurface soil.

Defecate in intertidal zones away from streams or ponds or use a shallow hole on land at least 200 feet away from any water source. Burn toilet paper completely and carry out, or burn, all sanitary napkins or tampons. Wash and brush teeth on beaches away from tidal pools or streams. Use a good sun screen. Carry mosquito repellent and antidote for bug bites in a first aid kit.

Hypothermia

Even in temperatures above freezing, hypothermia could be possible. Hikers exposed to wet, cold, and windy conditions can suffer hypothermia. Hypothermia is caused when body heat is lost faster than it is produced. Continued decline of internal temperature will lead to stupor, collapse, and possibly death. Hypothermia symptoms are: severe shivering, slurred speech, incoherence, clumsiness, lack of control of hands and feet, drowsiness, and exhaustion.

If hypothermia is suspected, get dry and warm immediately. Remove all wet clothes and put on dry ones. Get in a warm sleeping bag and drink something hot.

Littering

Alaska's beauty can be greatly blemished by paper, cans, and other litter. Dispose of litter in roadside receptacles. Littering is punishable by a fine of not more than $1,000, imprisonment of up to 90 days, or both.

Planning

Planning will make hiking a pleasant experience with comfortable flexibility. Much of Alaska is untamed wilderness. A short drive from a city and just a few steps from the trail put hikers in real wilderness situations. Know your limitation, rest when required, relax, and enjoy the trail. The attraction of hiking is the lack of schedule to be at a certain place at a certain time.

Be prepared by carrying the following essential items: extra clothing, map, waterproof matches, or a cigarette lighter, first aid kit, insect repellent, drinking cup, tide book, extra food, compass, knife, flashlight, rain gear, and water supply.

Plants

Opolopanex horridus, the scientific name for devil's club, explains much about this shrub. It is one plant all backcountry travelers learn to recognize and avoid. It grows to 10 feet tall with huge maple-shaped leaves and stems covered with sharp, barbed spines. When a spine touches skin it feels much like a bee sting, and causes swelling. Because of the barbs, the spines are difficult to remove and continue to irritate. Gloves and long-sleeved shirts should be worn in areas where devil's club is abundant.

A number of poisonous plants occur in Alaska but illness from them is uncommon and reports of death are extremely rare. Be careful to correctly identify berries before eating them as some are poisonous. The most serious danger is to children, who may eat plants out of curiosity or because plants, flower, or berries look tasty.

There is one very poisonous berry found in Alaska. The baneberry (acteaea rubra) has either white or red berries and is commonly found in forests and thickets. It is a perennial that grows 2-3 feet tall. The leaves are large and lobed and coarsely toothed. Water hemlock, death camas, and certain species of mushrooms should be avoided.

Some individuals may develop severe allergic reactions from coming in contact with such plants as indian rhubarb and nettles. Learn and avoid the common poisonous plants and eat only those known to be safe. In case of known or suspected poisoning from plants call the nearest hospital which will provide information regarding proper treatment.

Purchase and use, either: Verna's Pratt's, field Guide to Alaska Wildflowers, available in most bookstores, or a small guide titled, Wild, edible, and Poisonous Plants of Alaska, available for $1.00 from local offices of the University of Alaska cooperative Extension Service.

Water

Crystal clear rivers and streams give the false impression that water is pure and safe to drink. Water clarity is not an indication of the presence or absence of bacteria or parasites. Beaver fever, Giardia lamblia, may be present in all streams and lake water, especially near beaver ponds or swampy rivers. It is carried by animal feces, including those of humans and dogs. It is not possible to guarantee which streams have not been contaminated. Whenever surface water is used for drinking or cooking, steps should be taken to purify it through either of the following methods of treatment. Bring to a full rolling boil, not simply steaming. If the water has a flat taste, pour it back and forth between clean containers two or three times; or add four drops of household bleach such as clorox or purex containing 5.25% available chlorine to each quart of water. Mix thoroughly and allow to stand 30 minutes before drinking; or treat water with tetraglycine hydroperiodide; or use a purification system with pore sizes of less than two micrometers.

Weather

Summer temperatures average 55° to 60° degrees fahrenheit, and on bright, sunny days it may reach 70° to 80° degrees. Alaska weather is unpredictable. Even in summer months it can turn cold, wet, and windy. Hikers must be prepared for heat and sunburn and at the same time carry raingear, and warm clothing. Never enter Alaska wilderness without gloves, hat, warm coat, and raingear.

Winter travel

When traveling through snow-covered mountains, know about avalanches. Avalanche deaths have increased in recent years in Alaska as more people head to the hills for recreation. Educate yourself and have a safe trip. Avalanche awareness classes are held in Anchorage, Fairbanks, Juneau, on the Kenai Peninsula, and at Hatcher and Thompsom Pass. Before going into the backcountry, find the current avalanche conditions by calling the Avalanche and Mountain weather forecast recording.

ANCHORAGE, CITY OF TRAILS

It has been said that Anchorage is only 30 minutes from Alaska. Alaska is not in the city or along the highway. Alaska, the real Alaska, is only 30 minutes away from these. Alaska is wilderness. It is hiking the wild, fishing in unpolluted water, sighting a bear, tracking a moose, tricking a fish, or as Robert Service put it "standing in some mighty mouth hallow that's plumb full of hush to the brim, and watching the big husky sun wallow in crimson and gold and grow dim." Anchorage is only 30 minutes away.

Anchorage sprawls on the edge of Cook Inlet between Knik River and Turnagain Arm. It has been growing steadily by jerks since the 1930s. About one half of Alaska's 500,000 people live and work in Anchorage. Anchorage boasts a zoo, three universities, a performing arts center, two military bases, a complex bicycle path system, two excellent ski valleys, glaciers within 40 miles and hiking trails in the Chugach Mountains to the east. She brags about her weather, her people, her winter carnival, her summer fishing, and fall harvest.

Visitors to Anchorage and residents who do not frequent the wilderness remind us of the man who went to a buffet, ate his fill at the hors d'oeuvre table, and told everyone how great the food was. Alaska is not just hors d'oeuvres. It's not even soup and sandwiches. Alaska is a banquet. It's a seven-course meal with dinner music, mood lighting, and a Carnegie Hall all star cast performance and Anchorage is only 30 minutes away.

Thirty minutes from Anchorage and hikers can see, feel, touch, taste, hear, and smell Alaska. They can get away from the city and onto an uncrowded trail within 30 minutes. They can leave behind the concrete and the artificial and be in wilderness within a half hour of their job or home.

Anchorage, bordering on the Chugach State Park and Chugach National Forest, is a city of trails. Take any road off the Glenn or Seward Highway and it will lead to a trailhead. It would take a hiker at least one summer of constant hiking to trek all of the trails from Portage to Knik. Part of the old Johnson Trail and the Iditarod Trail pass through the mountains near Anchorage. New trails are constantly being developed and old ones upgraded and maintained. Yes, Anchorage is the city of trails. Wilderness Trails.

After hiking the Bird Creek Trail and then continuing to the headwaters of Ship Creek we camped on a open knoll at the base of one of the area's highest peaks. It was raining when we pitched the tent and sometime during the night it cleared and the stars came out. I awoke to a tent filled with light. It seemed to be almost dawn, but the light was different. I checked my watch, which I could easily read, and it said 1:47 a.m. I unzipped the tent and looked out. Just over the horizon was the source of the light. It was the moon. The largest, brightest moon I have ever seen. Moonlight reflected through clear, unpolluted air was bright enough to read by, and a night hike would have been possible.

When morning arrived, and we awoke to begin the day's activities, we had a strange feeling come over us. We felt like we were being watched. Quietly opening the tent flap we discovered that we were not alone. Our tent was

Sometimes Alaska's grand views cause hikers to ignore small visual pleasures.

surrounded by Dall sheep. They had taken a midnight hike in the light of the moon and were feeding at our doorstep. We remained where we were until they fed to full and wandered over the hill to their day beds.

Across the valley other sheep wandered the slopes, grazing as they went. Blueberries were ripe and in abundance. We picked and ate until our fingers were stained and our lips and tongues were blue. Blueberry pancakes, more blueberry than pancake, were cooked and consumed. Later in the day we discovered bear tracks along the trail and watched a bunch of moose doing their thing in the valley below our camp. We could see, feel, touch, taste, hear, and smell Alaska. And all within 30 minutes of the state's largest city.

HIKE 1: *ANCHORAGE COASTAL TRAIL*

General description: A city trail with views of Cook Inlet, Mt. Susitna, Alaska Range, and Mt. McKinley.
General location: From downtown Anchorage to Point Campbell area along the coast of Knik Arm of UPer Cook Inlet.
Trail begins: Elderberry Park, Westchester Lagoon, Earthquake Park, Pt. Woronzof, and Point Campbell-Kincaid Park
Trail ends: Kincaid Park
Maps: USGS Anchorage B7
Difficulty: Easy to moderate
Length: 17.7 miles
Elevation: Fifty feet
Special attractions: Knik Arm tide extremes, Earthquake Park, paved trail, city sites, vistas of Alaska Range
Best season: All year
For more information: Municipality of Anchorage Parks and Recreation, PO

HIKE 1: ANCHORAGE COASTAL TRAIL

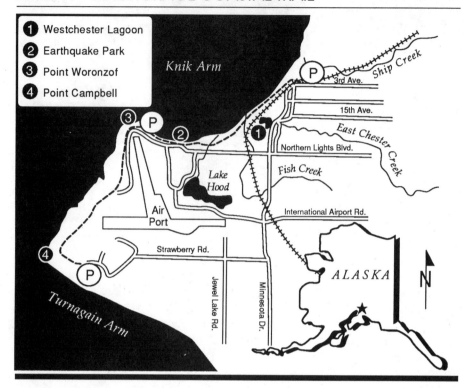

① Westchester Lagoon
② Earthquake Park
③ Point Woronzof
④ Point Campbell

Knik Arm

Ship Creek

3rd Ave.

15th Ave.

East Chester Creek

Northern Lights Blvd.

Lake Hood

Fish Creek

Air Port

International Airport Rd.

Strawberry Rd.

Jewel Lake Rd.

Minnesota Dr.

ALASKA

N

Turnagain Arm

Box 196650, Anchorage, Alaska 99516 (907) 343-4335

Finding the trailhead: Elderberry Trailhead is at the end of Third Avenue and L Street. Park here. This trailhead is within easy walking distance of major hotels and businesses. The Westchester Lagoon is off 15th Avenue and L Street. The trailhead is marked and there is parking.

The Earthquake Park trailhead is along Northern Lights Boulevard. At the intersection of Northern Lights and Aircraft Drive, turn right into parking area. The Kincaid trailhead is South on L Street to Minnesota Drive to Strawberry Road. Follow Strawberry through Jewel Lake Road then follow the signs to Kincaid Park.

The hike: Hiking or walking along Anchorage Coastal Trail is rewarding. The trail is clean, well ordered, paved, and marked. Hikers may jog, run, walk, or hike. Upper Cook Inlet's Knik Arm's scenic views invites frequent photography stops. Beginning at Elderberry Park trailhead, the Coastal Trail takes hikers through Anchorage's neighborhoods and among stands of birch and spruce on the route to Earthquake Park. Along the way to Earthquake Park the trail passes by Westchester Lagoon trailhead. Westchester Lagoon is the in-town site for windsurfing activity and wild duck feeding. The hike can end or begin here, go back to Elderberry Park trailhead or on to Earthquake Park, where hikers may observe the area which slid into the inlet during the 1964 Great

Alaska Earthquake.

Earthquake Park trailhead allows hikers to end their trek here or continue on to Kincaid Park on the edge of Point Campbell. Along Point Woronzof views of the perpetual sno- covered Alaska Range may be seen reaching to the sky. 180 miles north, Mt. McKinley grants hikers and camera enthusiasts splendid views on clear days. The Coastal Trail continues along the bluff to Kincaid Park where summer motorcross races and winter cross-country ski races are held. Around the corner, vistas change to Turnagain Arm and views of Fire Island, Kenai Peninsula, and volcanos of the northern end of the Pacific Rim of Fire.

Anchorage Coastal Trail allows residents and visitors to be in relative wilderness by taking just a few steps from their home or hotel room. Hikers not accustomed to virgin backcountry will find this trail as wild as their imagination wants it to be. More experienced wilderness trekkers enjoy Anchorage Coastal Trail year around as a way to remain in touch with wilderness and a quick hike to stay in shape. Anchorage Coastal Trail is the flagship trail for urbanites who live, work, and play in the 49th State's largest city, Anchorage, city of trails.

HIKE 2: *EAGLE LAKE TRAIL*

General description: Access route to an alpine lake setting
General location: In the canyon above Eagle River, north of Anchorage
Trail begins: 7.5 miles up Eagle River Road
Trail ends: Eagle Lake with trails beyond.
Maps: USGS Anchorage B7
Difficulty: Easy to moderate
Length: six miles
Elevation: 2,400 to 2,650 feet
Special attractions: Views of Eagle river Valley, Cook Inlet, and Alaska Range.
Best season: June through September
For more information: Chugach State Park Ranger District Headquarters, HC 52 Box 8999, Indian, Alaska, 99540 (907) 345-5014
Finding the trailhead: Twelve miles northeast on the Glenn Highway take the Hiland Road exit. Turn right after exiting, and drive 3.5 miles to end of the state maintained road. At the end of maintained road, take the right hand fork and travel another 1.5 miles. Again, stay on Hiland Road by taking the right fork for .4 mile, go left, and follow Hiland Road downhill and across the South Fork of Eagle River. Continue another 1.5 miles, turn right onto South Creek Road and follow it across the river, turning right onto West River Drive. The trailhead and parking is on the left.

The hike: The trail, beginning on a boardwalk, climbs to and follows a bench for about a mile, then descends to a bridge across South Fork. Cross the creek and follow the trail across the valley up the east side to Eagle Lake.

The lake, 2,600 feet, may be a final destination or the jumping off spot for other

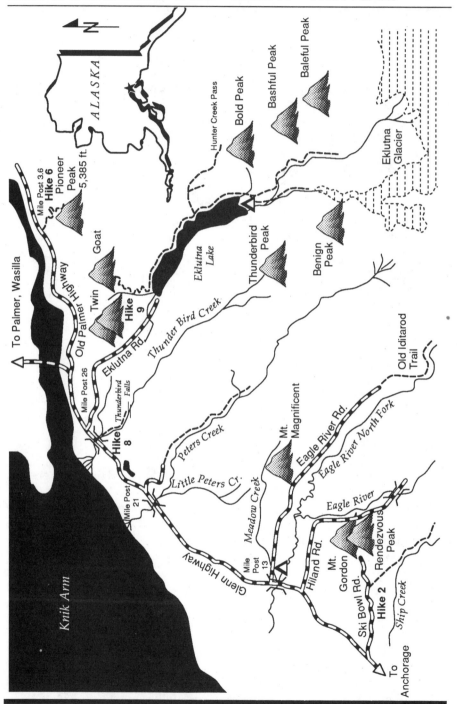

interesting hikes. Symphony Lake and the tarns beyond are a prime location. Between the tarns a ridge leads to a 4,500-foot-high plateau overlooking Ship Creek. Along the trail watch for moose, black bear, and Dall sheep.

An alternate hike from the same trailhead is Eagle River Overlook. Do not go south when the trail goes toward Eagle Lake, but continue straight up the slope to a hanging valley. Follow game trails for about 2.5 miles from the river and climb the steep, grassy slope on the left to a 3,950-foot pass. From the pass it is an easy climb to the overlook and spectacular views of Eagle River Valley. This alternate is about a .5 mile longer than the hike to the lake.

HIKE 3: *FLAT TOP MOUNTAIN*

General description: Because of its proximity to Alaska's largest city, Flattop is possibly the most frequently climbed peak in Alaska. The short, climbing hike to the top, at the edge of Anchorage, grants hikers a view that extends from Mt. McKinley to the northwest to Mt. Redoubt Volcano in the southwest.
General location: Flattop is at the edge of Hillside Subdivisions and easily accessed.
Trail begins: Gravel area just beyond power line off Upper O'Malley Road
Trail ends: Top of Flat Top
Maps: USGS Anchorage A8
Difficulty: Moderate to difficult; some rock scrambling, steep areas over broken rock.
Length: 3.5 miles
Elevation: 1,300 to 3,550 feet
Special attractions: Views of Anchorage, Alaska Range, Kenai Peninsula, stunted mountain hemlock trees and classic alpine plant communities.
Best season: June through October
For more information: Chugach State Park Ranger District Headquarters, HC 52 Box 8999, Indian, Alaska, 99540 (907) 345-5014
Finding the trailhead: Drive south on Seward Highway to O'Malley Road, drive four miles to the intersection with Hillside Drive. Turn left onto Upper O'Malley Road. Chugach State Park trailhead sign and the beginning of the hike is in the gravel area.

The hike: After walking up the stairway in the southeast corner of the parking lot, take the trail through a grove of mountain hemlock and continues until it emerges in alpine tundra. The trail parallels the ridge up Flat Top Mountain. Hikers find the trail by hiking on the road paralleling the powerline and following it for about 100 yards. It is easy to follow the track over a rough road and through scrub hemlock to a large open area past the trees. A low saddle at 2,500 feet separates Flattop from the long, low mound at the beginning of the ridge. Do not climb to the saddle, but angle left and hike up the slope to the crest of the ridge and follow it along to the second saddle and up the east side of Flattop's northwest ridge to the crest, then on to the top and the end of the trail.

Flat Top is a good hike for youngsters. Like any wilderness setting it is necessary to closely supervise children. There have been incidents of injury and at least one death when a young child became separated from adults.

One spring morning before daylight we journeyed to Flat Top. Our purpose was to witness the sunrise over the mountains behind us and watch the first light of morning illuminate Anchorage. We received much more than expected. It was a clear morning. The first rays touched the top of Mt. McKinley while Anchorage remained in total darkness. Perennial snows on top on North America's highest peak, turned from light pink to stark white in dawn's first light. Soon the eastern slopes of the Alaska Range received light and reflected it across Matanuska/Susitna Valley and Cook Inlet; turning first from black to light pink, and then red down to the black line of undergrowth and timber. Next, the valley floor awakened to the sun, and finally the tops of Anchorage's highest buildings mirrored the sun in their glass windows. Finally, the entire city caught the light until our perch up Flat Top was embraced by the warmth. Warm rays penetrating our outside could not compare to the glow we felt inside. We would have hiked further but few sights will exceed seeing Anchorage, with her surrounding wilderness, bursting into light.

HIKE 4: *KNOYA AND TIKISHLA PEAKS TRAIL*

General description: Difficult in spots, a trail for the hardy.
General location: Chugach Range above Anchorage.
Trail begins: At the end of Prospect Heights Road in the Hillside above Anchorage.
Trail ends: At the base of Knoya and Tikishla peaks.
Maps: USGS Anchorage A7, A8
Difficulty: Moderate to difficult
Length: six miles
Elevation: 1,000 to 5,050 feet
Special attractions: Excellent alpine scenery, wild flowers, berries in Autumn.
Best season: June through September
For more information: Chugach State Park Ranger District Headquarters, HC 52 Box 8999, Indian, Alaska, 99540 (907) 345-5014
Finding the trailhead: Drive five miles south on the Seward Highway to O'Malley Road. Turn east and drive about four miles to the intersection with Hillside Drive. Turn left onto Upper O'Malley Road, go .5 mile to a "T" intersection. Going left for .1 mile leads to the Prospect Heights entrance to Chugach State Park and the trailhead.

The hike: This is a hike in real wilderness. It is for the hardy and physically prepared. The summit of Knoya is gained by ascending three miles past three notches. Going southeast up-valley gives access to Tikishla one mile further. Elevation gain 2,950 feet to Tikishla. Hiking Tikishla is best done as an overnighter.

HIKE 5: *OLD JOHNSON TRAIL*

General description: Old Johnson Trail, now called the Turnagain Arm Trail is on the south side of the Turnagain arm and receives the first spring sun. The trail is a popular May and June hike.

General location: Turnagain Arm, south of Anchorage

Trail begins: At four trailheads: Mile 115 Potter Section House, Mile 112, McHugh Creek Picnic Area, Mile 108 Rainbow Creek Valley, and Mile 106 Windy Corner Trailhead.

Trail ends: At any one of the trailheads

Maps: Anchorage A8, Seward D6, D7

Difficulty: Easy to moderate

Length: Six miles

Elevation: 2,400 to 2,650 feet

Special attractions: Historical remains of by gone era. Views of animals and Turnagain Arm

Best season: April through October

For more information: Chugach State Park Ranger District Headquarters, HC 52 Box 8999, Indian, Alaska, 99540 (907) 345-5014

Finding the trailhead: Drive south on the Seward Highway to any one of the four trailheads and begin hiking.

The hike: The trail was used to deliver mail between Anchorage and Seward. With the coming of the railroad and highway much of the original trail was covered or destroyed by construction. Beginning at Potter, the trail goes uphill then levels off and follows a bluff through birch, aspen, and cottonwoods. The trail is wide and mostly downhill as the trailhead to McHugh Creek is reached. McHugh Peak is to the north and Suicide to the northeast. Spruce dominate this portion of the trail. The trail sign at the Y directs hikers north to Table Rock and south to McHugh Creek trailhead and picnic area.

McHugh Creek trailhead is in the lower parking lot at the stairs. The trail crosses a bridge and heads uphill. A sign at the Y guides hikers east to Rainbow and northeast to McHugh Peak. The trail levels off and crosses a scree slope and avalanche area. It then narrows down. Views are excellent with vistas of the Arm and Kenai Peninsula. The trail is rocky in spots. The trail turns inland winding behind a knoll and Beluga Point. Beluga Point was used by prehistoric hunters as a view point to search for beluga whales and sheep. As the trail switchbacks downhill into Rainbow Valley there is a three-log bridge crossing a gully, and another bridge crossing Rainbow Creek near the trailhead. The wide rocky trail continues to the trailhead at Windy corner Mile 106 Seward Highway.

HIKE 6: *PIONEER RIDGE-KNIK RIVER TRAIL*

General description: A climbing hike to the Pioneer Peak Ridge
General location: Old Palmer Highway Mile 3.6
Trail begins: Mile 3.6 on the Old Palmer Highway
Trail ends: AT the top of the ridge one mile from Pioneer Peak
Maps: USGS Anchorage B6
Difficulty: Moderate to difficult
Length: Six miles
Elevation: 180 to 5,300 feet
Special attractions: Mountain terrain, flora, and vistas where sheep, moose, black bear, and eagles can be seen.
Best season: June through September
For more information: Chugach State Park Ranger District Headquarters, HC 52 Box 8999, Indian, Alaska, 99540 (907) 345-5014
Finding the trailhead: Driving north from Anchorage about 35 miles, turn to the right and enter the Old Palmer Highway. There is a small parking area at Mile 3.6.

The hike: The trailhead area and part of the twenty-five-foot trail right-of-way is on private land. Trail users should stay within the right-of-way to avoid trespass. From the trailhead to about 1,000 foot elevation, the trail passes through open, old growth white spruce, birch, and cottonwood trees. The well-defined trail goes through patches of devil's club, wild rose, elderberry, alder, and grasses. The next 1,300-foot gain is through alder thickets intermingled with small grass patches. Above the alder zone to about 3,200 feet, the vegetation consists of low shrubs and grasses with scattered patches of low willow brush. The trail switches back and forth up the steep nose of the ridge and is marked with three- to four-foot-high orange and red fiberglass stakes. Above 3,200 feet, the route is less steep and travels through alpine tundra with shorter trail markers placed on the ridge crest.

The base of South Pioneer Peak is just over one mile from the trail end and is about another mile to North Pioneer Peak. Climbing North and South Pioneer peaks should be attempted only by persons experienced and equipped for this type of rock climbing. Anyone traveling in this area should have appropriate topographical maps, a good compass, and be skilled in their use. To the southeast and south, Pioneer Ridge leads to the south ridge of Goat Creek and toward Bold Peak, Eklutna Lake, and the Hunter Creek drainage.

HIKE 7: *RABBIT LAKE TRAIL*

General description: Rabbit lake is a family hike into some of the most beautiful alpine scenery in the Anchorage area.
General location: In the upper reaches of the Chugach Mountains Southeast of Anchorage.

Trail begins: At a gate at the end of Canyon Road.
Trail ends: Rabbit Lake four miles away.
Maps: USGS Anchorage A7, A8 (SE)
Difficulty: Easy to moderate.
Length: eight miles
Elevation: 2,000 to 3,082 feet.
Special attractions: Vistas, small animals, rolling hills, pristine lake, view of Suicide Peaks, and unparalleled photography.
Best season: June through September.
For more information: Chugach State Park Ranger District Headquarters, HC 52 Box 8999, Indian, Alaska, 99540 (907) 345-5014
Finding the trailhead: Drive south on Seward Highway to O'Malley Road, drive four miles to the intersection with Hillside Drive. Turn left onto Upper O'Malley Road. Chugach State Park trailhead sign and the beginning of the hike is in the gravel area. This is the trailhead for Flat Top Mountain. Rabbit Lake Trail follows the same route as Flat Top Mountain Trail to the base of Flat Top Mountain and then continues on to Rabbit Lake.

The hike: Hikers find the trail by hiking on the road paralleling the powerline and following for about 100 yards. It is easy to follow the track over a rough road and through scrub hemlock to a large open area past the trees. At this point the trail moves right, and away from Flat Top Mountain Trail. Rabbit Lake Trail has largely been ignored due to an earlier route dispute with local landholders and because of local popularity of Flat Top. It is used moderately and is well marked and open in most areas. On calm days there is no other place prettier than the Rabbit Lake area. The country is open and free of trees. This is an excellent area for personal discovery. The trail is easy to follow, but hikers may take any of many routes to the lake. It is also possible for a change of mind as the hike progresses. As hikers wander along the trail or beyond the marked track they are free to hike to Powerline Pass and cross over to The Wedge, The Ramp, or Ship Lake. Take lots of pictures as new discoveries are made.

HIKE 8: *THUNDERBIRD FALLS TRAIL*

General description: Thunderbird Falls Trail presents families and small children an opportunity for a pleasant outing and a hike to a beautiful waterfall.
General location: Twenty five miles north of Anchorage on the Glenn Highway
Trail begins: On Thunderbird Falls Road
Trail ends: Thunderbird Falls
Maps: USGS Anchorage B7 NE
Difficulty: Easy
Length: One mile
Elevation: 120 to 330 feet
Special attractions: Picnic grounds, waterfalls
Best season: May through October
For more information: Chugach State Park Ranger District Headquarters, HC

Thunderbird Falls. Photo by Curtis Hight

52 Box 8999, Indian, Alaska, 99540 (907) 345-5014

Finding the trailhead: From Anchorage drive northeast on the Glenn Highway to Thunderbird Falls exit at mile 25.2. Then travel .4 mile to a parking area on the right just before the Eklutna River bridge. The trailhead in the parking lot is well marked.

The hike: After leaving the trailhead the trail leads through woods to Eklutna River's waterfall and picnic area. The hike may be enjoyed as soon as snow leaves the ground in May and is a trail enjoyed until winter weather prevents a comfortable walk. The hike allows city dwellers easy access to birch trees, wild, roses, ferns, devil's club, and other plants associated with the forest.

There are two seasons during summer on Thunderbird Falls Trail: dusty and slick. If it's wet the trail is slick. In dry weather it is dusty. In either season, the view of the falls is worth the short hike. A picnic lunch on the banks of the stream is a bonus. Salmon run up the river and can be seen in the water. Hidden in the back of a narrow gorge, Thunderbird Falls receives sunlight only a few hours each day.

The hiking trail is in dense woods but the undergrowth is sparse. The atmosphere is quiet, serene, and natural. One cannot hike here without a feeling of rejuvenation.

Dividing near the end, the left fork leads down to the creek and a picnic area. The right fork travels to the falls viewing area. Do not go beyond the end of the foot path and do not allow children to explore the cliffs above the falls. The cliffs are inviting but dangerous.

Thunderbird Falls, only a mile from the highway, is still in a wilderness setting and reminds hikers to always obey safety rules. A fall from the cliffs above the falls can cause just as much injury as slipping into a crevasse on Mt. McKinley. Warning signs are placed for the protection of all. Only the foolish ignore the caution.

HIKE 9: *TWIN PEAKS TRAIL*

General description: Fall foliage is dynamic on this trail. The blaze of color is worthy of any camera.
General location: In mountains above Eklutna Lake
Trail begins: Second parking lot by lake at marked trailhead
Trail ends: Trailhead
Maps: USGS Anchorage B6 NW
Difficulty: Easy to moderate
Length: 3.5 miles
Elevation: 900 to 5,050 feet
Special attractions: Birch forests, Eklutna Lake vistas, flowers in season
Best season: July through September
For more information: Chugach State Park Ranger District Headquarters, HC 52 Box 8999, Indian, Alaska, 99540 (907) 345-5014
Finding the trailhead: Drive northeast from Anchorage on the Glenn Highway to mile 26, the Eklutna exit. Turn right, onto road coming across the overpass. Southbound traffic should cross the overpass to west side of the freeway. Turn immediately right onto frontage road and go .4 mile. Turn left at a "T" intersection, following signs for Chugach State Park. Follow this road about ten miles to its end at the lake. Drive through the first parking area, past the walk-in boat launch, to the second parking area and trailhead.

The hike: Although the trail name is Twin Peaks, the hike is below the peaks and few hikers climb them. Climbing the peaks requires mountaineering experience and special equipment. Hikers properly equipped, properly trained, and in good physical condition and desiring to hike the peaks usually approach from passes along Twin Peaks Trail.

The hike begins in the southeast corner of the parking area where the trail leads across a short bridge. Hikers then turn left on marked Twin Peaks Trail, cross a road, and follow the trail signs. As the trail climbs and winds through the woods it affords occasional views of Eklutna Lake below.

When hiking Twin Peaks Trail, hikers must make a route decision about .25 mile from the campground. Here the trail forks and is divided for about .5 mile. Those taking the right-hand trail will climb the hill along a series of switchbacks. The shorter, steeper left fork requires a hiker to be in good shape.

Under two hours of hiking will put most hikers at the brush line, at about 2,700 feet. Below the trail and through patches of high grass, is the first water along the trail. At this small, sparkling stream, which drops through the small canyon to an alpine bowl below, is an attractive camping or picnicking site. Many hikers stop here and return to the trailhead.

An outstanding vista of Matanuska Valley is the compensation for those who follow the ridge crest to the 5,050-foot pass and then down the steep south slope, staying west of the stream below the pass. The pass is reached by heading diagonally down to the stream and taking the path leading from the end of the trail and across the first draw coming down from the peak to the northeast. A hiker may lose the path in tall grass but don't worry, it is easy to find again. Just head for the low 4,450-foot pass to the northeast. Soon the high grass is left behind and the scene worth the 3.5-mile hike opens to view.

HIKE 10: *WILLIWAW NATURE TRAIL*

General description: Easy, interesting short nature hike among representative flora and along a stream of Portage Valley.
General location: Williwaw Campground two miles west of Begich, Boggs Visitor Center at Portage Glacier.
Trail begins: Between site 5 and 6 of the Williwaw Campground.
Trail ends: Loops back to the trailhead.
Maps: USGS Seward D5.
Difficulty: Easy.
Length: .5 mile.
Elevation: 100 to 150 feet.
Special attractions: Spawning salmon, scenery, glaciers, flowers, and small animals.
Best season: June through September.
For more information: Chugach National Forest, Glacier Ranger District, P.O. Box 129, Monarch Mine Road, Girdwood, Alaska 99587 (907) 783-3242.
Finding the trailhead: At Mile 79, Seward Highway, forty-nine miles south of Anchorage, turn onto Portage Valley Road. Travel four miles to Williwaw Campground. Trailhead begins between campsites 5 and 6.

The hike: Although the hike begins in Williwaw Campground, hikers should visit Begich, Boggs Visitor Center at Portage Glacier before taking this easy .5-mile trail. Numbered posts are set along the trail. A helpful trail guide is available at the visitor center. The numbered trail posts correspond to information in the guidebook to assist hikers understand and enjoy vegetation and natural features of the trail and Portage Valley.

Spawning salmon are part of the attraction of Williwaw Nature Trail and a viewing platform is near the entrance of Williwaw Campground. Spawning salmon may be seen from mid-August through September. The flat loop trail is a wide, well surfaced path entering an area that is representative of Portage Valley flora. The first section, to a thirty-foot span bridge, is wide enough for

Fields of Alaska cotton, not cotton at all, may be found in low, wet areas along road or trail.

handicapped access. Beyond the bridge, the trail is narrow and wet part of the time. Even if your feet get damp the interesting things discovered on this short hike make it worth while. Wildflowers grow along the trail and edible berries abound in late summer. Beyond the bridge are many spur trails, a waterfall, and a cascading creek. Wildlife in Portage Valley include moose, eagles, black and brown bear, and migratory birds in spring and fall.

Additional glacier information and data about Portage Valley may be obtained by visiting the Begich, Boggs Visitor Center. Portage Glacier icebergs float close to the viewing platform of the center. Portage Valley is subject to high winds and driving rain. Be prepared for rapid weather changes.

HIKE 11: *WOLVERINE PEAK TRAIL*

General description: Picturesque hike into wilderness near Anchorage. The trail goes through white spruce, birch, mountain hemlock, and alpine tundra into high country.
General location: Chugach Range above Anchorage

HIKE 3: *FLAT TOP MTN.*   HIKE 4: *KNOYA PEAK*
HIKE 5: *OLD JOHNSON*   HIKE 7: *RABBIT LAKE*
HIKE 10: *WILLIWAW NATURE*   HIKE 11: *WOLVERINE PEAK*

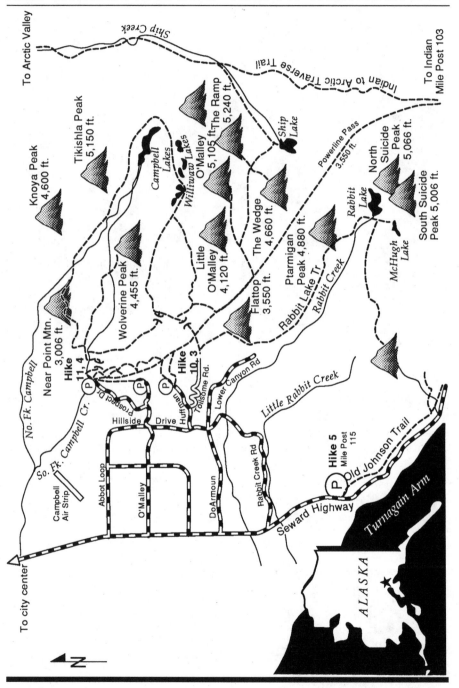

Trail begins: End of Prospect Heights Road
Trail ends: Wolverine Peak Country
Maps: USGS Anchorage A7, A8
Difficulty: Moderate to difficult
Length: Six miles
Elevation: 1,500 to 4,455 feet
Special attractions: Views of Alaska Range, Anchorage, and Cook Inlet
Best season: June through September (all Year)
For more information: Chugach State Park Ranger District Headquarters, HC 52 Box 8999, Indian, Alaska, 99540 (907) 345-5014
Finding the trailhead: Drive from Seward Highway onto O'Malley Road. After four miles turn right onto Hillside Drive. Turn right onto Upper O'Malley Road. Trailhead is at end of Prospect Heights Road.

The hike: The area behind Wolverine Mountain, the broad triangular mountain east of Anchorage, is a lake-dotted wild country. The trail to the lakes offers many views of Anchorage, Cook Inlet, and Alaska Range. The trail, an old homesteader's road, is part of the Chugach State Park trail system.

Watch for ground squirrels, spruce grouse, moose, and, on rare occasions, a wolverine. Pick blueberries and cranberries in season.

The trail leaves the trailhead on the old road and 500 feet into the hike the trail meets Powerline Trail. Take Powerline Trail to the left and continue to the South Fork of Campbell Creek. Cross a bridge and continue around a sharp switchback and up a hill. An old road, marked Middle Fork Loop Trail, turns sharply to the right. The second old road to the right is the trail to Wolverine Peak. The trail leaving Powerline is a mile beyond the creek crossing and two and one third miles from the trailhead. The peak is three miles ahead.

The old road, at an elevation of 1,330 feet, angles uphill and soon becomes a narrow foot path through blueberry bushes and underbrush. It then emerges above the brush line, paralleling the north side of the ridge. Climb the crest and continue to the 4,455 foot peak.

A network of about twenty miles of trails is accessed from Prospect Hights and three other entrances to Chugach State Park. The Loop Trail connects this entrance with Upper O'Malley, Upper Huffman, and Glen Alps Park entrances and can be hiked as a circular trip using the Powerline Trail. Maps of the trail system are available from the Park office, or posted at the trailheads.

DENALI NATIONAL PARK AND HIGHWAY

Denali, The High One, is the name given by Athabascan Indians to the massive peak, Mt. McKinley. The expansive landscape surrounding the peak is habitat of large caribou, moose, and grizzly bear, and lies adorned with miniaturized plants. The miniaturized beauty of tundra plants and itinerant wandering of nomadic mammals are striking counterpoints to the lofty, isolated, and often cloud-hidden grandeur of the Mount McKinley massif. These hikes are in the shadow of North America's highest peak and among its largest animals.

More visitors to Alaska go to Denali National Park than any other Alaska visitor destination. Most of these visitors do not see the park and what little the others do see, they see while sitting on a bus. Many park visitors never get far from park headquarters and those venturing into the park's interior never get off the road. By contrast, hikers in Denali National Park see spectacular scenery and are given excellent opportunities to view and photograph wildlife.

Denali National Park is on the Parks Highway 237 miles from Anchorage or 121 miles from Fairbanks. The park can also be reached from Richardson Highway via Denali Highway, 159 miles from Paxson. The Denali Highway, a gravel road paralleling the Nenanna River and crossing the upper Susitna River Valley, was the original highway into Denali National Park. Running from Paxson on the Richardson Highway it connects to the George Parks Highway near Cantwell, near the entrance to Denali National Park.

All hiking in Denali National Park begins on Denali National Park Road. Two trails in this section begin and end on the Denali Highway. All trails eventually return to Denali National Park Road. National Park Road runs from the park entrance to within twenty-seven miles of Mt. McKinley and free shuttle bus service drops hikers off anywhere they desire. The buses start at Riley Creek Visitor Center near the park entrance. Riley Creek Visitor Center issues the permits required for overnight camping in backcountry. Other helpful information such as free maps, information about bears, drinking water, and backcountry regulations may be obtained. Obtain as much data as possible from Park Rangers, but I have found that other hikers are a better source of current information and what I really need to know. Morino Campground, used as a staging area by many backcountry hikers, is a good source of information. Camping at least one night at Morino gives hikers an opportunity to gain from other's experiences.

Bears in Denali are wild and dangerous. Protection and avoiding unpleasant encounters with bears and all park wildlife is the hiker's responsibility. Following the Park Service rules and advice on bear safety, and using care and precaution, allows hikers a rewarding and exciting experience to watch and photograph bears.

HIKE 12: *ANDERSON PASS TRAIL*

General description: This strenuous twenty-six-mile hike leads through the Alaska Range. Bears, caribou, and sheep are common along the way, and the view from the pass is an extraordinary panorama of mountains, glaciers, and valleys on both sides of the Alaska Range. The Denali fault system runs through Anderson Pass, making this one of the best places to see a region shaped by the forces of plate shifting .

General location: Denali National Park

Trail begins: The hike begins on Denali National Park Road at Milepost at Milepost 65.

Trail ends: Denali National Park Road Milepost 65.

Maps: Mount McKinley National Park (the park on one map for convenience) Bradford Washburn, "A Map of Mount McKinley, Alaska"

Difficulty: Easy to moderate

Length: twenty-six miles round trip

Elevation: 3,733 to 5,000 feet

Special attractions: The thrill of hiking through the Alaska Range and viewing wildlife along the way.

Best season: Mid-June through mid-September

For more information: Denali National Park Headquarters, P. O. Box 9, Denali Park, Alaska, 99755. (907) 683-2294

Finding the trailhead: The hike begins at Milepost 65 about two miles west of Eielson Visitor Center where the road abruptly swings to the right away from the bluffs overlooking Thorofare River.

The hike: The trail, beginning at the "Rocks" sign on the Park Road, drops down a brushy bluff to the gravel bars of the Thorofare River, crosses it and

View of McKinley from the air.

Camp Creek, and then climbs a 200-foot bluff to a bench overlooking Glacier Creek. A backcountry overnight camping permit is required. Water must be carried in. Bears are very common in this area.

Hikers must pick a trail on the edge of the bluff leading about two miles south to where Intermittent Creek flows in from the left. The route descends the bluffs and cross Intermittent Creek, Crystal Creek (both clearwater streams) and Glacier Creek. Hikers should follow the right side of Glacier Creek to its source at the snout of an unnamed glacier descending from Sunset Peak. Dall sheep may be located on the vegetated lower glacier moraines.

Further south .5 mile, a freshwater stream flows out of the mountains to the left into a pristine little meadow thick with marmots. This creek is incorrectly indicated as the head of Glacier Creek on the map. This is the last good grassy camping spot before beginning the climb into the pass. The route follows rugged lateral moraines to the left of the glacier to 5,300-foot Anderson Pass. Near the summit, freshwater streams flow out of the mountains to freshen a hiker's water supply. Please boil all drinking water.

The view from the pass is exceptional. A 2,000-foot wall of granite is on the right and left is a row of 9,000- to 12,000-foot peaks. Muldrow Glacier extends twenty-five miles west to its source high on McKinley. To the Northeast stretches the Alaska Range, topped by Scott Peak. To the Southeast is a clear view, thirty miles down the valley, of the West Fork of the Chulitna to the Parks Highway at Broad Pass.

There are places to camp in the pass. Winds in the pass can reach gale force and spring up suddenly so camping should either be in mountaineering-quality tents or in protected areas. Return to the trailhead by the route you came.

It is possible to walk the thirty miles to the Parks Highway, but numerous sizable rivers must be crossed, making it a difficult and dangerous trip and is not recommended.

HIKE 13: BUTTE LAKE TRAIL

General description: A short hike to a good fishing lake
General location: Denali Highway
Trail begins: Mile 93.3 Denali Highway
Trail ends: At Butte Lake
Maps: USGS Healy A2
Difficulty: Easy to moderate
Length: 3.5 miles
Elevation: 3,000 to 3,400 feet
Special attractions: Good trout, grayling, and whitefish, fishing and views of the Susitna River Basin
Best season: June through September
For more information: State of Alaska, Division of Parks and Recreation, HC32 Box 6706, Wasilla, Alaska 99687, (907) 745-3975
Finding the trailhead: The trailhead is located in a large gravel pit off the

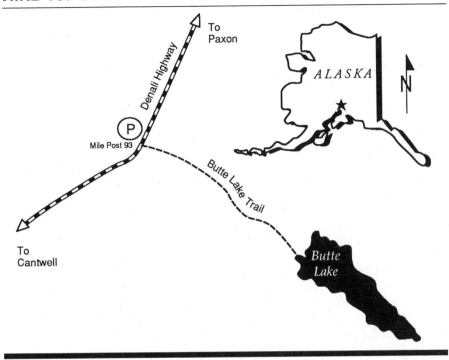

Denali Highway at Mile 93.3. It can be located, if driving from Paxson, thirteen miles beyond the highway's Susitna River crossing. It is 41.4 miles from the George Parks Highway junction.

The hike: Although this is a short hike it may be advisable to plan on a multi-day stay. Butte Lake, the largest lake in this section of the Denali Highway, contains good stocks of lake trout, grayling, and whitefish and one of the best fishing spots in the area. Over two miles long and .5 mile wide, the lake invites hikers to carry a small inflatable boat or raft to use as a platform from which to conduct fish catching experiments.

Traveling through high rolling tundra, the trail takes hikers through an area of small lakes. Many have never been fished or at least fished very little. There are three private cabins on Butte Lake but hikers will still have the feeling of wilderness as fox, bear, moose, and caribou are seen.

Generally speaking, the Denali Highway is built atop a ridge. The southern slopes of the ridge provide a perfect setting for blueberry patches. I enjoy the Denali area in August and early September when blueberries are ripe. These tasty tidbits have occupied many a pleasant hour on sunny fall days. A particularly good berry year produced them in such profusion that I gorged myself for an hour without moving further than a few feet. The down side of this pleasant gluttony was pants with blue stained knees and fingers to match.

HIKE 14: *BUTTE CREEK TRAIL*

General description: The trail takes hikers off the Denali Highway at Mile 80.7, fifty-six miles from the George Parks Highway, into an area rich in wildlife and good fishing.

General location: The Denali Highway, a gravel road paralleling the Nenana River and crossing the upper Susitna River Valley and River, was the original highway into Denali National Park. Running from Paxson on the Richardson Highway it connects to the George Parks Highway near Cantwell, near the entrance to Denali National Park. It has many turnouts for camping and wildlife viewing. Butte Creek Trail runs south from the highway.

Trail begins: Mile 80.7 Denali Highway west side of Susitna River Bridge

Trail ends: Butte Creek

Maps: USGS Healy A2

Difficulty: Easy to moderate

Length: 11.5 miles

Elevation: 2,500 to 3,000 feet

Special attractions: Fishing, wildlife viewing, scenery along the Nenana River

Best season: June through September

For more information: State of Alaska, Division of Parks and Recreation, HC32 Box 6706, Wasilla, Alaska 99687, (907) 745-3975

Finding the trailhead: Follow the Denali Highway to a gravel pit on the west side on the Susitna River Bridge at milepost 80.7, 56 miles from the junction with George Parks Highway. The highway crosses the Susitna River at Mile 80.

The hike: This is a hike where hikers should leave their pack rods out and handy. I suggest an early morning start without eating. Only two miles from the trailhead is a small stream flowing from Snodgrass Lake. Grayling fishing with a small fly is excellent. With a little luck and reasonable skill the hiking angler can capture breakfast. Chances are while the day's first meal is being prepared and consumed, caribou will wander into view, maybe even a bear or moose. The route, following an old mining trail, parallels the Susitna River for the first two miles to Snodgrass Lake. Grayling fishing in the lake is generally good and if luck was absent at the creek, breakfast can be caught here. The trail begins in high tundra and turns to alpine forest near Butte Creek. Seven miles from the trailhead, the trail crosses Wickersham Creek where the pack rod may again be exercised. Another small stream is crossed before the trail reaches Butte Creek. I have not dropped a fly in either Butte Creek or the small stream but suspect that if a fresh fish lunch or dinner was desired it could be gathered here. Grizzly, moose, and caribou roam these hills and may be seen at any time. There are many inactive mining claims on this trail. Some mines are active further back in the valley.

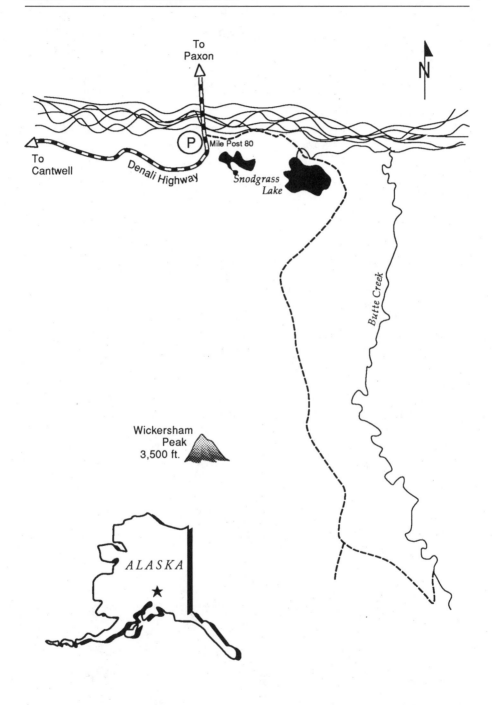

HIKE 15: *MT. EIELSON TRAIL*

General description: Circling Mt. Eielson, this hike goes into one of the best places in the Park to see bear, sheep, and caribou. Traversing a mixture of terrain, this strenuous dayhike, or easy overnighter, includes river bars, glacial rivers, low bush, grassy tundra, rocky canyons, and alpine tundra.

General location: Denali National Park

Trail begins: Eielson Visitor Center, Denali National Park Road Milepost 65.

Trail ends: The trail is a circular route ending back at Eielson Visitor Center

Maps: Mount McKinley National Park (the park on one map for convenience) Bradford Washburn, "A Map of Mount McKinley, Alaska"

Difficulty: Easy to moderate

Length: fourteen miles

Elevation: 3,778 to 5,000 feet

Special attractions: Photograph grizzly bears and view of Mt. McKinley

Best season: Mid-June through Mid-September

For more information: Denali National Park Headquarters, P. O. Box 9, Denali Park, Alaska, 99755. (907) 683-2294

Finding the trailhead: Get off the shuttle bus at Eielson Visitor Center, Milepost 65.

The hike: Left of Eielson Visitor Center take a trail down to and across Gorge Creek. Pick up the trail and climb a fifty-foot bluff to a high bench of rolling tundra, and then hike south. Sunrise Creek enters the Thorofare River two miles from the trailhead. Drop down off the bench and cross Sunrise Creek, and then the Thorofare. The Thorofare fans into numerous braids and makes for a safe crossing. Dall sheep are often seen on mountains to the left. This is a good place to set up a spotting scope and watch the animal's antics. Bears frequent this area.

Contact Creek enters from the right about a mile south of the confluence of Sunrise Creek and the Thorofare River. Follow Contact Creek up a steep, mile long, rocky canyon. The pass at the head of the canyon, 1,300 feet above

Free shuttle bus service drops hikers off anywhere they desire along the National Park road.

Thorofare River, has excellent camping spots with great views of Mt. Mckinley and Scott Peak. Headwaters of Wolverine Creek are just over the pass. Replenish your water here. A backcountry overnight camping permit is required.

Hikers reaching this point may elect to climb Mt. Eielson. Sheep trails go up a ridge running directly north of the pass. It is a fairly easy climb until just below the summit. Obtaining the summit requires climbing over rocks. Views of the Alaska Range and surrounding territory is the hiker's reward.

Hikers continuing from the pass move along the southern flank of Mt. Eielson to a gap in the mountains leading to Intermittent Creek. Drop to

HIKE 12: *ANDERSON PASS*   HIKE 15:   *EIELSON MTN.*

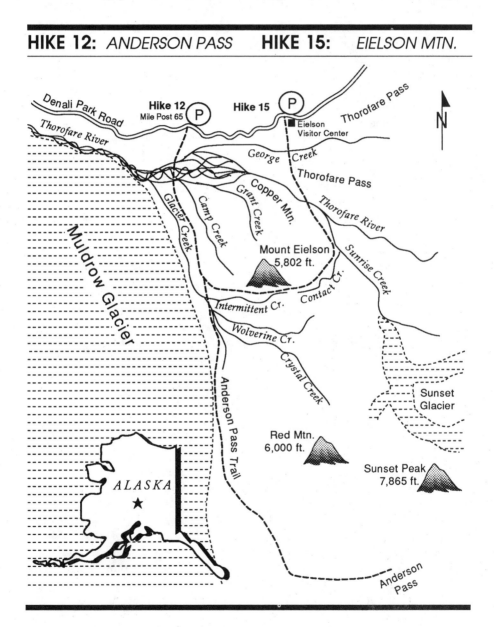

Intermittent Creek and follow it to its confluence with Glacier Creek. The trail to Camp Creek (watch for bears) and Thorofare River is reached by climbing a bluff on the right to a high bench overlooking Glacier Creek. Follow the trail leading north. Cross Camp Creek and the Thorofare River. The trail ends by returning up Gorge Creek to Eielson Visitor Center or climbing a steep brushy ravine up the bluffs to the road.

HIKE 16: *EAST BRANCH OF THE TOKLAT TRAIL*

General description: This day, or overnight, hike into the Alaska Range, offers beautiful scenery and opportunities to see and photograph fox, bear, sheep, wolves, caribou, and other wildlife.
General location: Denali National Park.
Trail begins: Denali National Park Road, Milepost 51.
Trail ends: Nine miles inland at the head of Thorofare River Valley.
Maps: Mount McKinley National Park (the park on one map for convenience) Bradford Washburn, "A Map of Mount McKinley, Alaska."
Difficulty: Easy to moderate.
Length: Nine miles one way.
Elevation: 3,500 to 6,300 feet.
Special attractions: Wildlife photo opportunities.
Best season: Mid-June through Mid-September.
For more information: Denali National Park Headquarters, P. O. Box 9, Denali Park, Alaska, 99755. (907) 683-2294.
Finding the trailhead: At Riley Creek Visitor Center, catch the Park Service, shuttle bus and the driver will let you off at Mile 51. Just ask.

The hike: The hike is fairly easy and does not require crossing any glacial or dangerous streams. It is an excellent Denali National Park sampler of pristine backcountry and wildlife. Hikers with limited time may stop at any point and return to the road and still feel they have seen more Denali wilderness than most of the annual half million visitors.

It's an eighteen-mile round-trip hike to the head of the valley. Wildlife may be seen anywhere along the way. Hikers remaining overnight must have a backcountry overnight camping permit.

Milepost 51 is about six miles past Polychrome Overlook rest stop. The hike begins by climbing down a brushy bank to a ravine which opens to the broad Thorofare River Valley. The trail heads south on glacial bars. Grizzly bears may be seen in this lower part of the valley. Caribou are common here and wolves can be glimpsed.

Three miles in the valley begins to narrow. Sheep are often seen on a high bench to the left. Beyond and to the left hikers see strikingly colored, volcanic rock mountains. Millions of years ago volcanos erupted and buried the area under lava. For the next two miles there are several good camping spots where creeks flow out of the mountains to the left.

Two miles from the end of the valley, the river splits into two forks. The

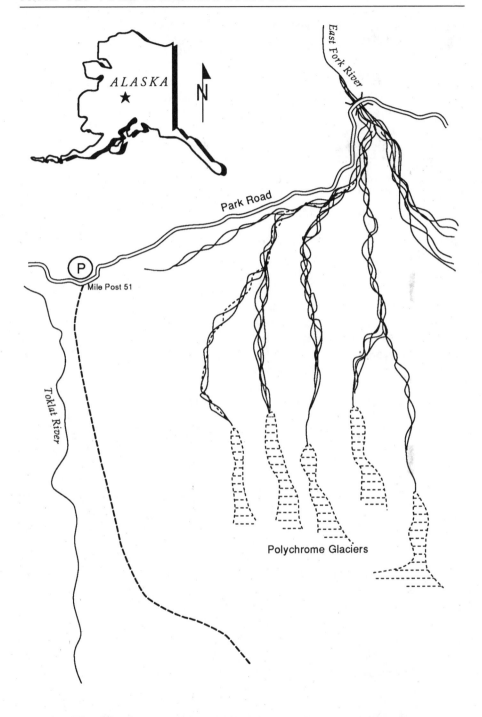

ALASKA

N

East Fork River

Park Road

P
Mile Post 51

Toklat River

Polychrome Glaciers

small, scenic valley to the left is a good place to see Dall sheep. These valleys are subject to strong night winds. If you camp overnight, be prepared.

HIKE 17: *UPPER TEKLANIKA-SANCTUARY RIVERS TRAIL*

General description: This hike goes into the home of Dall sheep. Bear are abundant and caribou roam the valley floors. Much of the way is on unmarked trails where hikers must make their own way.

General location: Denali National Park.

Trail begins: Just before the Sable Pass Restricted Area sign on Denali National Park Road at Milepost 37.

Trail ends: Sanctuary Campground, Denali National Park Road Milepost 22.

Maps: Mount McKinley National Park (the park on one map for convenience) Bradford Washburn, "A Map of Mount McKinley, Alaska."

Difficulty: Easy to moderate.

Length: Thirty-two miles roundtrip.

Elevation: 1,200 to 5,400 feet.

Special attractions: Photograph Dall sheep, other wildlife, the Alaska Range.

Best season: Mid-June through Mid-September.

For more information: Denali National Park Headquarters, P. O. Box 9, Denali Park, Alaska, 99755. (907) 683-2294.

Finding the trailhead: Use the shuttle bus from Riley Creek Visitor Center and get off just before the Sable Pass Restricted Area sign at Milepost 37. The trail begins by dropping down a steep bank to Igloo Creek.

The hike: The trail crosses Igloo Creek and moves east following the southern flank of Cathedral Mountain. Care must be taken to avoid the restricted area. The route follows game trails leading across a grassy divide and down a brushy bank to Teklanika River Valley.

An Athabascan word, Teklanika means "much river bed, little river." Teklanika River, heavily laden with glacial silt created from glaciers grinding rocks into fine powder, flows north. Quickly clogging the stream channels, this silt causes the river to change course. Each year the river shifts back and forth across the valley floor, laying down broad, braided river bars, hence "much river bed, little river."

The trail follows gravel bars south for six miles to a large bowl where the river breaks into three branches. Dall sheep are often seen here feeding on the slopes above the valley floor. This is an area visited by bears and a good spot to set up a photo location.

Continuing, the trail goes to the headwaters of the Teklanika River until it branches left into a clearwater stream, and then up a steep, rocky ravine to an unnamed 5,400-foot pass. This pass is a major caribou migration route. July is the best summer month to see caribou in this area.

The trail on the east side of the pass is steep and follows caribou trails down to a creek which flows east through a canyon to Refuge Valley. Do not follow the creek itself. Stay high and right and follow a grassy bench above the canyon to avoid ravines which drop down to the creek. The canyon is blocked by waterfalls. Refuge Valley is an excellent place to camp and set up a spotting scope or long lens camera to catch Dall sheep rams, often seen at the head of the valley.

It is eighteen miles to the road from where Refuge Valley meets the main valley of the Sanctuary. There are no trails except for the last two miles. Either hike through low bush tundra on the mountain's edge or along river banks and bars. Willow and alder thickets grow along the latter route. Be extremely alert for bears, as visibility is limited. Once the river leaves the mountains, there are restricted areas on either side of the river. Hiking is limited to the river banks. Again, watch for bears. The river leads to the Sanctuary Campground at mile 22.

HIKE 17: *UPPER TEKLANIKA-SANCTUARY RIVERS TRAIL*

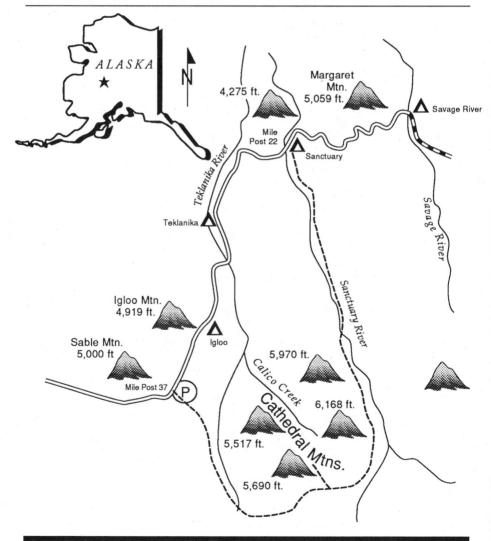

KACHEMAK BAY TRAIL SYSTEM

The trail system takes a hiker from ocean beaches to glacier lakes, from alpine meadows to rocky crags and glacier outwashs, and from tide flats to clear streams and fishing lakes. The system could keep a hiker interested for a week and a single trail could a hiker occupied for an afternoon.

There are many trailheads in the system. One begins north of Glacier Spit at the east end of Kachemak Bay, another at Right Beach in the same area, several in Halibut Cove Lagoon, and others where trails join. Access is by water or air and your charter boat captain or pilot will locate your preferred trailhead. See individual trails for directions to finding each trailhead.

The Kachemak Trail system includes trails in Kachemak Bay State Par, which is undeveloped. There are no roads to, or in, the park. It is accessible only by air or water from Homer, at the tip of Kenai Peninsula. Alaskans rate this park extremely high for its scenic, wild mountain terrain, fjords, coves, and vast glacier fields. Boating, fishing, and beachcombing are outstanding. There are primitive campsites along trails to high mountain lakes and glaciers. The trails include Grewingk Glacier, Saddle, Alpine Ridge, Lagoon, Goat Rope Spur, China Poot Lake, Poot Peak, and Wosnesenski Trails. The area lends itself to hiking established trails above timberline and out of the brush.

Kachemak Bay is opposite Homer Spit, the northern end of the Pan American Highway beginning in Argentina. The Spit, 230 road miles south of Anchorage, is the jumping off spot for many Kachemak Bay State Park trails. Access to the park may be accomplished by boat or aircraft. There is boat taxi service at reasonable rates from The Spit. Aircraft charter is more expensive than water taxi, but faster, and gives hikers an opportunity to review the trail by air. Boat rental is also available. Several air charter services and water taxies specialize in transporting hikers into the park at affordable prices.

China Poot Lake (locally knows as Leisure Lake) is at the base of Poot Peak better known as Chocolate Drop Mountain and is a small 2,100-foot-high peak set in the center of a large valley. Looking east from the tip is a vista of glaciers. The view west encompasses Kachemak Bay, Cook Inlet, and active volcanos in the Alaska Range.

Halibut Cove Lagoon is connected to Halibut Cove by a short, narrow salt water river, which changes direction with tide flow. Admittance to the lagoon is achieved by boating the incoming or slack high tide. Exit from the lagoon takes the same kind of planning. Many a boater has tried to buck the incoming or outgoing tide, only to find the current too much for their craft.

HIKE 18 : *ALPINE RIDGE TRAIL*

General description: A two hour hike to get above timberline
General location: Kachemak Bay State Park
Trail begins: Northeast end of Halibut Cove at the same location as Lagoon and Saddle trails.
Trail ends: Two miles inland and above timberline
Maps: USGS Seldovia C4
Difficulty: Moderate to difficult
Length: Two miles one way
Elevation: Sea level to 400 feet
Special attractions: View and photo opportunities
Best season: June through September
For more information: State of Alaska, Division of Parks and Recreation, P.O. Box 321, Homer, Alaska 99603, (907) 235-7024
Finding the trailhead: Steep Alpine Ridge Trail branches off at the high point on Saddle Trail and follows a ridge up through spruce and alder stands to alpine tundra and its abundant wildflowers.

The hike: Once above timberline, views of glaciers on one side and a deep glacial valley on the other are outstanding. Rock cairns mark the alpine part of the trail, but picking out landmarks will make it easier to find the end of the trail for the trip back down. Slippery vegetation clinging to steeper slopes may make footing difficult. Alpine areas, especially steep slopes, are extremely delicate. Use care when hiking and please practice minimum impact camping.

HIKE 19: *CHINA POOT LAKE TRAIL*

General description: An easy two-hour hike to three alpine lakes
General location: Kachemak Bay State Park
Trail begins: Ranger Station at the southeast end of Halibut Cove Lagoon
Trail ends: China Poot Lake
Maps: USGS Seldovia C4
Difficulty: Easy to moderate
Length: 2.5 miles one way
Elevation: Sea level to 200 feet
Special attractions: Wild flowers and fishing
Best season: June through September
For more information: State of Alaska, Division of Parks and Recreation, P.O. Box 321, Homer, Alaska 99603, (907) 235-7024
Finding the trailhead: This trail begins at the south end of Lagoon Trail near the Rangers Station. If you are not hiking Lagoon Trail you can locate the trailhead from the beach just west of the ranger station.

Most Kachemak Bay trails give hikers access to good fresh or saltwater angling.

The hike: China Poot Lake Trail begins at Halibut Cove Lagoon and passes three lakes beneath China Poot Peak. You reach the first lake after fifteen minutes of uphill hiking. The trail crosses the lake outlet stream just before reaching the lake and continues through forest and bog for thirty minutes to the second lake, Two Loon Lake. It is not a spectacular hike, but the trail ends at beautiful China Poot Lake, thirty minutes beyond Two Loon Lake through more spruce and muskeg. Highlight of the trail is the number of different species of wild flowers along the trail. Occasional breaks in the trees give hikers their first view of China Poot Peak, more commonly called Chocolate Drop Mountain. China Poot Lake, known locally as Leisure Lake, sports good camping sites on a gravel and sand beach near Inlet Stream. Pan- size rainbow trout may be taken at the stream's mouth and in the lake.

On one hike to China Poot Lake my son, Lars, and I pitched our tent twenty yards from the small, clear-water inlet stream. Our companions, Cindy and Kevin Sidelinger, said other hikers had done well fishing for rainbow trout at the mouth. Lars and I unpacked our fly rods before the tent was up. My first cast with a polar shrimp brought a tug to the line. The bow made several small runs, always staying in the current. Finally I maneuvered him out of the fast water. By the time I had him beached, an audience had gathered. "Trout for supper," Cindy announced. "Catch three more." The first one had been so easy I readily accepted the challenge. Supper was late that night as Lars and I labored for the next three hours to accomplish our task. I learned again to never judge a fishing hole on the first cast. Later, Kevin took us out in the canoe where we were able to even the score on rainbow trout.

HIKE 20: *CHINA POOT PEAK TRAIL*

General description: China Poot stands as a singular peak surrounded by views of lakes, streams, glaciers, mountains, alpine meadows, and Kachemak Bay.
General location: Kachemak Bay State Park
Trail begins: China Pook Lake
Trail ends: China Poot Peak
Maps: USGS Seldovia C4
Difficulty: Moderate to difficult
Length: two miles one way
Elevation: Sea level to 2,100 feet
Special attractions: View of Kachemak Bay and photo opportunities.
Best season: June through September
For more information: State of Alaska, Division of Parks and Recreation, P.O. Box 321, Homer, Alaska 99603, (907) 235-7024
Finding the trailhead: Inlet Stream enters China Poot Lake on the northeast side at the lake's narrowest point. There is a bridge crossing the stream. China Poot Peak Trail begins at the bridge.

Outcroping overlooking Homer Spit, from summit of China Poot Peak.

The hike: The climb to 2,100-foot China Poot Peak is over a steep, slick, unmaintained route. Beginning at Inlet Stream Bridge, the trail travels to timberline, through alder patches, and finally over rocks to the peak. Be cautious near the top. There is shifting scree and rotten rock. Hand and foot holds are poor and worse in wet weather. When you reach the top your labor will be rewarded with an outstanding view of Wosnesenski Glacier and a magnificent, lofty look at Kachemak Bay. Looking back and down toward China Poot Lake gives the impression you are suspended above your camp. China Poot Peak, known to the locals as Chocolate Drop Mountain, is a small, 2,100-foot-high peak set in the center of a large valley. Looking east from the top of the peak, hikers have a vast view of glaciers. The view west encompasses Kachemak Bay, Cook Inlet, and active volcanos of the Alaska Range.

In the early days of Kachemak Bay Park, I climbed China Poot Peak using llamas as pack animals. They are quiet, docile, intelligent animals, and extremely sure-footed. Because of padded feet, they are able to travel over a wide variety of terrain, steep mountain sides and precipitous trails. On my return to the Homer Small Boat Harbor, I remembered the Homer Spit is the northern end of the Pan American Highway beginning in Argentina. This road passes through Peru, Bolivia, and other South American countries, the ancient home of the llama. I suppose it is only fitting that one of the world's oldest domestic animals should be earning its keep at the end of this road.

Concerning the llamas' reputation, the only spit I saw was the HomerSpit.

HIKE 21: *GOAT ROPE SPUR TRAIL*

General description: A half mile, difficult trail to photo opportunities
General location: Kachemak Bay State Park
Trail begins: Highest point on Lagoon Trail
Trail ends: Alpine areas above timberline
Maps: USGS Seldovia C4
Difficulty: Moderate to difficult
Length: .5 mile one way
Elevation: 100 feet to 1,200 feet
Special attractions: Photo opportunities
Best season: June through September
For more information: State of Alaska, Division of Parks and Recreation, P.O. Box 321, Homer, Alaska 99603, (907) 235-7024
Finding the trailhead: Goat Rope Spur Trail begins at the highest point on Lagoon Trail.

The hike: It is a short, steep trail through alders leading hikers through a 'notch' in alpine area where the trail ends. Take your camera. Photos of scenery will be worth it.

General description: A trail over flat terrain and glacier outwash. The easiest hike in Kachemak Bay State Park.

General location: Kachemak Bay State Park

Trail begins: North of Glacier Spit at east end of Kachemak Bay. Many hikers begin their hike at the favorite water taxi drop off point at Right Beach.

Trail ends: Grewingk Glacier Lake. Hikers may return by connecting with Saddle Trail and ending at Lagoon Trail trailhead in Halibut Cove Lagoon.

Maps: USGS Seldovia C4

Difficulty: Easy

Length: 3.5 miles one way

Elevation: Sea level to 1,100 feet feet

Special attractions: Glacier viewing, wildlife, and flora

Best season: June through October

For more information: State of Alaska, Division of Parks and Recreation, P.O. Box 321, Homer, Alaska 99603, (907) 235-7024

Finding the trailhead: North of Glacier Spit at east end of Kachemak Bay

The hike: Grewingk Glacier hike is over flat terrain, through stands of spruce and cottonwood, and across the outwash of Grewingk Glacier. It is an easy hike offering top-drawer views of the glacier and surrounding area. There is a small campground about ten minutes from the trailhead, and another at Right Beach, a favorite water taxi drop-off point. Right beach is accessible by land only from the north and only at low tide. Rock cairns mark the trail across the outwash of the glacier and you can't get lost. You may even want to wander off the trail among the small trees and shrubs that are trying to get a foothold on the outwash. Access to glacial ice is difficult and hazardous due to the slide area on the south and steep cliffs on the north. Camping or picnicking on the

Boys floating on a ice berg on Grewingk Lake. Even on a warm day the water is near freezing.

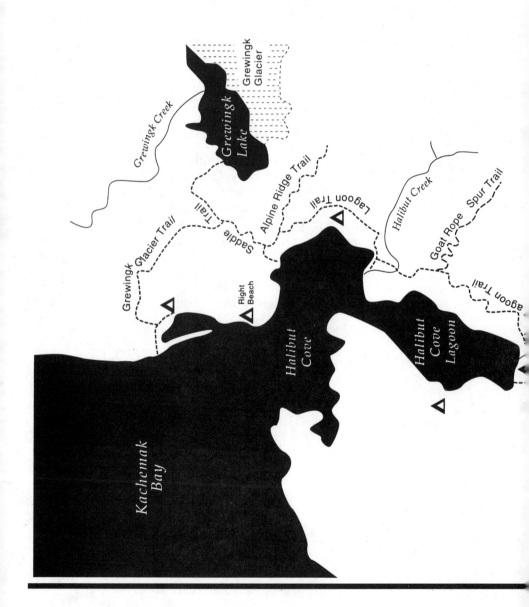

glacier's lake beach is enjoyable. Icebergs float across the lake to the beach when the wind is just right. There is a small stream near the junction of this trail and Saddle Trail.

HIKE 23: *LAGOON TRAIL*

General description: A one-day hike from Halibut Cove to the Ranger Station in Halibut Cove Lagoon.
General location: Halibut Cove in Kachemak Bay State Park
Trail begins: North east end of Halibut Cove; same location as Alpine Ridge and Saddle Trail trailhead
Trail ends: Ranger Station at south east end of Halibut Cove Lagoon
Maps: USGS Seldovia C4
Difficulty: Moderate to difficult
Length: 5.5 miles one way
Elevation: Sea level to 1200 feet
Special attractions: Variety of terrain, spruce forest, tide flats, and streams
Best season: June through September

Fishing for salmon is a bonus for hikers in Kachemak Bay State Park.

For more information: State of Alaska, Division of Parks and Recreation, P.O. Box 321, Homer, Alaska 99603, (907) 235-7024

Finding the trailhead: Lagoon, Alpine Ridge and Saddle trails have a common trailhead in the northeast corner of Halibut Cove Lagoon.

The hike: From the junction with Alpine Ridge Trail, Lagoon Trail winds along Halibut Cove and passes through a wet, boggy area to Halibut Creek Delta. You may be able to ford the river at low tide but water can be high, depending on weather. Pick up the trail again by walking upstream for about 200 yards on the south side or walk around the delta on the tide flats. A series of steep switchbacks then lead through a spruce forest to where the trail intersects Goat Rope Spur Trail at 1,200 feet. The trail continues downhill and south, across Falls Creek to the end of the lagoon and to the Ranger Station. Here you may take the stairs down to the stream where a sign directs you to China Poot Lake Trail.

HIKE 24: *SADDLE TRAIL*

General description: A steep trail connecting three other trails in Kachemak Bay Trail System.

General location: Kachemak Bay State Park.

Trail begins: Northeast end of Halibut Cove and same spot as Lagoon and Alpine Trails trailhead.

Trail ends: By intersecting Grewingk Glacier Trail.

Maps: USGS Seldovia C4.

Difficulty: Moderate.

Length: one mile one way.

Elevation: Sea level to 400 feet.

Special attractions: Access to three other trails.

Best season: June through September.

For more information: State of Alaska, Division of Parks and Recreation, P.O. Box 321, Homer, Alaska 99603, (907) 235-7024.

Finding the trailhead: Saddle Trail accesses Alpine Ridge and Lagoon trails and also connects with Grewingk Glacier Trail.

The hike: Saddle Trail leads over the saddle between Halibut Cove and Grewingk Glacier and is steep on the Halibut Cove side. No transportation is available from the trailhead to Glacier Spit or Halibut Cove unless you have made prior arrangements. It is not possible to hike the beach from the trailhead to Right Beach campsite due to steep cliffs. Saddle Trail trailhead is a popular spot to land boats during bad weather. Please respect private property near this trail.

HIKE 25: *WOSNESENSKI TRAIL*

General description: A short hike and a glacier river fording.
General location: Kachemak Bay State Park.
Trail begins: China Pook Peak trailhead at the south east end of China Poot Lake.
Trail ends: Wosnesenski Valley.
Maps: USGS Seldovia C4.
Difficulty: Easy to moderate.
Length: Two miles one way.
Elevation: 200 feet to 300 feet.
Special attractions: Geologic fault formed lakes.
Best season: June and September.
For more information: State of Alaska, Division of Parks and Recreation, P.O. Box 321, Homer, Alaska 99603, (907) 235-7024.
Finding the trailhead: Begin the Wosnesenski Trail where it meets the China Poot Peak Trail, about ten minutes after crossing Inlet Stream Bridge at China Poot Lake.

The hike: This easy trail winds along the shoreline of three lakes formed by a geologic fault. After about thirty minutes on the trail, you will find a good camping area in a stand of cottonwood by the lake. In another half hour, the trail climbs over a low saddle and drops down into the valley. Be careful if you decide to cross the rivers while exploring the valley. Glacial rivers are murky and you cannot see the bottom. They vary in depth and current depending on weather. Water level is usually lower in early summer and much higher in July and August when glacier melting is greater. Choose a slow-moving, shallow spot to cross. Water above thigh level is too hazardous to cross. A pair of tennis shoes will make crossing these icy, cloudy rivers easier.

Several kinds of berries can be found growing along the edge of trails.

KENAI PENINSULA TRAILS

The Kenai Peninsula is the outdoor playground for over half of Alaska's residents. Old trapper, mining, explorer, and Native trails extend off the peninsula's road system to wilderness areas. Hikes as short as .5 mile and others over one hundred miles long attract hikers. Almost every skill level, climatic condition, and personal interest is covered.

The Kenai Peninsula includes the communities of Kenai, Homer, Seward, Soldotna, and small villages. The peninsula begins forty miles south of Anchorage at Portage and extends to Seward and Homer, seventy-seven miles beyond Soldotna. Nearly all Kenai Peninsula hike trailheads are located immediately off the road system, and either terminate at another road or converge with another trail.

Kenai Peninsula hikes are designed, administered, and maintained with the recreation hiker in mind. The trailheads are well marked and easy to find. Adequate parking is readily available at the trailheads.

The Kenai Peninsula has well-developed and maintained hiking trails and numerous forest service cabins to help you achieve your desired wilderness hiking experience. The eastern half of the Kenai Peninsula lies within the 5.8 million-acre Chugach National Forest. Almost 200 miles of trails, most of Chugach National Forest's hiking trails, are on the Kenai Peninsula. These trails lead to backcountry cabins, and popular fishing spots.

The peninsula is a miniature Alaska. Some of all habitat types can be found: tundra, mountains, wetlands, and forests play host to wolf, lynx, beaver, coyote, caribou, wolverine, black bear, Dall sheep, mountain goat, grizzly bear,

This old Kenai Peninsula cabin was built as an overnight stop for dog mushers carrying mail from Seward to old Kenai.

and small birds and mammals. It is a mixture of ice fields and flatlands, rugged mountains and rocky shoreline, sandy beaches and glaciers, and is within easy weekend driving distance of Anchorage. It is a popular recreation destination with the trails spread out to adequately offer delightful backcountry and wilderness experiences.

Summer temperatures on the Kenai Peninsula generally range in the sixties and seventies. The region enjoys up to nineteen hours of daylight in summer. Kenai Peninsula annual precipitation ranges from nineteen inches at Kenai to twenty-three inches at Homer and on the mountainous eastern section, precipitation exceeds forty inches annually. Late summer and fall weather is wet, and raingear is recommended for hiking. The first snow normally falls in October and spring breakup on low lakes is in May, and on high lakes in July.

The Seward and Sterling highways trisect the heart-shaped land mass and almost all hiking and other outdoor recreation is achieved from these roads and secondary access roads: Skilak Lake Loop Road, Swanson River Road, Swan Lake Road, and Funny River Road.

Hundreds of trails, too many to be covered by one book, administered by various state and government agencies cover the peninsula. There are nine trails in the Skilak Lake area alone that are not included here. The hikes here represent the wide variety and number of hikes available to peninsula hikers.

HIKE 26: *CARTER LAKE TRAIL*

General description: Carter Lake Trail allows hiking recreationists to penetrate sub-alpine and alpine country with only 1.5 miles of travel. A good trail for a dayhike or multi-day trip with tent camping at Carter or Crescent Lakes.
General location: Johnson Pass, thirty-four miles out of Seward on the Seward Highway
Trail begins: Mile thirty-four of Seward Highway
Trail ends: Northeast of Crescent Lake
Maps: USGS Seward B7, C7
Difficulty: Moderate to difficult
Length: 3.3 miles
Elevation: 300 to 5,000 feet
Special attractions: Wildflowers, scenery, fishing
Best season: June through September
For more information: Chugach National Forest, Seward Ranger District, P.O. Box 390, 334 4th Avenue, Seward, Alaska 99664 (907) 224-3374
Finding the trailhead: Trailhead is easy to find at Mile 34, Seward Highway.

The hike: Carter Lake Trail is on the roadbed of an old jeep road originally built by the City of Seward as part of a now defunct plan for water development. Although the first 1.5 miles is steep, it is a good trail for families and young, beginning hikers. The last half of the trail is level and all of it is well maintained. Some areas above tree line may be muddy in places.

On the first and steep half of the trail, hikers move through hemlock forests.

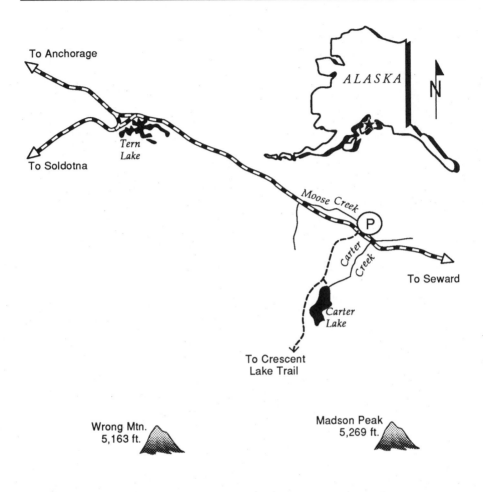

Wetter areas are overgrown with alder and willow. As the trail levels out, vegetation changes to sub-alpine with low-growing shrubs and a multitude of wildflowers: lupine, columbine, chocolate lilies, and forget-me-nots. This level terrain offers good camping sites and excellent vistas.

The creek flowing into Carter Lake is wide and without a bridge but not too deep. Expect to get wet. Steep and bushy terrain around the west end of Crescent Lake makes summer access is difficult. There is a Forest Service public recreation cabin on Carter Lake for use by hikers and may be reserved by mail or at any Chugach National Forest Service office as much as 179 days in advance of planned stay. Occupancy is by permit only for a cost of $20 per night per party. Carter Lake Trail is closed to saddle and pack animals from April 1 to June 30. Snow machines may be used during winter months from November 30 through May 1.

HIKE 27: *CRESCENT CREEK TRAIL*

General description: A good family trail traveling through birch and sub-alpine terrain between Right and Wrong Mountains.

General location: Trailhead is off the Sterling Highway at Mile 3.5 of Quartz Creek Road

Trail begins: Mile 3.5 of Quartz Creek Road, Mile forty-five Sterling Highway

Trail ends: Crescent Lake

Maps: USGS Seward B7, C7, C8

Difficulty: Easy

Length: 6.5 miles

Elevation: 300 to 1,500 feet

Special attractions: Fishing, cabin, scenery, mining activity

Best season: June through September

For more information: Chugach National Forest, Seward Ranger District, P.O. Box 390, 334 4th Avenue, Seward, Alaska 99664 (907) 224-3374

Finding the trailhead: Seven miles west of the Seward/Sterling junction, at mile forty-five of the Sterling Highway, turn south onto Quartz Creek Road. Take the left fork. Drive past Quartz Creek and Crescent Creek campgrounds to the trailhead at Mile 3.5 Quartz Creek Road.

The hike: The trail follows a small creek gradually upwards through birch-aspen forests, climbs over a low ridge, and drops into scenic Crescent Creek Canyon. It alternates between meadows and forested areas. The meadows appeal to hikers who are interested in wildflowers because of the variety and abundance.

Crescent Creek Trail is a well-maintained level path with long gradual grades. Crescent Lake lies just below the tree line and there are good camping sites located near the lake. Snow on the trail in shady areas persists into late spring. Winter winds and snow loads down trees and hinder travel in winter and spring. There mayalso be times of extreme avalanche danger on the trail in winter and early spring.

Wildlife include moose, black and brown bear, and Dall sheep. Hunting for these species is in designated seasons. Grayling fishing in Crescent Lake is excellent with trophy-size fish available in the western half. Grayling are also in Crescent Creek.

My teenage daughter and her friends hiked Crescent Creek Trail and camped at the lake. It was her first overnight hike without her parents. She expressed concern about getting lost, so I obtained a USGS map of the area and went over it thoroughly with her. I knew the trail was well marked and there was little danger she and her friends would not find the way.

The night before she left I helped her load her pack and put the map in the map pocket. I drew special attention to my placing the map in her pack. I told her that when she got out on the trail she could impress the other girls by bringing out the map and identifying their position. I suggested she not tell them she had a map until they were well into the hike.

After she had gone to bed I replaced the map with a three foot by five foot poster of her favorite football player. The girls got a good laugh when my daughter showed them her map. They hung the poster on a tree in their camp. It is probably the closest Joe Namath will get to Crescent Lake. My daughter's high school nickname was "The Happy Hiker."

There is a Forest Service public recreation cabin on Crescent Lake for use by hikers and may be reserved by mail or at any Chugach National Forest Service office as much as 179 days in advance of planned stay. Occupancy is by permit only for a cost of $20 per night per party. The cabin is available year-round. This is an excellent family hike, day hike, or a two-day trip with tent camping at the lake or stay in Crescent Lake Cabin. A boat is provided for those

HIKE 27: *CRESCENT CREEK TRAIL*

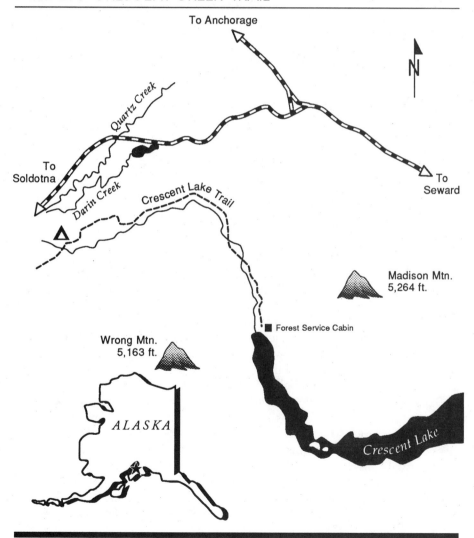

To Anchorage

Quartz Creek

To Soldotna

Darin Creek

Crescent Lake Trail

To Seward

Madison Mtn. 5,264 ft.

■ Forest Service Cabin

Wrong Mtn. 5,163 ft.

ALASKA

Crescent Lake

N

reserving the cabin. As a courtesy to hikers staying at the cabin, please camp in other areas out of sight of the cabin.

Crescent Creek Trail is closed to saddle and pack animals from April 1 to June 30. Snow machines may be used during winter months from November 30 through May 1. For winter access to the Crescent Lake Cabin use Carter Lake Trail and traverse across frozen Crescent Lake, except during extreme avalanche hazard. There are active mines in the area and miners may obtain permits and use motorized vehicles on the trail.

HIKE 28: *DEVIL'S PASS ACCESS TRAIL*

General description: Hiking into an area of good fishing, scenic environs, and connecting with Resurrection Pass National Recreation Trail at mile 21.4
General location: Off the Seward Highway to Devil's Pass near the summit of Resurrection Pass
Trail begins: Mile thirty-nine Seward Highway
Trail ends: Devil's Pass Cabin where the trail intersects with Resurrection Pass National Recreation Trail
Maps: USGS Seward C7, C8
Difficulty: Moderate
Length: ten miles
Elevation: 100 to 2,500 feet
Special attractions: Scenery, wildlife, cabin
Best season: June through September
For more information: Chugach National Forest, Seward Ranger District, P.O. Box 390, 334 4th Avenue, Seward, Alaska 99664 (907) 224-3374
Finding the trailhead: Trailhead is on west side of Seward Highway at Mile thirty-nine.

The hike: Well-maintained Devil's Pass Trail, established in the late 1800s by prospectors, has steep, uphill grades for the first eight miles and a slight decline after the pass. Snow in shady areas along the trail and at Devil's Pass may persist into early summer. Varied scenery includes: mountains, forests, streams, lakes, and alpine areas with spruce/birch forests at the lower elevations which blend into tundra with wildflowers. Along the trail hikers will observe reddish-gray colored dead trees killed by spruce bark beetles. These trees are a major fire hazard! Be extra careful with fire.

Devil's Pass Trail provides access to seldom-traveled alpine valleys fanning out from the main route. The valley trails connect with the Resurrection Pass National Recreation Trail for an extended trip. Cross-country hiking in these valleys is at or above tree line for easy travel. It is a good two-day trip with camping at the Beaver Pond tent site, two miles from the trailhead, or in Devil's Pass Cabin.

Wildlife includes moose, wolves, grouse, marmot, caribou, wolverine, and ptarmigan. Hunting for these species is allowed in appropriate season. Good fishing for Dolly Varden is in Devil's Pass Lake.

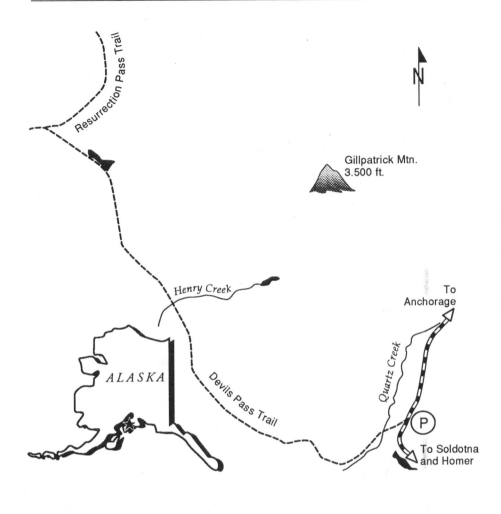

Winter storms and whiteouts are frequent above tree line, extreme avalanche hazard exists beyond Mile three, and winter travel is not recommended.

There is a Forest Service public recreation cabin, located above tree line, ten miles from trailhead, for use by hikers, and may be reserved by mail or at any Chugach National Forest Service office as much as 179 days in advance of planned stay. Occupancy is by permit only for a cost of $20 per night per party. As a courtesy to hikers staying at the cabin, please camp in other areas out of sight of the cabin.

Devil's Pass Trail is closed to saddle and pack animals from April 1 to June 30. Snow machines may be used during winter months from November 30 through February 16.

HIKE 29: *GULL ROCK TRAIL*

General description: A hiking trail just off the Turnagain Arm Beach near the old gold mining town of Hope

General location: Southwest of the small town of Hope

Trail begins: Porcupine Campground at the terminus of the Hope Highway

Trail ends: Gull Rock

Maps: USGS Seward D8

Difficulty: Easy

Length: 5.1 miles

Elevation: 300 to 750 feet

Special attractions: History, wildlife, scenery, berry picking

Best season: June through September

For more information: Chugach National Forest, Seward Ranger District, P.O. Box 390, 334 4th Avenue, Seward, Alaska 99664 (907) 224-3374

Finding the trailhead: At mile 56.5 Seward Highway, turn west onto the Hope Highway. Drive 17.5 miles to, and through, Hope and then to Porcupine Campground, west of Hope. Trail starts at the far northwest end of the campground.

The hike: The trail is a well-maintained, level path with long gradual grades. It follows a portion of an old wagon road built at the turn of the century and is very scenic as it parallels, well above high tide, Turnagain Arm of Cook Inlet. Ruins of an old sawmill and remains of a cabin and stable can be seen from Johnson Creek. Edible berries can be found along the trail. It is suitable for family outings and day hiking.

Trail passes through diverse vegetation: mosses, spruce forests, birch-aspen woods, alder-choked gullies, low bush cranberry patches, tundra with tiny spruce, and hemlock forests with a carpet of moss. The trail leads through the woods with many breaks through the stands of trees for views of the arm, the shoreline, and on clear days, Mt. McKinley. The destination, Gull Rock, protrudes into the water inviting the hiker to listen, look, and smell the splendor of water, sky, and land. Although the old road continues beyond Gull Rock, the trail is not maintained. Carry your binoculars to get an up-close look at bear, moose, white beluga whale, and birds.

Warning: Do not venture onto the tide flats. The glacial mud is like quicksand and can trap the unwary hiker. The composition of the mud is such that it will support a person's weight for a moment. When stopped, a person's boots will break through the top, drier surface and begin to sink into wet, sticky mud. An attempt to free one foot will invariably cause the other to sink deeper and in just a few seconds it is possible that a hiker could be trapped. This type of situation has led to drowning in incoming tides. If caught in inlet tidal mud the best thing to do is to act quickly. Don't be afraid to get wet and muddy. Fall forward, taking weight off your feet and break the suction hold of the mud on lower extremities. Roll out of the danger area before standing up. Yes, it is wet and dirty to roll around in Cook Inlet mud, but it will save your life.

HIKE 30: *HOPE POINT TRAIL*

General description: A two-mile hike on Turnagain Arm with vistas of surrounding mountains and ocean
General location: Hope, opposite Alyeska on Turnagain Arm
Trail begins: Porcupine Campground
Trail ends: Hope Point
Maps: USGS Seward D8
Difficulty: Moderate
Length: 2.5 miles
Elevation: 500 to 3,630 feet

HIKE 29: *GULL ROCK*   HIKE 30: *HOPE POINT*

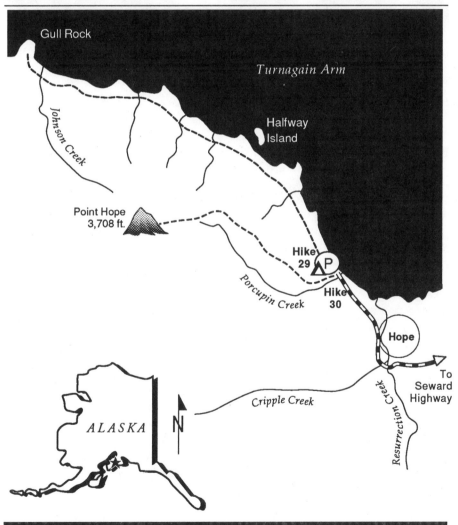

Hikers are never far from wildflowers to photograph.

Special attractions: Scenery, wildflowers, berry picking
Best season: June through September
For more information: Chugach National Forest, Seward Ranger District, P.O. Box 390, 334 4th Avenue, Seward, Alaska 99664 (907) 224-3374
Finding the trailhead: Drive seventy-one miles south of Anchorage on the Seward Highway to the Hope cut-off at mile 56.5. Follow the Hope Highway, past Hope to the road's end at the Chugach National Forest's Porcupine Campground. Walk the road back toward the entrance to tiny Porcupine Creek. The trail begins on the right-hand side of the stream.

The hike: The historic gold mining community of Hope, originally a mining camp, was established in 1896 as Hope City. It was founded by gold seekers working Resurrection Creek and its tributaries. Despite Hope's history, the trail itself does not offer any historical significance. A microwave tower along the trail was built in 1973 and is a landmark for cars driving on the Seward Highway along Turnagain Arm.

This scenic trail offers many good views of Resurrection Creek Valley. The trail's highlight, however, is the impressive views of Turnagain Arm, Cook Inlet, Fire Island, and the Chugach Mountains. The first mile or so is suitable for young children, but after this it may be too strenuous. Beginning in an alder/cottonwood forest the trail continues through alpine meadows lush with wildflowers in spring and early summer and eventually goes above tree line where the grassy mountainside is broken by rocky knolls. The first .3 mile meanders beside Porcupine Creek and is fairly easy going. After this, the trail is steep and strenuous as it climbs from the creek to above tree line and on to

Hope Point. Edible berries can be found along the trail. Wildlife in the area includes bear and moose, and look for beluga whale in Turnagain arm.

Although not marked with signs, the trail is clearly defined up to the microwave tower. From the tower to the summit, the trail is less clearly defined but still obvious. Some scrambling is required to reach the actual summit. This trail makes a great day hike, and adventurous hikers can fan out to other summits in the Kenai Mountains for possible overnight hikes.

HIKE 31: *PRIMROSE TRAIL*

General description: Forested hike to access Mt. Ascension.
General location: Seward highway in Johnson Pass area.
Trail begins: Mile 17 of the Seward Highway at Primrose Campground.
Trail ends: At the end of Lost Lake Trail.
Maps: USGS Seward B7.
Difficulty: Moderate.
Length: 6.5 miles to Lost Lake and eight miles to Lost Lake Trail.
Elevation: 300 to 1,800 feet.
Special attractions: Scenery, wildflowers, fishing.
Best season: June through September.
For more information: Chugach National Forest, Seward Ranger District, P.O. Box 390, 334 4th Avenue, Seward, Alaska 99664 (907) 224-3374.
Finding the trailhead: At Mile 17, Seward Highway, turn northwest and travel 1.5 miles to Primrose Campground. There is a trailhead sign in the campground.

The hike: The Primrose Trail follows an old mining road to historical Primrose Mine which is still active. After Mile 4, the well maintained trail becomes steep and eroded. The first 4.5 miles are through dense spruce forest with limited viewing spots. At Mile 3 there is a spur trail leading to a viewpoint overlooking Porcupine Creek Falls. There are no developed facilities at the viewpoint. It's just a place to see the falls and a good destination for a day hike or a family outing.

Once above tree line the trail may be boggy and the path with a steeper grade is not maintained. As the trail follows an old mining road, there remains evidence of past mineral exploration. An active mine can be seen at about 3.75 miles. Please respect the miner's private property and equipment. The last two to three miles are at timberline with dramatic views of mountains and lakes. After reaching timberline, follow the 4 X 4 pos-sight markers to Lost Lake. These sight markers are provided to give general direction to the lake during fog and whiteout conditions. A bridge is erected across Lost Creek for hiking beyond.

This is an excellent multi-day trip for fishing at Lost Lake and for enjoying spectacular scenery with good backcountry campsites near the trail and at Lost Lake.

Mt. Ascension, forming the west border of Lost Lake, requires mountaineering skills to climb to its 5,710-foot summit. By hiking along the north end of the lake and walking west up the valley, hikers get a view of the steep north side of Mt. Ascension and increase their possibility of seeing black bear and mountain goats. If a longer, but easy, cross-country trip is desired, follow the

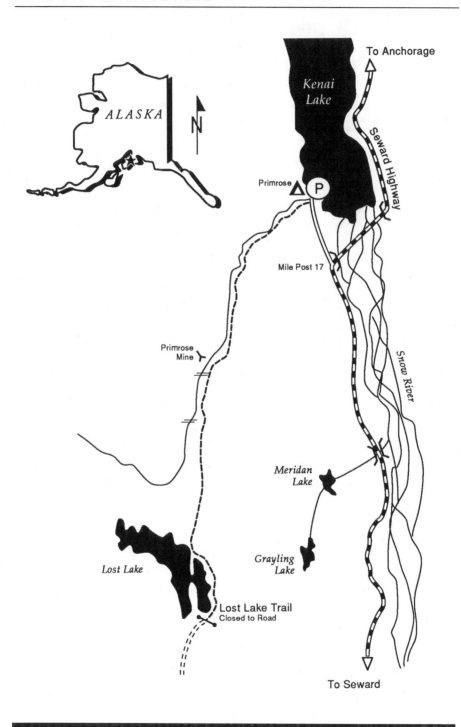

drainages to Cooper Lake.

This is a good place to see black bear in the spring. Wildlife includes moose, grouse, marmot, ptarmigan, black bear, mountain goat, and Dall sheep. Fishing for rainbow trout is good in Lost Lake and hunting is permitted in designated seasons.

Lost Lake Trailhead is closed. The trail crosses private property, hikers are not permitted at this time, and trespassers have been threatened. Do not return to the highway by the Lost Lake Trail.

This is an outstanding area for skiing or snowmobiling into the alpine areas. Winter travel is relatively safe, but whiteout conditions and disorientating fog may occur. Be prepared for rapid weather changes.

HIKE 32: *PTARMIGAN CREEK TRAIL*

General description: Hiking and camping in an azure lake region that is suitable for dayhikes and multi-day trips with backcountry camping by a lake.
General location: Kenai Peninsula.
Trail begins: Trailhead at Ptarmigan Campground.
Trail ends: East end of Ptarmigan Lake.
Maps: USGS Seward B6, B7.
Difficulty: Moderate.
Length: 3.5 miles to west end of Ptarmigan Lake and 7.5 miles to east end of Ptarmigan Lake.
Elevation: 300 to 900 feet.
Special attractions: Scenery, fishing, wildlife. Hikers spending the night at Ptarmigan Campground and hiking the first two miles of the steeper section of the trail will be rewarded with reflections in the turquoise lake.
Best season: June through September.
For more information: Chugach National Forest, Seward Ranger District, P.O. Box 390, 334 4th Avenue, Seward, Alaska 99664 (907) 224-3374.
Finding the trailhead: At Mile 23, Seward Highway, turn east into Ptarmigan Campground. The trail begins at the south end of the campground.

The hike: The west end of Ptarmigan Lake is 3.5 miles from the trailhead. The trail to the lake follows the creek upstream and leaves the spruce forest after the second mile, ascending to the left through a large meadow and back to wooded area. The path is in hilly terrain the first 2.5 miles but level for the remaining hike to the lake's east end. There are many good places for viewing the surrounding mountains and alpine areas. There are good campsites at both ends of the lake. It is four miles to the east end of the lake from the west campsite. Hikers may visit the remains of an old mining cabin on the eastern shore of Ptarmigan Lake.

For mountaineering, the trail provides access to Andy Simons Mountain which forms the southern boundary of Ptarmigan Lake. For longer, backcountry trips, twenty-five to thirty miles, follow an old, overgrown, un-maintained trail up the drainage beyond Ptarmigan Lake and over Snow River Pass to Lower

Paradise Lake. There is a Forest Service public recreation cabin on Lower Paradise Lake for use by hikers, and may be reserved by mail or at any Chugach National Forest Service office as much as 179 days in advance of planned stay. Occupancy is by permit only for a cost of $20 per night per party. A boat is provided for those reserving the cabin. As a courtesy to hikers staying at the cabin, please camp in other areas out of sight of the cabin.

Follow Snow River downstream along remains of Paradise Valley Trail back to railroad and eventually to Seward Highway.

Along the trail hikers may expect to see bear, moose, mountain goats, and

HIKE 32: *PTARMIGAN CREEK*   HIKE 37: *VICTOR CREEK*

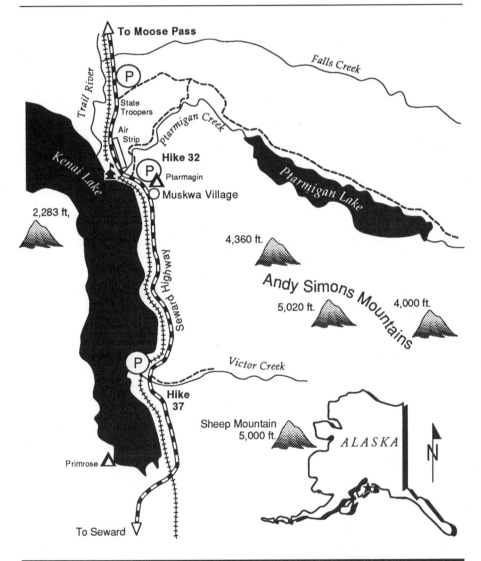

Dall sheep. Goats and sheep are on the mountains surrounding the lake. There is hunting for these species in designated seasons and fishing for Dolly Varden and rainbow trout in Ptarmigan Creek, and grayling in Ptarmigan Lake. Salmon fishing is prohibited in these areas, but it is an excellent spot for viewing many brilliant, red sockeye salmon if hiking after the first week in August.

HIKE 33: *RAINBOW LAKE TRAIL*

General description: A short hike to a valley lake for camping, resting, and fishing.
General location: Off Snug Harbor Road in the Russian Lakes area.
Trail begins: Rainbow Lake trailhead on Cooper Lake Road.
Trail ends: Rainbow Lake.
Maps: USGS Seward B8.
Difficulty: Easy.
Length: .5 mile.
Elevation: 100 to 150 feet.
Special attractions: Fishing, wildlife, scenery.
Best season: June through September.
For more information: Chugach National Forest, Seward Ranger District, P.O. Box 390, 334 4th Avenue, Seward, Alaska 99664 (907) 224-3374.
Finding the trailhead: At end of Kenai Lake at Mile 48 of the Sterling Highway, in the town of Cooper Landing, turn onto Snug Harbor Road. Travel eleven

If bears hear hikers, they will usually run away.

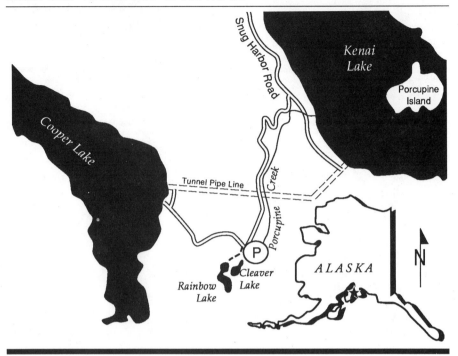

miles to Cooper Lake and the Rainbow Lake trailhead. Parking area capacity is three vehicles.

The hike: Rainbow Lake, nestled in a small valley with two other lakes, is an excellent place for campfires and tent camping. The level trail is without grade and travels through sub-alpine and hemlock terrain. Most of the trail is maintained and graveled to keep hikers out of mud in swampy areas. This small lake offers good rainbow trout fishing during the spring. Daisy, cinquefoil, lady's tresses, and flowering dogwood are common wildflowers. The trail's short length makes it an ideal family hike.

Many Anchorage suburbanites use Bird Creek Trail for a spring warm-up to summer's hiking. One lovely spring day we decided on a warm-up hike. The weather was so nice we drove past Bird Creek and on to the Kenai Peninsula and ended up at Rainbow Lake Trail. It looked like we would be the lake's first visitors for the year.

When we arrived at the lake we discovered three fishing rods propped up on forked sticks. Lines had been cast about twenty feet offshore as evidenced by three white bobbers. The mid-afternoon spring sun was radiating its heat and warming all solid objects. As we arrived one of the bobbers began bobbing and a young man came charging down the beach from a secluded area we were unable to see. We soon discovered that three young men had made Rainbow Lake their spring warm-up fishing, camping, and hiking spot. They were sitting out of the wind, on the beach, in the sun, reading and watching their fishing rods. The first young man grabbed the rod, set the hook, landed a small rainbow. From their conversation we determined that the fish ended up being part of the camping trio's dinner. We returned by hiking the half mile to our car and left the lake to the Three Musketeers and their trout dinner.

HIKE 34: *RESURRECTION PASS TRAIL*

General description: This trail was used in the 1890s by miners traveling from Seward to the gold fields at Hope, and is now the most popular hike in the Chugach National Forest. There are eight Forest Service cabins along the trail.
General location: If the hike begins at the northern trailhead, the trail goes over Resurrection Pass from the mining area south of Hope to Mile 52 on the Sterling highway near Cooper Landing. If the hike begins at the southern trailhead the trail goes over Resurrection Pass from Mile 52 on the Sterling highway near Cooper Landing to the mining area south of Hope.
Trail begins: The north trailhead is at the south end of Resurrection Creek, near Hope. The south trailhead is at Mile 52 on the Sterling Highway near Cooper Landing.
Trail ends: Traveling south from the trailhead at Resurrection Creek the trail ends at Mile 52 on the Sterling Highway near Cooper Landing. Traveling north from the trailhead at Mile 52 on the Sterling Highway near Cooper Landing the trail ends at Resurrection Creek, near Hope.
Maps: USGS Seward A7, A8, B8.
Difficulty: Easy.
Length: 38.6 miles.
Elevation: five to 2,100 feet.
Special attractions: Vegetation, scenery, wildlife, and following the trail of gold miners.
Best season: June through September.
For more information: Chugach National Forest, Seward Ranger District, P.O. Box 390, 334 4th Avenue, Seward, Alaska 99664 (907) 224-3374.
Finding the trailhead: The northern trailhead can be found by driving to Mile 15 of the Hope Highway, then turn South onto Resurrection Creek Road. Travel four miles to the trailhead parking area. The southern trailhead is found at The Resurrection Pass National Recreation Trail sign at Mile 52 of the Sterling Highway. There is a parking area at the trailhead.

The hike: Resurrection Pass National Recreation Trail, first used in the late 1800s by gold prospectors, is now a wel-maintained, level path, with gradual grades, and some steep places with switchbacks. It is the most-used trail in the Chugach National Forest and connects with Russian Lakes and Resurrection River Trails to complete a seventy-two-mile trek from Seward to Hope. It also connects with Devil's Pass Trail for twenty-eight or thirty-one-mile trip to Devil's Pass trailhead depending on which Resurrection Pass trailhead is used as a starting point. It incorporates spectacular scenery of spruce/aspen forests

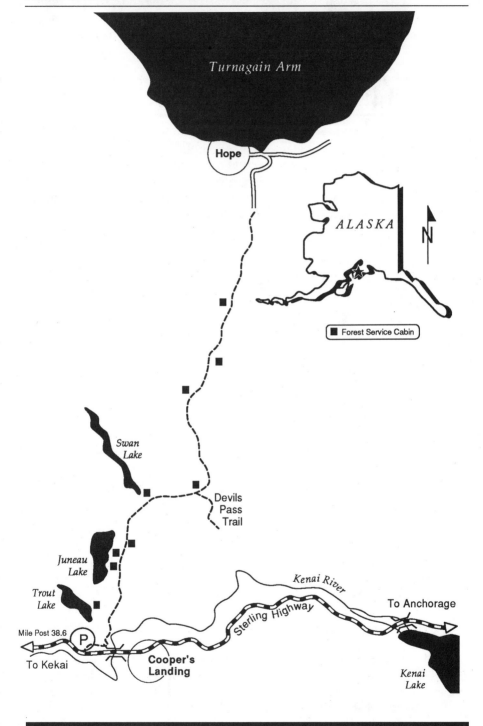

Turnagain Arm

Hope

ALASKA

N

■ Forest Service Cabin

Swan Lake

Devils
Pass
Trail

Juneau Lake

Trout Lake

Kenai River

To Anchorage

Sterling Highway

Mile Post 38.6

P

To Kekai

Cooper's Landing

Kenai Lake

Beaver Dam near Resurrection Pass.

at lower elevations and higher alpine tundra with wildflowers above the tree line. Heavy snow on Resurrection Pass persists into late spring.

Near Wolf creek, hikers pass through a Forest Service-prescribed burn area for improved moose habitat. Along the trail, hikers will observe reddish-gray colored dead trees killed by spruce bark beetles. These trees are a major fire hazard! Be extra careful with fire.

Wildlife includes moose, wolves, caribou, grouse, ptarmigan, Dall sheep, mountain goats, and black and brown bear. Hunting for these species is permitted during designated seasons. Fish for pink salmon during July and August in Resurrection Creek and Dolly Varden, rainbow, and grayling in Juneau Lake. Dolly Varden, red salmon, rainbow trout may be taken in Swan Lake, and Dolly Varden, rainbow trout, red, pink, and silver salmon are available in Kenai River. Red salmon spawn in Swan Lake outlet during July and August. Hikers can even pan for gold in designated recreational gold panning areas.

The Hope area is one of our family's special spots. Once when hiking along Resurrection Pass Trail we spotted our pick-up car and driver waiting near the road. My children decided to have some fun on the last steep slope of the trail by sliding on their sit-downs in the tall grass. The grass was well over their heads and it was impossible for them to see where they were going. The pick-up driver could only see the matted grass trails left behind them. They had a good time and laughed about their green behinds. Only after a thorough washing did they realize that they had permanently stained their hiking clothes green as a lasting memento of Resurrection Pass Trail.

The trail is used all year and winter travel is relatively safe, but may be icy in some areas. It is difficult to follow the trail from East Creek to Resurrection Pass during or after heavy snowfall and the same is true from Swan Lake to Resurrection Pass. Downed trees caused by wind and winter storms can hamper travel in winter and spring.

Eight Forest Service public recreation cabins are on Resurrection Pass National Recreation Trail for use by hikers, and may be reserved by mail or at any Chugach National Forest Service office as much as 179 days in advance of planned stay. Occupancy is by permit only for a cost of $20 per night per party. A boat is provided at lake side cabins for those reserving the cabin. As a courtesy to hikers staying at the cabins, please camp in other areas out of sight of the cabin. Numerous designated campsites with fire grates are located along the trail.

HIKE 35: RESURRECTION RIVER TRAIL

General description: This wilderness hiking trail, with occasional views of river and mountains, completes the seventy-two-mile trek from Hope to Seward.
General location: Travels from Seward and connects with Russian Lakes Trail and then the Resurrection Pass National Recreation Trail.
Trail begins: Mile 8 of Exit Glacier Road near Seward.
Trail ends: Junction with Russian Lakes Trail.
Maps: Seward A7, A8, B8.
Difficulty: Easy.
Length: sixteen miles.
Elevation: five to 1,050 feet.
Special attractions:
Best season: June through September.
For more information: Chugach National Forest, Seward Ranger District, P.O. Box 390, 334 4th Avenue, Seward, Alaska 99664 (907) 224-3374.
Finding the trailhead: At Mile 4 of the Seward Highway, turn northwest onto Exit Glacier Road. Trailhead is at Mile 8 on Exit Glacier Road. The area receives a large amount or rain during summer months and Exit Glacier Road is subject to closure due to flooding. During winter months Exit Glacier Road is only plowed for first 1.5 miles.

The hike: This trail has been used as a route between Seward and the rest of the Kenai Peninsula since prehistoric times. It is a level path with long gradual grades. The trail may be wet and boggy in places with poor drainage and is difficult to walk on when raining. Resurrection River Trail connects with Russian Lakes and Resurrection Pass National Recreation trails to complete a seventy-two-mile trek from Seward to Hope Alaska. The first eight miles of the trail passes through dense forest with the remainder gradually climbing and offering excellent vistas. Two metal bridges span Martin and Boulder creeks.

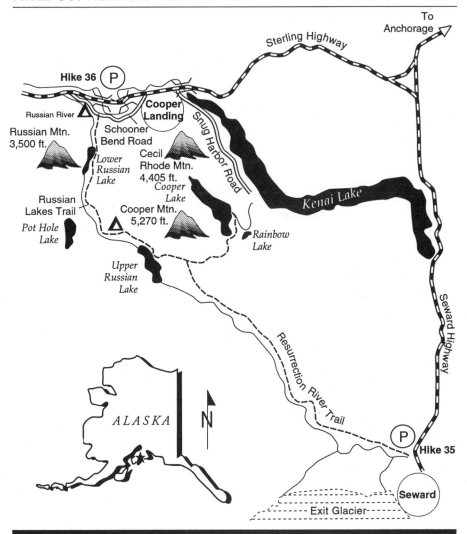

The forested areas along the trail provide excellent habitat for beaver and pine marten, and a high bear density offers possibility for viewing bears in natural environment. Wildlife includes bear, moose, wolves, coyotes, Dall sheep, and mountain goats. Hunting for these species in designated seasons is permitted. Fishing along the trail is exceptional. The area west of the Resurrection River is managed by the National Park Service which has special hunting and fishing regulations.

There is a Forest Service public recreation cabin, located one mile south of Boulder Creek at about 9.5 miles south of the junction with Russian Lakes Trail, for use by hikers, and may be reserved by mail or at any Chugach National Forest Service office as much as 179 days in advance of planned stay. Occupancy is by permit only for a cost of $20 per night per party. As a courtesy to hikers staying at the cabin, please camp in other areas out of sight of the cabin..

Special consideration should be given when planning winter travel on the trail because it is difficult due to steep side hills. Winter storms and whiteouts are frequent above tree line. Resurrection River Trail is closed to saddle and pack animals from April 1 to June 30. Snow machines may be used during winter months from November 30 through May 1.

HIKE 36: *RUSSIAN LAKES TRAIL*

General description: A trail popular with anglers, Russian Lakes Trail connects with Resurrection Pass National Recreation Trail and a portion of it is part of the seventy-two-mile hike from Hope to Seward.
General location: Kenai Peninsula.
Trail begins: Either at Cooper Lake or Russian River Campground.
Trail ends: If the hike begins at the trailhead at Cooper Lake it ends at the trailhead at Russian River Campground. If the hike begins at the trailhead at Russian River Campground it ends at the trailhead at Cooper Lake. The trail intersects with Resurrection River Trail.
Maps: USGS Seward B8 and USGS Kenai B1.
Difficulty: Easy.
Length: twenty-one miles.
Elevation: Five to 1,100 feet.
Special attractions: Fishing, scenery, and connecting trails
Best season: June through September.
For more information: Chugach National Forest, Seward Ranger District, P.O. Box 390, 334 4th Avenue, Seward, Alaska 99664 (907) 224-3374.
Finding the trailhead: The north-end trailhead is found at Mile 52 of the Sterling Highway in the Russian River Campground. Trailhead parking is one mile into the campground. The east-end trailhead is found by driving to Mile 48 of the Sterling Highway, and turning onto Snug Harbor Road. Then travel nine miles to Cooper Lake Road and three miles to parking.

The hike: This well-maintained, level and gradually-graded trail was established in the late 1800s by gold prospectors. The trail connects with the Resurrection River and Resurrection Pass National Recreation trails to complete the seventy-two-mile trek from Hope to Seward. Scenic overlooks of Russian River, panoramic views of mountains, and easy hiking for family outing are the outstanding features of Russian Lakes Trail. The first part of this trail provides an outstanding dayhike from Russian River Campground to Russian River Falls at Mile 2 and Lower Russian Lake at Mile 3.

From Russian River Campground the first three miles of the trail are heavily used for fishing access to Russian River and Lower Russian Lake. My first Alaska fishing cast was in the Russian River. Two or three of my children and I would hike the two miles to our favorite hole. Having great confidence in our ability to fish, and the river's capacity to provide, we would build a fire.

Brian Kneen fixes a shore lunch of lake trout.

Once the fire was set, we would break out our rods.

The fish were stacked on top of each other and it didn't take long to bring in the first salmon. Whoever was fortunate enough to draw first catch would immediately clean the fish, wrap it in foil, and put it under the coals of the fire. We'd then fish for a couple of hours, and fill our limit

By then the fire would be just a warm spot on the ground in a circle of rocks. The foil wrapped around our first caught salmon was now blackened by the coals. Someone would fish it out with a stick and unwrap the package. The perfectly cooked red would be laid out on a log. Each would then help themselves to gourmet "red-a-la-riverbank."

Along the trail, hikers will observe reddish-gray colored dead trees killed by spruce bark beetles. These trees are a major fire hazard! Be extra careful with fire.

There are three Forest Service public recreation cabins on Russian Lakes Trail for use by hikers, and may be reserved by mail or at any Chugach National Forest Service office as much as 179 days in advance of planned stay. Occupancy is by permit only for a cost of $20 per night per party. A boat is provided for those reserving a cabin. Handicapped accessible features at Lower Russian Lake Cabin include: ramps at door, large pit toilets, boat dock, and ramp for wheelchair users. As a courtesy to hikers staying at the cabin, please camp in other areas out of sight of the cabin.

Winter travel is not recommended. Snow on the trail can persist into late spring and downed trees can impede travel. Cooper Lake Road is not plowed in winter and Snug Harbor Road may be icy.

HIKE 37: *VICTOR CREEK TRAIL*

General description: Hiking in Glacial terrain into the mountains which surround Kenai Lake.

General location: Between Moose Pass and Seward at mile 19.7 of the Seward Highway.

Trail begins: Mile 19.7 of Seward Highway at Victor Creek.

Trail ends: Three miles up the Victor Creek Valley.

Maps: USGS Seward B7.

Difficulty: Moderate.

Length: three miles.

Elevation: 100 to 1,200 feet.

Special attractions: Wildlife, scenery.

Best season: June through September.

For more information: Chugach National Forest, Seward Ranger District, P.O. Box 390, 334 4th Avenue, Seward, Alaska 99664 (907) 224-3374.

Finding the trailhead: The trailhead is located on the east side, just north of Victor Creek, at Mile 19.7 on the Seward Highway. Parking is available at the gravelled turn out on the west side

The hike: This short, summer-only trail, takes hikers past the remains of old mine activity that can be seen on the lower portion of the trail. The first mile has steep grades with the remaining two miles fairly level. It is an excellent trail, when time is limited, to see wildlife. Mountain goats can be viewed along the slopes at the upper end of the trail and brown bear are occasionally seen in the drainage. The trail is sometimes used by mountaineers to access Andy Simon's Mountain.

Avalanche paths may continue to cover the trail into June and due to the avalanche hazard, winter travel is not recommended.

Children try to catch fish with a cup in Victor Creek.

FAR NORTH TRAILS

Summer season in the far north is short, but the days are extremely long. During summer, hikers enjoy over twenty hours of sunlight. Winter adventure seekers may find themselves hiking by moonlight or witnessing displays of the Aurora. The far north's geography and climate is distinct, different from Southeast Alaska as California is different from Maine. Hikers searching for the unusual and rarely accomplished, may want to look north.

Hikes in the far north demand a different attitude than more conventional hikes elsewhere. Hikers must adapt their mental makeup to cope with twenty-four-hour daylight and bugs. Insects can be more than just pesky, they can literally drive a person over the brink.

Once a hiker is properly outfitted with a good-qality bug-proof tent, head net, and lots of mosquito dope he can manage the bugs and they become just a mild annoyance. There is often a breeze blowing which keeps the bugs at bay.

Hiking in the land of the midnight sun can be a challenging, but satisfying, experience. Pitching a tent as the sun sets in the north at midnight, and watching it rise again in the north before last night's fire is cold, can be exciting. Sunsets blend into sunrises, and days are marked, not by darkness, but by twilight. A hiker taking a late afternoon nap on a warm hillside in the sun is often surprised when it cannot be determined if it is 10 a.m. or 10 p.m.

I once interviewed a young couple who went on a extended northern hike around June 21, the longest day of the year. They were not in a hurry and decided to refrain from using a watch and just go as they desired without constraint of time. They slept when tired, moved when the mood struck them, and ate when hungry. Because of the expanded amount of daylight and twilight with no darkness, they lost all track of time and could not determine which day it was or if it was morning or afternoon. Getting back to civilization's time-controlled environment required some adjustment.

These are hikes at the top of the world, where the air is clean and clear. A visitor, getting off the airline, looked around and said, "There's something wrong with your air. I can't see it." Pilots receiving current weather reports before taking off, often hear the flight service attendant describe visibility as CAVU, clear and visibility unlimited. Someone from, even a mildly smog infested area, cannot comprehend having visibility unlimited. Air so clear and unpolluted that mountain peaks 200 miles distant appear to be an afternoon's jaunt away. Distances seem greater because of the isolation. Not only do hikers go back to a time not governed by clocks, but they journey to a land where even the air allows freedom to look to the horizon and beyond.

HIKE 38: *ANGEL ROCKS TRAIL*

General description: An easy, loop walk into ancient plant beds, granite tors, and scenic view of Interior Alaska in the Chena River State Recreation Area
General location: Chena Hot Springs Road north east of Fairbanks
Trail begins: Mile 48.9 Chena Hot Springs Road
Trail ends: Trail loops back to the trailhead
Maps: USGS Big Delta D5, Circle A5
Difficulty: Easy
Length: 3.5 miles
Elevation: 100 to 1,750 feet
Special attractions: History, geology, plants, and wildlife
Best season: June through September
For more information: State of Alaska, Division of Parks and Recreation, 3700 Airport Way Fairbanks, Alaska 99709 (907) 451-2695
Finding the trailhead: The trail begins in the parking lot at Mile 48.9 of Chena Hot Springs Road. Enter the parking lot by turning at the Chena River Bridge

HIKE 38: *ANGEL ROCKS TRAIL*

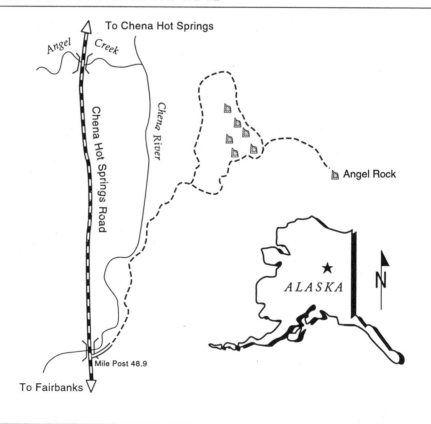

and follow the trail upstream along the river's north fork.

The hike: Constructed in 1984 and 1985 by the Alaska State Parks Youth Conservation Corps, this easy 3.5-mile loop trail leads to large granite outcroppings near the north boundary of the recreation area. Hikers can reach the top of the rocks less than two miles from the trailhead.

The first 1.25 miles of the trail is uneventful until a fork in the trail is reached. Take the right fork to a small stream bubbling over mossy rocks. Turning sharply, the trail moves uphill for a short distance. Soon the first rocks are reached where the trail starts a moderately steep ascent. After weaving through giant rocks it emerges onto the upper rock ridge.

Leaving the upper rock ridge is accomplished by either returning on the same trail or continuing down a steep unimproved trail through rocks on the north ridge. This trail goes down to the base of the hill, follows along a small slough, returns to the fork, and back to the trailhead. A worthy side trip is to scramble up the treeless alpine ridge for views of the Butte, Chena Dome, Alaska Range, and Far Mountain.

Granite outcroppings, called tors, were formed millions of years ago when molten rock pushed upward, cooling before reaching the surface. The surrounding earth slowly eroded, leaving the rock pinnacles.

Plants in this area are remnants of the vegetation covering Interior Alaska during the Pleistocene era, 10,000 to 20,000 years ago. Sage, poppies, arnicas, dogbane, and other plants peculiar to steep, south-facing slopes in Interior Alaska are found. Plant communities of broomrape and witches-broom are the first part of the trail. The stream is home to purple and yellow violets. Moss campion, saxifrage, and bunchberries are found on north-facing slopes, sometimes just a few feet from completely different vegetation of the south slopes.

HIKE 39: *CHENA DOME TRAIL*

General description: A hike for the hardy into a wilderness area with plenty of scenery, and photography opportunities.
General location: Northeast of Fairbanks on the Chena Hot Springs Road
Trail begins: Mile 50.5 Chena Hot Springs Road
Trail ends: Trail loops back to Mile 49.3 Chena Hot Springs Road
Maps: USGS Big Delta D5, USGS Circle A5, A6
Difficulty: Moderate to difficult
Length: twenty-nine miles
Elevation:1,000 to 4,421 feet
Special attractions: Views of Alaska Range tors
Best season: May through September
For more information: State of Alaska, Division of Parks and Recreation, 3700 Airport Way Fairbanks, Alaska 99709 (907) 451-2695
Finding the trailhead: The trail begins in the parking lot at Mile 50.5 of Chena Hot Springs Road or at Mile 49.3. Maps and information are on a bulletin board at the trailhead

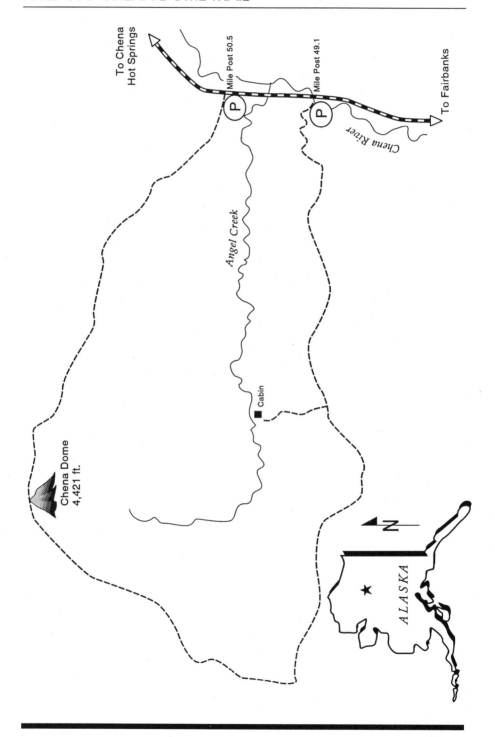

To Chena
Hot Springs

Mile Post 50.5

Mile Post 49.1

To Fairbanks

Chena River

Angel Creek

Cabin

Chena Dome
4,421 ft.

N

ALASKA

The hike: Constructed by the Youth Conservation Corps between 1981 to 1985, this twenty-nine-mile trail loops around the entire Angel Creek drainage. The first three miles of each end of the trail cut through forest until reaching timberline. Tundra ridge tops marked by rock cairns complete the loop. Three days should be planned to cover the entire loop, however steep, scenic day hikes are worthwhile if a longer hike cannot be done. If hiking the entire loop, it is recommended to begin at the upper trailhead at Mile 50.5.

Tundra wildflowers abound in July and blueberries in August. Birds, characteristic of high tundra, ptarmigan, golden plovers, and horned larks may be seen along with grouse, thrushes, warblers, and other songbirds. Bear, wolverine, and other wildlife may also be seen.

For the convenience of hikers, there is a public-use cabin on Angel Creek which may be reserved in advance for an overnight fee. Make reservations by contacting: State of Alaska, Division of Parks and Recreation, 3700 Airport Way Fairbanks, Alaska 99709 (907) 451-2695.

The trail is open to mountain bikes and horses but closed to motorized vehicles.

HIKE 40: *CREAMERS FIELD NATURE PATH*

General description: An easy nature walk into a vegetation sampler of Interior Alaska. Creamers Nature Path in the Migratory Waterfowl Refuge was built by cooperative efforts of the Alaska Department of Fish and Game, the Alaska State Division of Parks Youth Conservation Society using funds provided by the Alaska Bicentennial Commission.
General location: Inner city Fairbanks near the Fish and Game Building on College Road
Trail begins: College Road near Fish and Game building
Trail ends: Trail loops back to the trailhead
Maps: None
Difficulty: Easy
Length: Two miles
Elevation: 450 feet
Special attractions: Witnessing how plant life progresses in the far north
Best season: May through October
For more information: State of Alaska, Department of Fish and Game, 1300 College Road, Fairbanks, Alaska 99709 (907) 452-1531
Finding the trailhead: The Alaska Department of Fish and Game has an office near the University of Alaska off College Road. The trail begins from the fish and game parking lot. In addition to the trailhead there is undeveloped access available at several points off of Farmers Loop Road.

The hike: 200 years after our country was founded, Alaska Bicentennial Commission provided funds for the Alaska Department of Fish and Game, State of Alaska, Division of Parks and Recreation, and the Youth Conservation Society to construct Creamers Nature Path. Literature about the path proclaims, "Welcome to to Creamer's Nature Path," and most hikers are reluctant to leave.

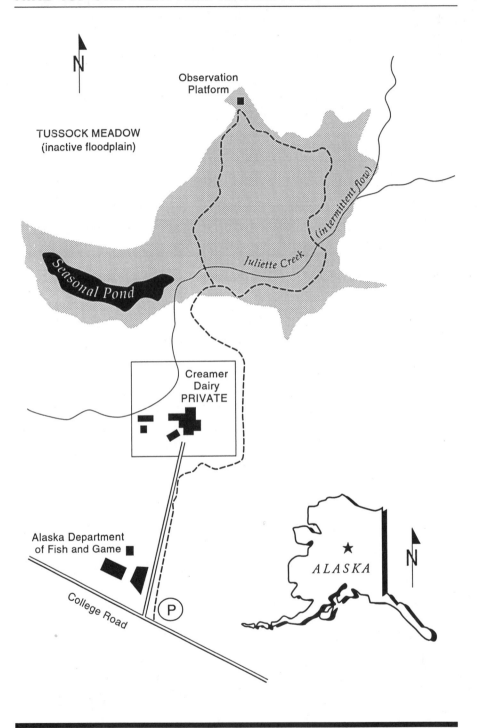

Geese are a common sight at Creamers Field.

Looping two miles, this unique, short trail passes through most vegetation types common to Interior Alaska. It allows hikers to observe wildlife species associated with Alaska's lowlands and permits first-hand observation of many geological processes common to northern latitudes. Otherwise impenetrable to all but moose and other wild creatures, the trail allows hikers to walk through areas which would be nearly impossible without a trail. Creamers Nature Path visitors claim there are only two seasons along the trail: wet and mosquito. Waterproof boots are recommended during April and early June and insect repellent is advisable from June through August.

Creamer's Field, a 1,776-acre Migratory Waterfowl Refuge, is located within two miles of downtown Fairbanks. It is best known for its spring concentrations of ducks, geese, and cranes stopping on the refuge fields during their spring migration.

Managed by the Department of Fish and Game, the former dairy farm field, is for the benefit of public and waterfowl. Over 150 different species of birds have been seen on the refuge. Twenty are residents, fifty-seven are migrants, and the rest are breeders and occasional visitors. In late April thousands upon thousands of waterfowl arrive, stopping to rest and feed before continuing to their summer nesting grounds. Canada geese, white-fronted geese, pintails, wigeons, mallards, shovelers, and green winged teal are most abundant. Sandhill cranes, Lapland longspurs, sandpipers, dowitchers, and plovers stop in the refuge. Rough-legged hawks, northern harriers, and short-eared owls patrol the fields and muskeg for voles.

Moose may be seen on the refuge in addition to voles, shrews snowshoe hare, woodchuck, red squirrel, red fox, pine marten, and muskrat. Even black bear have been seen.

Wildlife viewing in spring is fantastic. Visitors either stop at the fields to watch feeding waterfowl or take the two-mile long self-guided nature path, complete with moose viewing tower. The old farmhouse is an interpretive center for visitors and meeting place for refuge-related groups. Other activities on the refuge are dog-mushing, cross-country skiing, snowmobiling, retriever training, hunting, and trapping.

HIKE 41: *PINNELL MOUNTAIN HIKING TRAIL*

General description: A Far North hike with wildlife, wildflowers, sweeping mountain vistas, and the midnight sun.

General location: Steese Highway between Fox and Circle, north of Fairbanks.

Trail begins: Mile 85.6 Steese Highway.

Trail ends: Mile 107 Steese Highway.

Maps: USGS Circle B3, B4, C3, C4.

Difficulty: Moderate to difficult.

Length: 27.3 miles.

Elevation: From 3,100 feet to 4,721 feet.

Special attractions: Wildlife, scenery.

Best season: June through September.

For more information: United State Department of the Interior, Bureau of Land Management, Steese/White Mountain District Office, 1150 University Avenue Fairbanks, Alaska 99709 (907) 474-2200. For current recorded trail condition information call (907) 474-2372.

Finding the trailhead: Trailheads are off the Steese Highway at Twelve Mile Summit, Mile 85.6 or Eagle Summit, Mile 107.3. Give BLM your input about the trail at trailheads registers. Parking areas are provided at both trailheads.

The hike: Pinnell Mountain National Recreation Trail, 27.3 miles long, offers challenges and unforgettable rewards. The trail traverses alpine ridgetops entirely above timberline. Wooden mileposts and rock cairns clearly mark the trail. Benched switchbacks provide safe access over steep talus slopes. Wood planks provide passage over wet muskeg.

Action begins just a few steps from either trailhead with spectacular views. Any length of hike, an hour, a day, or overnight, is enjoyable for hikers of any ability or condition. Beyond the first few miles the trail is steep and rugged in many areas and hikers should be physically prepared or go slow and rest often. Three days should be allowed for the entire trail.

Farther north, Pinnell Mountain National Recreation Trail, grants the hiker sweeping mountain vistas, bountiful and beautiful wildflowers, wildlife, and an opportunity to capture on film the midnight sun hovering above the horizon.

Weather along Pinnell Mountain Trail is unpredictable. A calm sunny day

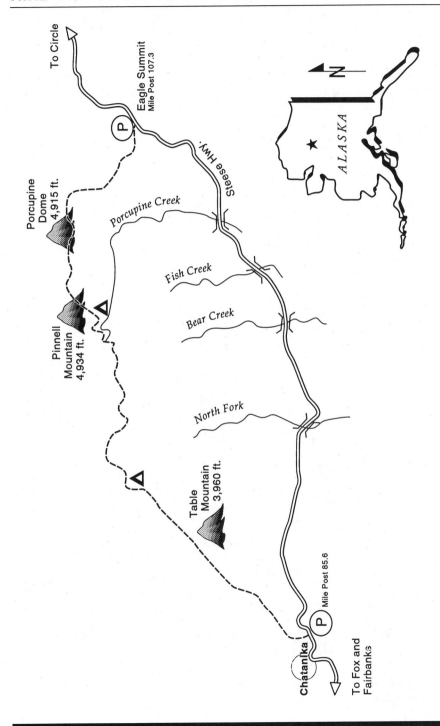

can quickly turn to rain, heavy fog and cold high winds over fifty-mile-per-hour, or all of the above. Small log shelters, reminiscent of an earlier age, are located between mileposts 10 and 11, and 17 and 18. Fully enclosed, they have no improvements, such as bunks or stoves and only offer protection from the elements. They are welcome sights, however in the face of a sudden wind-driven rain or snow storm.

Generally clear of snow from June to September, the trail's summer temperatures range from twenty to eighty. Wind chill creates the effect of much lower temperatures and low clouds and fog can obscure the trail, making travel difficult and dangerous. Carry your own drinking water or plan to boil it as good water is scarce.

Visitors to the area are immediately struck with the lack of facilities along the Steese Highway. They are reminded to start with a full tank of gas, spare tire, and tools for minor repairs. Gasoline and food can only be counted on in Fox, Mile 11, Central, Mile 127, and Circle, Mile 162. Most of the road is gravel surface, but in good condition and suitable for all vehicles. Telephones are in Fox and Central. Campgrounds are at miles 39, 60, 119, and 162 on the Steese Highway.

MATANUSKA SUSITNA TRAILS

The Matanuska-Susitna Valley takes its name from the two major rivers cutting across the flat-lands beneath the mountains. The area has been the scene of much mining activity and many of the trails follow paths taken by prospectors and supply trains. The valley was introduced to modern settlers when, in 1935, the United States Government moved farmers from poverty stricken Minnesota to Palmer and surrounding region. These homesteaders created a productive farming and dairy industry out of wilderness. Families of these homesteaders, new citizens, residents of Anchorage, and visitors from outside use the valley as a major recreation area. Recently, hiking has become popular and old trails have been restored and new ones constructed.

There seems to be something that tugs back to the days of '98: days when rugged men scratched the land in search of gold; days when the lucky struck it rich; days carefree and without the constraints of traffic jams, television news updates, cellular phones, and regular employment; days of closeness with the land and those hiking by our side, days where the supersonic speed of living was slowed to the pace of mist forming a dewdrop on the bottom of a red berry.

When Anchorage residents and those traveling from even bigger and faster, more unfriendly cities yearn to get away, when the craving to leave it all—even for only a moment—strikes, they can get get into the outback in moments. From the forty-five-yard hike in Matanuska River Park in Palmer to following the steps of miners to Lucky Shot Mine, the Matanuska-Susitna Valley trails can satisfy the urge and restore harmony to an unbalanced life.

HIKE 42: CREVASSE MORAINE TRAIL

General description: A series of five trail loops ranging from .2 to 1.4 miles providing outdoor opportunities include hiking, running, cross-country skiing, equestrian riding, and an assortment of other leisure time activities. The trails are available year-round.

General location: Midway between Palmer and Wasilla

Trail begins: At the end of Loma Prieta Drive off mile 1.9 Palmer-Wasilla Highway

Trail ends: Back at the trailhead

Maps: None

Difficulty: Easy

Length: Nine miles of hiking trails

Elevation: 150 feet to 200 feet

Special attractions: Bird life, flora, scenery

Best season: June through September

For more information: Mat-Su Borough Parks and Recreation Division P.O. Box 1608, Palmer, Alaska 99645 (907) 745-9963

Finding the trailhead: From Palmer, drive West on the Palmer-Wasilla Highway until you reach Loma Prieta Road on your left. At the end of this road there is a parking area and trailhead signs. Two picnic tables and fire grills are at the trailhead. The trail

Trail marker on Crevasse Moraine Trail.

begins at the parking area and follows ridges, slopes, and valleys.

The hike: The trail system consists of four irregular loops and a connecting link to Long Lake Trail in the Kepler-Bradley Lakes State Recreation Area. The area may be referred to as "kame and kettle" topography resulting from glacier ice that once occupied the valley. Mound-like hills, kames, were created by ice melting. Basins, kettles, were formed by melting blocks of ice buried in the moraine.

HIKE 42: *CREVASSE MORAINE TRAIL*

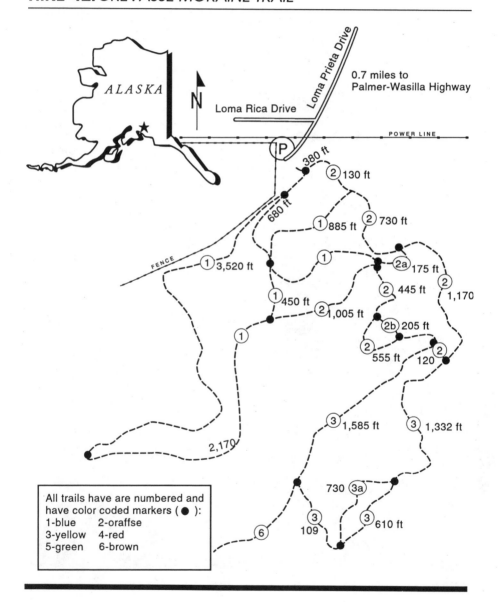

The ecosystem primarily consists of a hardwood forest featuring white spruce, mature birch, interspersed with cottonwood. Ferns, highbush cranberry, and red raspberries are also common. Wildflowers seen during summer include: violets, fireweed, monkshood, bunchberry, dwarf dogwood, Jacob's ladder, chiming bells, and prickly wild rose. Moose, red fox, snowshoe hare, and red squirrels can be seen throughout the forest. Black bear may be encountered. During spring and summer, robins, Swainson's thrush, yellow-rumped warblers, and orange-crowned warblers may be observed. Year-round residents include: black-capped chickadees, spruce grouse, bohemian waxwings, and pine grosebeaks. The great horned owl, a common resident, may also be sighted.

HIKE 43: *FERN MINE TRAIL*

General description: Hatcher Pass, one of the most popular recreation areas of the Matanuska-Susitna Borough, provides alpine scenery views and year around recreational opportunities. The gold mining area north of Palmer is accessible to Southcentral Alaska's population centers. This is an easy hike into the Hatcher Pass area.
General location: Hatcher Pass north of Palmer
Trail begins: The end of Archangel Road
Trail ends: Fern Mine
Maps: USGS Anchorage D6
Difficulty: Easy
Length: Four miles
Elevation: 3,000 to 4,000 feet
Special attractions: Vistas, scenery, history
Best season: June to September

On the trail in Hatcher Pass. Remains of old mines can be spotted in this area.

For more information: State of Alaska Division of Parks and Recreation, HC32 Box 6706, Wasilla, Alaska 99687, (907) 745-3975

Finding the trailhead: Travel from Glenn Highway, along Palmer-Fishhook Road for nineteen miles to the Motherlode Roadhouse. Immediately past the roadhouse the road makes a sharp left hook giving the road its name. Continuing past the hook for one mile, the road is steep to Archangel Road. Turn right on Archangel Road and go for 2.5 miles to the trailhead. There is ample parking at the trailhead.

The hike: Among these mountains are scenes of pristine splendor. Craggy mountains to your left guard the wilderness along Susitna River and Gold Mint Glacier. Ravines and slopes filled with flowers in spring and dramatic foliage in fall add to the distinction of this easy hike. Along the trail you will find remains of a long-ago mining era. Names like Archangel, War Baby, and Lucky Shot will spark your interest and have you resting later in the library learning the history of such places. As you climb you will be able to turn around and look down the pass to the farming flatlands of Matanuska Valley. With a pair of binoculars you will be able to have a clear view of the Chugach Mountain Range and Kink River Flats, forty miles away.

We carried in all the trappings for breakfast along the trail in Hatcher Pass, prepared a morning feast and still haven't forgotten the enjoyable day of hiking and exploring.

HIKE 44: *GOLD MINT TRAIL*

General description: A short, or all day, hike includes land and mountains on both sides of the upper reaches of Little Susitna River into the Gold Mint Glacier country.

General location: To the north of the Mother Lode Roadhouse at the junction of Hatcher Pass Road and the Palmer-Fishhook Road.

Trail begins: Trailhead parking lot across the road from Motherlode Roadhouse

Trail ends: Mint Glacier

Maps: Anchorage C6, C7, D6, D7

Difficulty: Easy to moderate

Length: 4.5 miles

Elevation: 3,000 to 4,000 feet

Special attractions: Scenery, moraines, and history

Best season: June through September

For more information: State of Alaska Division of Parks and Recreation, HC32 Box 6706, Wasilla, Alaska 99687, (907) 745-3975

Finding the trailhead: The trail, which begins in the parking lot just beyond the Motherlode Roadhouse, follows and crosses the Little Susitna River. At the roadhouse, do not take the sharp left hook of Hatcher Pass Road, but continue straight ahead into the parking lot to the marked trailhead.

The hike: The first 1.5 miles, to Archangel Creek, is gentle and fairly level. No need to portage this swift creek as there is a bridge. Past Archangel Creek

HIKE 43: *FERN MINE TRAIL*
HIKE 44: *GOLD MINT TRAIL*
HIKE 45: *INDEPENDENCE MINE TRAIL*
HIKE 51: *REED LAKES TRAIL*

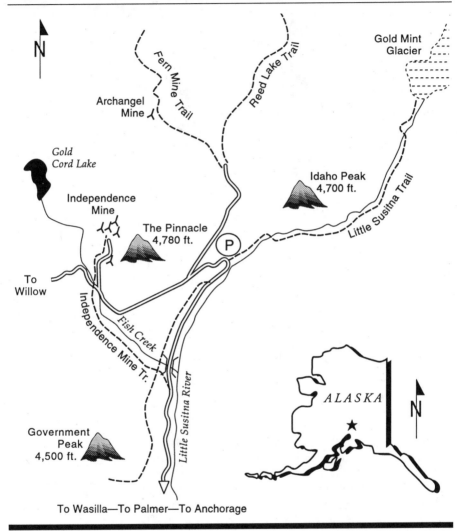

Bridge, the trail follows the west side of the Little Susitna River for approximately 1.5 miles where it crosses the river, here you will have to boulder hop. It then approaches Lonesome Gold Mine. The flat trail is open to mountain biking to the river but is too brushy beyond. During flooding, due to excessive rain or spring run off, fording may be dangerous. Generally, during summer, the water is low and rivers and streams are safe to cross. Hikers can verify crossing condition with the Park Ranger. Lonesome Mine is one mile from the

Panoramic views await hikers on the Fern Mine Trail.

crossing. The trail follows the Little Susitna River to its source at Mint Glacier and end of the trail. The Mountaineering Club maintains a cabin at Mint Glacier.

The trail is used in all seasons of the year. A gold panning and sightseeing trail in summer, the trail is used by cross country skiers, snow machiners, and dog mushers in winter.

Wildflower fields, along and beyond the trail, can be visited and photographed. Arising early from our camp I visited an area of wildflowers. It was about an hour before sunup. I wanted to photograph flowers as they were opening to receive life nourishing rays of the sun. The Hatcher Pass sunrise captured my interest and I nearly forgot about the flowers. Before the sun poked above the eastern horizon, brilliant rays drove across the valley and illuminated the taller western peaks.

I happened to catch the very first splash of sunlight as old sol slipped into view. There was a momentary flash of blue just as the sun came into sight. I have since learned that it was not a phenomenon of the morning, but it happens each sunrise. I confirmed this while taking an early morning flight in my old Stinson. As the sun came up I dropped the nose of the plane below the horizon and then let it slowly rise. Each time I repeated the test, there was a flash of blue just before the sun became visible.

Remembering my reason for being in the Hatcher Pass wildflower meadow I returned to my photo session. Growing proudly in the meadow's middle was a patch of blue flowers. As I set up my tripod and snapped a few frames, I wondered if there was a correlation between dawns first color and the meadows early risers.

HIKE 45: INDEPENDENCE MINE

General description: A one-day hike to an old gold mine and its environs. Explorers of the Independence Mine area are rewarded with breathtaking scenic vistas of Matanuska Valley and majestic tundra terrain, as well as a peek at Alaska's old gold mining past.

General location: Above Independence Mine Camp in Hatcher Pass sixty miles north of Anchorage

Trail begins: Independence Mine Camp

Trail ends: Hatcher Pass Road mile 17.3

Maps: USGS Anchorage D6,D7,D8

Difficulty: Easy

Length: four miles

Elevation: 3,000 to 4,000 feet

Special attractions: Recreation and visit to old gold mining area

Best season: All year

For more information: State of Alaska Division of Parks and Recreation, HC32 Box 6706, Wasilla, Alaska 99687, (907) 745-3975

Finding the trailhead: Travel from Glenn Highway, along Palmer-Fishhook Road for nineteen miles to the Motherlode Roadhouse. Immediately past the roadhouse the road makes a sharp left hook giving the road its name. Continuing past the hook drive 2.5 miles to Independence Mine and the trailhead.

Hikers encounter a great deal of brush on the Independence Mine Trail, much like miners of old.

The hike: In 1979, geologist-owner Starkey A. Wilson, donated the lower half of Independence Mine to the State Division of Parks. Now, a 227-acre State Historical Park, it includes the assay building, bunkhouses, a tipple, and other old mine buildings. Summer hikers will get an idea of what prospectors and miners met when they first visited this valley as the trail is only brushed out in the most extreme brushy areas. A trail is not clearly established. Hikers must pick and choose their way. It is not difficult to find good footing and it is impossible to get lost. One of the desirable features of this trail is that it is all downhill from the trailhead at Independence Mine, across Hatcher Pass Valley, down the North side of Fishhook Creek, and beyond to Hatcher Pass Road.

In winter, the upper end of the trail is used extensively by cross-country skiers. Downhill skiing, snow boarding, sledding, and advanced cross-country skiing are favorite uses of the trail's lower ends.

HIKE 46: *KNIK RIVER-JIM CREEK TRAIL*

General description: This is a year-round playground for outdoor enthusiasts. Fall fishing is excellent, summer swimming superb, and hiking unstructured.
General location: On north shore of Knik River Outwash Plain below Knik Glacier, near Bodenburg Loop
Trail begins: Jim Creek
Trail ends: Anywhere the hiker chooses to stop along Knik River outwash plain
Maps: USGS Anchorage C6, C6 SE
Difficulty: Easy
Length: Unlimited
Elevation: 100 feet
Special attractions: Swimming, vistas, fishing, four-wheeling, boating.
Best season: June through September
For more information: Mat-Su Borough Parks and Recreation Division P.O. Box 1608, Palmer, Alaska 99645 (907) 745-9963
Finding the trailhead: At Milepost 11.5 on the Old Glenn Highway turn east on Plumley Road, go 1.4 miles to Caudill Road, turn right and proceed approximately 0.7 mile to the trailhead on the east side of the road. The hike may begin here but most people take the 1.7-mile old logging road directly to Jim Creek.

The hike: Seth Cook, a logger, pioneered the road in about 1949 to reach timber on both sides of Jim Creek and on the north side of the Knik River to Friday Creek. Still visible is evidence of the bridge he built across Jim Creek and of the rough road along the north shore of Knik River.

Jim Creek, a slow moving, clear water stream, wanders out of Jim Lake and warms in the summer sun. Near its junction with Knik River it narrows to deep sand-lined pools ideal for swimming. Big birch trees line one bank of the creek where enterprising youth have tied a rope to one of the high branches overhanging the creek. Both young and old thrill to climbing the creek's bank, swing rope in hand, and then swinging out over the creek and dropping into the deep pool below.

HIKE 46: *KNIK RIVER-JIM CREEK TRAIL*

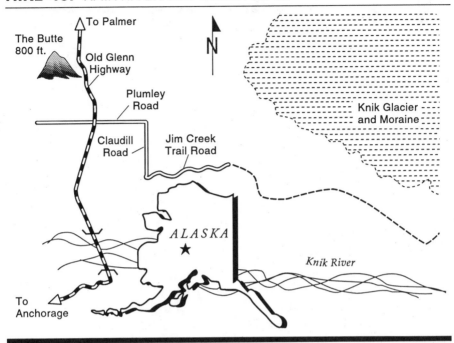

Sand covers the near bank where would-be hikers, turned swimmers, throw out a beach blanket, enjoy a picnic lunch, and obtain a tan on sunny days. Near the swinging tree a scrub-tree covered, sand ridge terminates at the river. The high sand ridge provides fun for the young, where they run down the ridge and jump as far as they can into open space and then land in the sloping sand hill of the ridge.

Until the 1964 Alaska earthquake, active, moving Knik Glacier sealed off a steep-walled canyon each winter creating Lake George behind the glacier. In spring, as the glacier melted and calved, crashing into the river gorge below, the glacier would become rotten and recede. When the glacier deteriorated enough that the water pressure of Lake George broke down the glacier wall, the lake emptied in one mighty rush to the sea. The quick flood left the river bottom flat and strewn with debris.

The Alaska earthquake changed the topography of the land and the lake no longer fills and empties as it did previously. The riverbed is now wide and flat and provides hikers an opportunity to beachcomb the area from Jim Creek to Friday Creek and beyond.

The area never lacks for ready, seasoned firewood. Piles of tree stumps and branches similar to that found along the seashore can be used. One evening we visited the area, crossed Jim Creek, and traveled a short distance up the riverbed. After gathering a substantial amount of dry driftwood, we built a fire and enjoyed watching the sun, as Robert Service wrote in his poem, The Spell of the Yukon, "wallow in crimson and gold and grow dim." In the fire's dying embers we roasted hot dogs and returned to Jim Creek after dark.

HIKE 47: *LAZY MOUNTAIN TRAIL*

General description: An easy to moderate climbing trail into scenic vistas.
General location: In the eastern hills above Palmer.
Trail begins: At the end of Huntley Road.
Trail ends: Trailhead or connecting hikes.
Maps: Anchorage C6, C6 SE.
Difficulty: Easy moderate.
Length: Two miles.
Elevation: 800 to 3,720 feet
Special attractions: Views, vistas, vegetations.
Best season: June through September.
For more information: Mat-Su Borough Parks and Recreation Division, P.O. Box 1608, Palmer, Alaska 99645 (907) 745-9963.
Finding the trailhead: Turn east off the Glenn Highway at Arctic Avenue in Palmer. Arctic Avenue becomes the Old Glenn Highway after two miles. After crossing the Matanuska River turn left on the Clark-Wolverine Road. Proceed to the 'T' intersection and turn right onto Huntley Road. Go to the end of Huntley Road and follow the signs.

The hike: This popular hike begins in stand of cottonwood-birch and then goes

HIKE 47: *LAZY MOUNTAIN TRAIL*

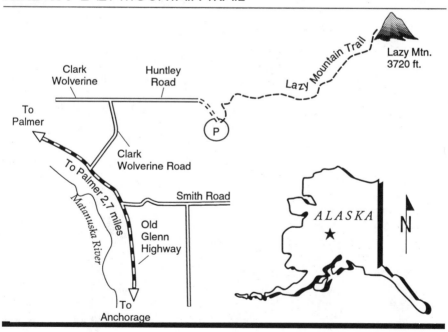

straight up the ridge to the top of Lazy Mountain. The trail consists of approximately a four-hour round trip to the 3,720-foot mountain top. The entire Matanuska Valley from Sutton to Anchorage can be viewed from here. Hikers can venture over to Matanuska Peak and other ridges or loop back down to the McRoberts Creek Trail. Access to Wolverine Creek and other hiking trails can be gained from Lazy Mountain. Little evidence of earlier copper mining claims remain on the mountain.

Planning and construction of Lazy Mountain Trail was cooperatively done by Palmer-Wasilla Trail Association, volunteers, and Matanuska-Susitna Borough Parks and Recreation Division.

HIKE 48: *MAT-SU COLLEGE NATURE TRAIL*

General description: An afternoon hike for socializing and learning about nature.
General location: Off the Trunk Road between Wasilla Highway and the Palmer-Wasilla Highway.
Trail begins: Student parking lot at Mat-Su College.
Trail ends: Trailhead.
Maps: None.
Difficulty: Easy.
Length: three miles of hiking trails.
Elevation: 100 feet.
Special attractions: Panoramic views, flora, fauna tranquility, camera views.
Best season: All year.
For more information: State of Alaska Division of Parks and Recreation, HC32 Box 6706, Wasilla, Alaska 99687 (907) 745-3975.
Finding the trailhead: In Palmer turn west off the Glenn Highway onto the Palmer-Wasilla Highway. Travel about four miles and turn right onto Trunk Road. Travel to the Matanuska Susitna College and trailhead is in parking lot.

The hike: This trail is a 1.5-mile education, exercise, and aesthetic pleasure. Part of Mat-Su College's 280-acre campus, the trail system winds through sixty-acres dedicated to agricultural research in Alaska. For horticultural buffs, plants have been identified, and soil pits display Alaska's various soil structures. An experimental tree planting area is another point of interest. The trails are designed to attract seasoned hikers, strollers, even wheelchair ramblers. Wood chip-covered paths make walking easy, but vigorous exercisers may want to challenge steeper paths.

Summer and winter the trail presents uncommon opportunities for artists and photographers. Benches at scenic spots invite one to rest and admire the valley's splendid mountain panorama: Three Sisters, Pioneer Peak, Knik Glacier, Bodenburg Butte, The Talkeetnas. The observation deck, a short easy walk from Snograss Hall, overlooks peaceful Okeson Pond. Schools and the general public are encouraged to use and enjoy the trails.

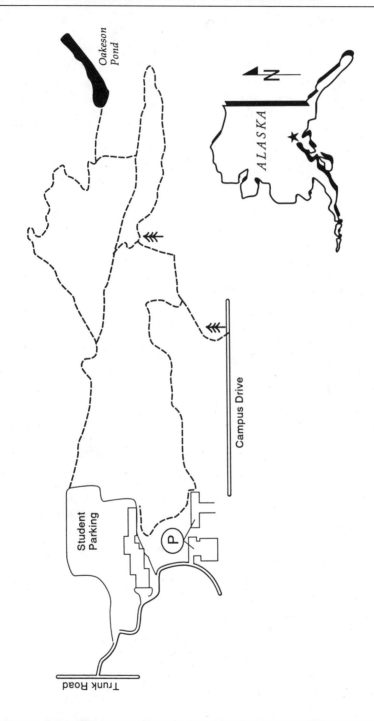

HIKE 49: *MATANUSKA RIVER PARK TRAILS*

General description: Short, well defined hiking trails near Matanuska River.
General location: Near the Old Matanuska River Bridge just northeast of Palmer.
Trail begins: Park camping area.
Trail ends: Trailhead.
Maps: Furnished free by the park.
Difficulty: Easy.
Length: Two miles of hiking trails.
Elevation: 100 feet
Special attractions: Bird life, scenery, Matanuska River Camping, ponds.
Best season: June through October.
For more information: Mat-Su Borough Parks and Recreation Division, P.O. Box 1608 Palmer, Alaska 99645 (907) 745-9663
Finding the trailhead: Park entrance is on the north side of the Old Glenn Highway .4 mile east of Gulkana Street in Palmer.

The hike: Matanuska River Park Trail system can claim the shortest hiking trail in the largest state in the union. This trail system includes recently constructed paths as short as forty-five yards. Cleared paths begin at four trail heads in the park camping area. A fifth trailhead near the fenced softball complex is the start of another trail. All of the trails loop into or connect with the trails of the system. This is an ideal group of trails to take youngsters—even toddlers—to give them a beginning appreciation for wilderness. Although the trails are never far from the camping area they give the impression of backcountry, especially to the young and those familiar only with city life, sidewalks and paved streets. These short trails are good hikes to introduce kids to backpacking, but never let them go on their own. Trails near the icy cold, fast moving Matanuska River could be dangerous for young inexperienced hikers.

Following the trails of the system will take hikers along paths leading to and paralleling the Matanuska River. For the young, following a map, furnished free by the park, to areas with exciting names is a never-to-be-forgotten thrill. Names like Long Pond Trail, Duck Pond Trail, Duck Pond Spur, Swan Pond, and River Spur Trail conjure up images in their minds of backcountry and wilderness intrigue.

My eight-year-old grandson, Trent, and I hiked the system on a July afternoon. It was a special thrill for him to talk to the park director and obtain a map and instructions. He listened intently and plotted our course on the map with a pencil. It took less than an hour, under Trent's leadership, to complete the trails he had marked. He carefully guided us from loop to loop and safely past the dangerous Matanuska River. We saw birds and dog tracks closely resembling those of a big wolf.

Hearing Trent explain to his grandmother about all the things we did along the miles of backcountry, wilderness trails, I think he thought we had been gone for weeks not minutes. I look forward to being guided again in the wilderness by Trent Lewis and Clark Clawson.

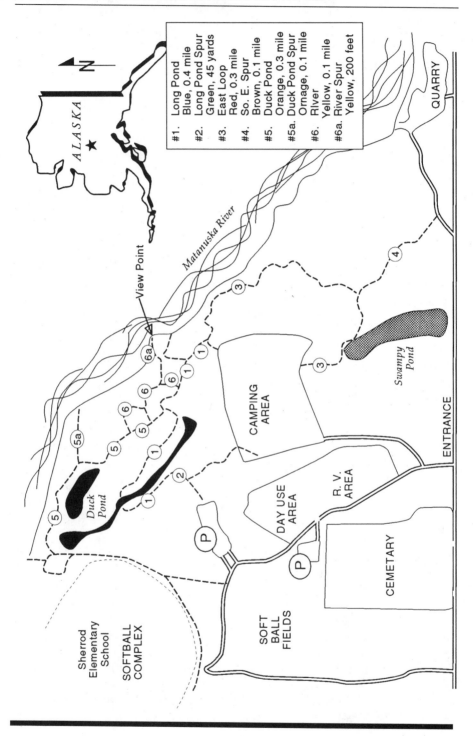

#1. Long Pond
     Blue, 0.4 mile
#2. Long Pond Spur
     Green, 45 yards
#3. East Loop
     Red, 0.3 mile
#4. So. E. Spur
     Brown, 0.1 mile
#5. Duck Pond
     Orange, 0.3 mile
#5a. Duck Pond Spur
     Ornage, 0.1 mile
#6. River
     Yellow, 0.1 mile
#6a. River Spur
     Yellow, 200 feet

HIKE 50: *McROBERTS CREEK TRAIL*

General description: McRoberts Creek Trail is a backcountry hike leading to the summit of Matanuska Peak where hikers gain a birds-eye view of the an area where nearly one half of the state's residents live.

General location: A mountain hike east of Palmer.

Trail begins: End of Smith Road at Harmony Avenue.

Trail ends: Matanuska Peak, called Byers Peak and also known as Mt. Vigor.

Maps: Anchorage C6, C6 SE.

Difficulty: Moderate to difficult.

Length: nine miles.

Elevation: 450 to 6,115 feet

Special attractions: Vistas of basin, animals, scenery.

Best season: June through September.

For more information: Mat-Su Borough Parks and Recreation Division, P.O. Box 1608, Palmer, Alaska 99645 (907) 745-9963

Finding the trailhead: Leave the Glenn Highway at Arctic Avenue in Palmer. Drive along the Old Glenn Highway to Smith Road. Smith Road is 2.7 miles from the junctions of the Old and New Glenn highways. Turn left onto Smith Road and follow it for 1.4 miles until it turns onto Harmony Avenue. There isn't a parking area, but the wide corner provides ample parking off the roadway. From the trailhead to the base of 3,800-foot Summit Ridge is a three-and-one-half hour hike.

The hike: The best way to get an eagle's-eye view of the Palmer, Matanuska-Susitna Valley, Wolverine Creek drainage, Talkeetna and Chugach mountains, Upper Cook Inlet, and distant views of the Alaska Range, including Mt. McKinley, is to take an airplane ride. The next best way is to climb Matanuska

Picking salmon berries, a favorite activity for hikers and bears.

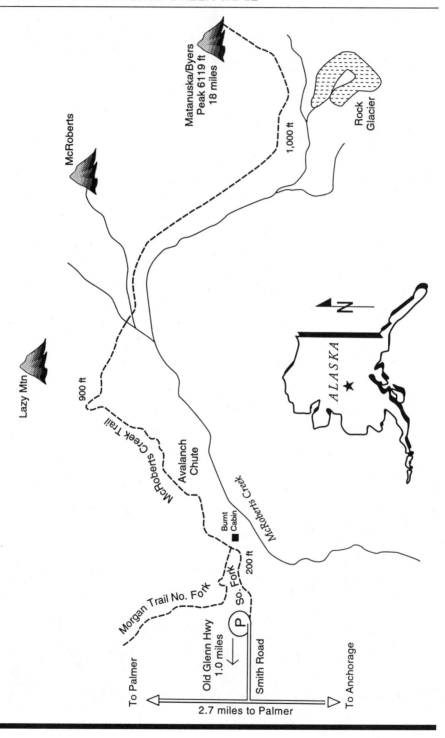

Matanuska/Byers
Peak 6119 ft
18 miles

McRoberts

Rock
Glacier

1,000 ft

Lazy Mtn

N

ALASKA

900 ft

McRoberts Creek Trail

Avalanch
Chute

McRoberts Creek

Burnt
Cabin

Morgan Trail No. Fork

So. Fork

200 ft

P

Old Glenn Hwy
1.0 miles

Smith Road

To Palmer

To Anchorage

2.7 miles to Palmer

Peak. Those who are not content to see their scenery sitting down, but find magic in walking the land, should take McRoberts Creek Trail. The trail, leading to Upper McRoberts Creek Valley, is an easy approach for climbing 6,119-foot Matanuska Peak. In addition to an outstanding, sweeping view of a large area, an unusual, active rock glacier can be seen. A rock glacier is a mixture of permafrost and rock debris.

The trail starts in a decadent cottonwood stand then changes to cottonwood-birch with areas of grass and scattered alder clumps at the middle elevations and a narrow strip of younger cottonwood ending at treeline. Dryas, geraniums, and chocolate lilies can be viewed along the way. Above the treeline, alpine bearberry, which turns a bright red in late fall, and blueberry, dark red in late fall are conspicuous, along with dwarf birch, dwarf willow, and a variety of alpine forbs and grasses. At upper elevations the vegetation is reduced to mainly lichens growing on the more stable boulders. Moose, black and grizzly bear, Dall sheep, ground squirrel and Ptarmigan are seen occasionally.

Six hundred feet from the trailhead, on an old jeep road, the trail crosses an equestrian trail. This crossing is in the corner of four townships marked by a General Land Office Survey metal post. The hike's final destination, the summit of Matanuska Peak, is visible from this spot. The jeep trail continues for .2 mile and is washed out at a steep section of the trail. Another .2 mile brings the hiker to a burned out cabin. For the next .2 mile the trail is along the east edge of a small grassy ridge at elevation 1,300 feet. A distinct path leads forty feet to the brink of a deep canyon. Another 440 feet puts the hiker on a second bench. Then a few hundred yards beyond and the hiker is standing on the edge of McRoberts Creek Canyon. From here the trail gradually swings away into tributary draws.

At total distance of .8 mile from the burned cabin, the trail crosses a draw where snow avalanches occur in winter. Less than 1.5 miles from the burned cabin the trail reaches treeline at 2,160 feet elevation. From here the balance of the hike can be viewed and the route planned. A distinct route continues only for a short distance and beyond this the route is wherever the hiker chooses.

At a ridge rising 3,800 feet, a clear view of McRoberts Rock Glacier can be seen across the canyon. From here to the summit of Matanuska Peak, hikers will want to go slow and enjoy the scenery. Once standing on the summit, hikers feel the thrill of gaining ground while not sitting down.

HIKE 51: *REED LAKES*

General description: High Mountain Lakes hiking with scenery and glaciers.
General location: Gold Mint Glacier area in mountains high above Hatcher Pass.
Trail begins: 2.5 miles up Archangel Road. Trail sign on right.
Trail ends: Upper Reed Lake.
Maps: USGS Anchorage D6,D7,D8.
Difficulty: Easy to moderate.
Length: 4.5 miles.
Elevation: 2,400 to 4,200 feet.

Special attractions: Scenery, glaciers, camping, animals.

Best season: June through September.

For more information: State of Alaska Division of Parks and Recreation, HC32 Box 6706, Wasilla, Alaska 99687, (907) 745-3975.

Finding the trailhead: Travel from Glenn Highway, along Palmer-Fishhook Road for nineteen miles to Motherlode Roadhouse. Immediately past the roadhouse the road makes a sharp left hook giving the road its name. Continuing past the hook for one mile, the road is steep to Archangel Road. Turn right on Archangel Road and go 2.5 miles to the trailhead just beyond Archangel Creek. There is ample parking at the trailhead.

The hike: The trail passes Snowbird Mine, is steep in one section, crosses one creek, and terminates at Upper Reed Lake. Snowbird Mine is reached about .5 mile along the trail, and Upper Reed Lake is three miles from there. Just past Snowbird Mine, it is necessary to cross a small creek. The old bridge is washed out requiring hikers to boulder hop to keep from getting wet. There are plenty of boulders and it is an easy crossing. Continuing from the creek the trail turns steep with switchbacks to a boulder field. Beyond the boulder field is a grassy meadow bisected by Reed Creek. Huge boulders dot this grassy area and is quite scenic.

Heart-shaped, turquoise colored Lower Reed Lake is at elevation 3,750 feet. Gentle sloping meadows surrounding the lake make it is a good place to camp and for children to play and picnic. One of the outstanding scenic features of the area is waterfalls in Reed Creek between Upper and Lower Reed Lake. Granite spires beyond the lakes and meadow rise to an elevation of 6,536 feet and are a popular destination for local mountaineers.

HIKE 52: *WILLOW CREEK SLED TRAIL*

General description: A long hike paralleling a scenic road at the edge of the Talkeetna Mountains and includes land and mountains on both sides of Willow Creek.

General location: Fifty eight miles south of Anchorage beginning at Houston, off the Parks Highway, and traveling into the Hatcher Pass area, North of Palmer.

Trail begins: Houston.

Trail ends: At numerous places along the Willow-Hatcher Pass Road.

Maps: USGS Anchorage D6,D7,D8.

Difficulty: Moderate to difficult.

Length: 15.5 miles.

Elevation: 3,000 to 4,000 feet.

Special attractions: Camping, scenery, wild animals.

Best season: June to the last of September for summer hikers and October through May for winter enthusiasts.

For more information: State of Alaska Division of Parks and Recreation, HC32 Box 6706, Wasilla, Alaska 99687, (907) 745-3975

Finding the trailhead: Travel from Anchorage on the Parks Highway for 58.4 miles to Houston and turn on Fire Hall Road. Park on the north side of the road, gear up, and start hiking. For the comfort of hikers there is the Willow Creek

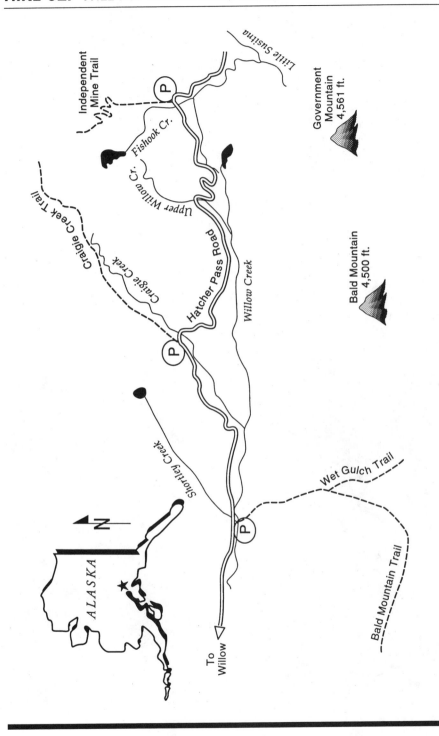

Wayside public recreation site at Mile 48, one mile east of the Parks Highway.

The hike: Historically, War Baby and Lucky Shot mines on Craigie Creek in the Talkeetna Mountains, and mines on Willow Creek, received supplies freighted in on Willow Creek Sled Trail. The site of the trail was a winter supply route from Knik to the Hatcher Pass mining district. Today the trail is a winter dog mushing trail and summer hiking trail.

Hiking the trail includes camping, gold panning, rock collecting, observing small animals, exploring old mining sites, and identifying and photographing alpine tundra flowers. As the trail parallels the road and can be exited almost any time, hikers can hike for an hour or a day, year round.

In addition to good places to pitch a tent, there are old miner and prospectors cabins along the trail. My first visit to the area was in winter. It was -39° as night fell. Our day ended at one of the old mining cabins. Windows had been broken out and the stove lacked a stove pipe. In the darkening twilight we located pieces of stove pipe in the area above the ceiling and nailed old boards over the windows. A fire was built and the cold was driven from the room as we prepared supper.

There was a wood box full of small logs near the door. During the night we fed the fire from the wood box intending to refill it when it got light. By morning, the box was almost empty. In the light of day we discovered several old sticks of dynamite mixed in with like-sized willow sticks in the bottom of the wood box. I have wondered since, what would have happened if we had loaded the stove with willow sticks mixed with dynamite.

Old cache found along the Willow Creek Sled Trail.

NELCHINA-KNIK-CHICKALOON TRAIL SYSTEM

Hiking the entire Chickaloon-Knik-Nelchina Trail System, with its accompanying activities, probably could not be accomplished in one season. Nearly all of the hikes are above timberline and travel through wide, open valleys. Each trail in the system has its own specific characteristic and interesting features; however, someone could hike three or four of these trails and have a representative look at the entire area. None of these trails were established for recreation, but created mainly by footsteps of Indians, miners, trappers, explorers, and freight haulers. The system contains hikes of various lengths and difficulty with enough variety to capture the interest of any hiker.

There are numerous trailheads in the system. Nearly all the trails in this system have trailheads along the Glenn Highway and most are clearly marked. These are long established trails and some trailhead markers are old and in disrepair. The trailhead markers' age and condition give these trails an air of nostalgia. See individual trails for directions to finding each trailhead.

The Chickaloon-Knik-Nelchina Trail System includes trails off the Glenn Highway between King Mountain, Mile 66 and the Matanuska Borough Boundary to the Northeast, Mile 136.6.

Rushing milky-white waters of the Matanuska River flow from the melting Matanuska Glacier. Retreating ice age combination of grinding glacier and cutting river water carved this valley. Heading north, the first good view of the Matanuska Glacier is at a pullout at Mile 101.7. Following the meandering river, the Glenn Highway offers access to dozens of hikes.

Predominate landmarks along the highway include, Pinnacle Mountain, rising southeast of the highway at Mile 68, Kings Mountain, elevation 5,809 feet, is at mile 80, Castle Mountain with its white anthracite ridges, elevation 5,291, and the turnout by Caribou Creek Bridge at mile 107 offer good views of the Matanuska Glacier and the 5,000 foot Fortress Ridge. Sheep Mountain, visible from the highway for elevan miles beginning at mile 112.5, grants travelers sightings of Dall sheep lingering on the 6,200-foot-high slopes.

Many trails are segments of the Chickaloon-Knik-Nelchina Trail connecting with trailheads along the Glenn Highway. Originally an Indian route, the Chickaloon-Knik-Nelchina Trail was used in the 1890s by prospectors, and United States Government surveyors. Trails in this area lead into big game country of rugged Talkeetna Mountains, home of sheep, moose, caribou, black and grizzly bear.

The first part of the Chickaloon-Knik-Nelchina Trail was also called the Matanuska Trail. It followed the north side of the Matanuska River to Sheep Mountain. The Glenn Highway follows this route except where the old trail is in the river bottom. The road is now at higher elevations.

Construction of a railroad in 1929 from Matanuska to Chickaloon coal fields changed freighting habits. Freight now moved on the railroad to the coal fields,

This old cabin built before the turn of the century has seen continuous use.

then up the Nelchina Trail to Nelchina. With the beginning of World War II in 1942 gold mining was terminated and old trails had very little use. In the early 1970s there was a renewed interest in placer gold exploration and mining in the Nelchina area and trails north of Sheep Mountain were used again.

Early users of the Chickaloon-Knik-Nelchina Trail began their trek at Knik on the North shore of Knik Arm of Cook Inlet. Civilization, towns, farms, roads, and highways have replaced or covered the old trail. Hikers now access this historical trail at the Chickaloon Trailhead, other trailheads along the Glenn Highway, or Old Man Creek Trailhead, the trail's most northern access point.

Numerous other trails, too many to mention here, access the Chickaloon-Knik-Nelchina Trail from the highway system. This whole area is criss-crossed with animal and human trails that would fill a book if only a brief description was used for each trail. We've lived in Alaska and walked these trails for over three decades, and we're still discovering new paths and places to visit and new ways to get there. The trails mentioned in this section are only a sampling of what we've found, and hardly begins to represent the numbers of trails and exciting routes to the wilderness.

HIKE 53: *CARIBOU CREEK TRAIL*

General description: Caribou Creek Trail is a sixteen-mile trail leading north, east of the Glenn Highway beginning at Caribou River Bridge and connecting the Glenn Highway to Chickaloon-Knik-Nelchina Trail System
General location: 107 miles north of Anchorage on the Glenn Highway
Trail begins: Mile 107 of Glenn Highway
Trail ends: At Chickaloon-Knik-Nelchina Trail System
Maps: USGS Anchorage D1, D2
Difficulty: Moderate to difficult
Length: nineteen miles to Chickaloon-Knik-Nelchina Trail System
Elevation: 1,100 to 4,700 feet
Special attractions: Open alpine scenery, wild animals, especially caribou.
Best season: June through September
For more information: State of Alaska, Division of Parks and Recreation, HC32 Box 6706, Wasilla, Alaska 99687, (907) 745-3975
Finding the trailhead: The trailhead is located north of Anchorage at mile 107 of the Glenn Highway. There is a foot trail to the north, just east of Caribou Creek Bridge.

The hike: A spur of the Chickaloon-Knik-Nelchina Trail System, it is used by hunters and hikers. The trail joins Alfred Creek Trail, (sixteen miles) another spur of the Chickaloon-Knik-Nelchina Trail System. Alfred Creek Trail is behind Sheep Mountain. Prior to reaching Alfred Creek Trail, Caribou Trail becomes rough and indistinct. Caribou Creek Trail moves north, past its intersection with Alfred Creek Trail, and terminates when it becomes part of the Chickaloon-Knik-Nelchina Trail System. Then it joins Purinton Creek Trail at Chitna Pass. Moose, caribou, and brown bear frequent this area and are hunted along the north end of the trail. Dall sheep can frequently be seen on Sheep Mountain. Sheep cannot be hunted on Sheep Mountain.

One spring, my fifteen-year-old daughter and I spent two days and one night on Sheep Mountain observing and photographing a band of Dall rams. Sheep have excellent eyesight and can pick up the slightest movement if a hiker allows themselves to be seen. Once seen, however, don't move out of sight. As soon as sheep cannot see the person they have been looking at they will quickly move out of sight. We watched for an hour or more and they did not move. I told my daughter about sheep running if they saw us, then couldn't see us. She decided to test the theory. As soon as she moved out of sight the four big rams quickly stood up and walked over the hill and out of sight.

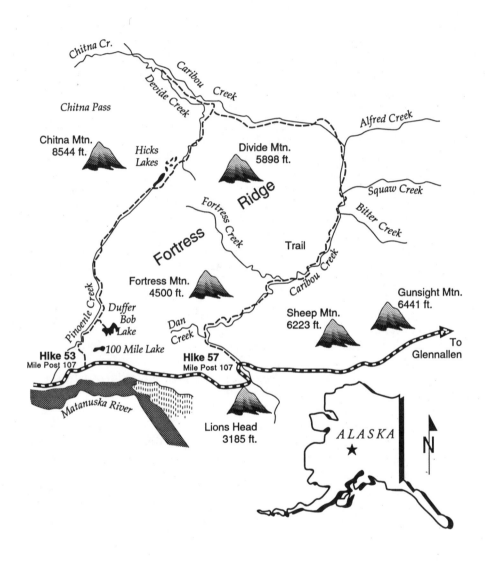

HIKE 54: CASTLE MOUNTAIN TRAIL

General description: Tiered ledges of Castle Mountain, consisting of almost pure limestone, can be seen from the Glenn Highway. The trail runs along the foot of Castle Mountain and then drops down into the King River Basin. It then travels above the river in dense trees as it further winds slowly down to the river. Once at the river, the trail crosses, then follows the east fork into a small steep-walled canyon.

General location: Seventy-two miles north of Anchorage on the Glenn Highway.

Trail begins: Mile 71.8 of Glenn Highway.

Trail ends: Kings River headwaters.

Maps: USGS Anchorage D5, C5.

Difficulty: Easy to moderate.

Length: Three miles to Chickaloon-Knik-Nelchina Trail, 18.8 miles to headwater of Kings River.

Elevation: 1,000 to 3,000 feet.

Special attractions: Good hiking, scenery, vistas of Kings Mountain.

Best season: June through September.

For more information: State of Alaska, Division of Parks and Recreation, HC32 Box 6706, Wasilla, Alaska 99687, (907) 745-3975.

Finding the trailhead: There are no signs, but the trailhead is easy to find. It is located north of Anchorage at mile 71.8 on the Glenn Highway where a dirt road turns left from the highway. Turn on this dirt road for a short distance to a cleared area which is used by the public for parking. This cleared area is on private property. Please respect the landowners and pack out what you pack in.

The hike: Castle Mountain Trail give hikers access to the historic Chickaloon-Knik-Nelchina Trail System. Sometimes called the Permanenti Road, Castle Mountain Trail intersects Chickaloon-Knik-Nelchina Trail three miles from Castle Mountain Trail trailhead. To this point it is a trail for the whole family. The trail to the left goes about a mile to a high cliff overlooking Kings River. The Chickaloon-Knik-Nelchina Trail is difficult to find beyond this point but begins again as Kings River Trail and continues to the trailhead at Mile 66.7 on the Glenn Highway.

Hikers may continue straight ahead on Castle Mountain Trail for another eighteen miles on a foot, four-wheel, and off-road vehicle trail. It climbs over a ridge and follows along the west flank of Castle Mountain. An excellent trail with majestic views of King River Basin. Near trails-end, hikers have a marvelous view of the Matanuska River and a number of small glaciers. My experience on Castle Mountain Trail was during a period of dry weather and the going was very good. There was evidence however, that the trail had been wet earlier in the year and those who had proceeded me had had a more difficult time. A popular hunting area during the month of September, hunters use the Castle Mountain Trail to gain access to game country. Hunter traffic is a mixed blessing. It keeps the trail free of brush and well defined, but it also makes bog holes in wet swampy areas.

HIKE 55: *KINGS RIVER TRAIL*

General description: Hiking to Kings River and the scenery of alabaster cliffs along the way. This is first trail in the Chickaloon-Knik-Nelchina Trail System.
General location: North of Anchorage into the Talkeetna Mountains
Trail begins: Mile 66.7 on the Glenn Highway
Trail ends: Kings River
Maps: USGS Anchorage D5, C5
Difficulty: Easy to moderate
Length: five miles one way
Elevation: 500 to 1,200 feet
Special attractions: Picnicking spots and scenery
Best season: June through September
For more information: State of Alaska, Division of Parks and Recreation, HC32 Box 6706, Wasilla, Alaska 99687, (907) 745-3975
Finding the trailhead: There is a dilapidated King River Trail sign at the trailhead at mile 66.7 on the Glenn Highway. If traveling from Anchorage the sign is on the north side of the highway. Parking is on the north side just before the highway crosses King River Bridge. The parking area, which continues all the way to river's edge, is a great spot for picnics, fishing, or exploring the beach where King River flows into Matanuska River.

The hike: Kings River Trail is part of the historic Chickaloon-Knik-Nelchina Trail System. The going is easy and is a good trail for youngsters. It will let them get a feel of the trail system and enjoy a one day outing or picnic.

In the beginning, the trail wanders over flat terrain through stands of big cottonwood trees. At 2.7 miles from the trailhead, there is a trail going to the left to Young Creek. Kings River Trail continues following the wooded banks of Kings River until the trail becomes lost and ends at Kings River. After crossing Kings River, about a mile further, Chickaloon-Knik-Nelchina Trail can be found again on a high cliff overlooking the river.

The Kings River Trail is a good one for youngsters.

HIKE 54: *CASTLE MOUNTAIN*   HIKE 55: *KINGS RIVER*
HIKE 58: *PURINTON CREEK*

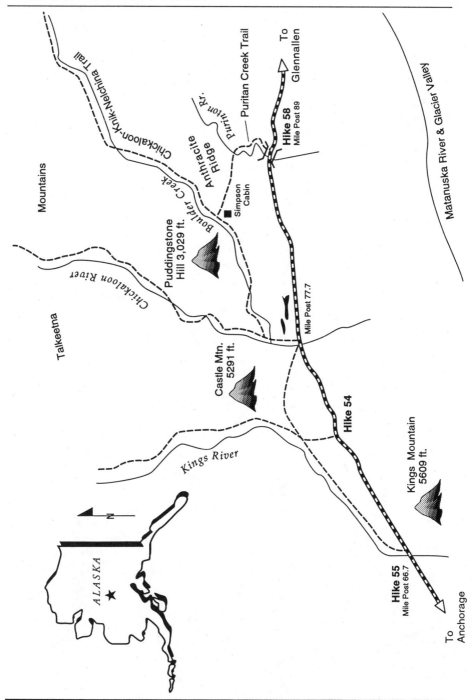

111

HIKE 56: OLD MAN AND CROOKED CREEK TRAIL

General description: These trails take hikers over high tundra country where wildlife abounds and very little timber exists. These trails comprise the northern end of the historic Chickaloon-Knik-Nelchina Trail System.

General location: 130 miles north of Anchorage on the Glenn Highway.

Trail begins: Mile 130 of Glenn Highway, 2.3 miles north of Eureka Lodge in a gravel pit.

Trail ends: Nelchina river and townsite.

Maps: USGS Anchorage D1, USGS Talkeetna A1.

Difficulty: Moderate to difficult.

Length: Twenty-seven miles round trip.

Elevation: 3,000 to 3,800 feet.

Special attractions: Scenery, animals, connections with other Chickaloon-Knik-Nelchina Trails.

Best season: June through September.

For more information: State of Alaska, Division of Parks and Recreation, HC32 Box 6706, Wasilla, Alaska 99687, (907) 745-3975.

Finding the trailhead: Old Man and Crooked Creek trails trailhead is in a gravel pit 2.3 miles north of Eureka Lodge. There is a Chickaloon-Knik-Nelchina Trail system sign visible from the Glenn Highway which reads, Old Man Trail-two miles, Crooked Creek-nine miles and Nelchina Town-14.5 miles.

The hike: Old Man and Crooked Creek Trail is part of the historic Chickaloon-Knik-Nelchina Trail System. In 1912, gold was discovered on Albert Creek, a tributary of Crooked Creek, by Fred Getchell, Dunkin McCormick, and O. D. Olson. The news got around and 100 men departed Valdez late in the year to stake their claim. By 1914, 400 men were active in mining the area and a small town became established known as Nelchina. Fifteen or twenty cabins and an assorted number of tents comprised the camp. Old Man and Crooked Creek

Sign at trailhead of Chickloon-Knik-Nelchina trail.

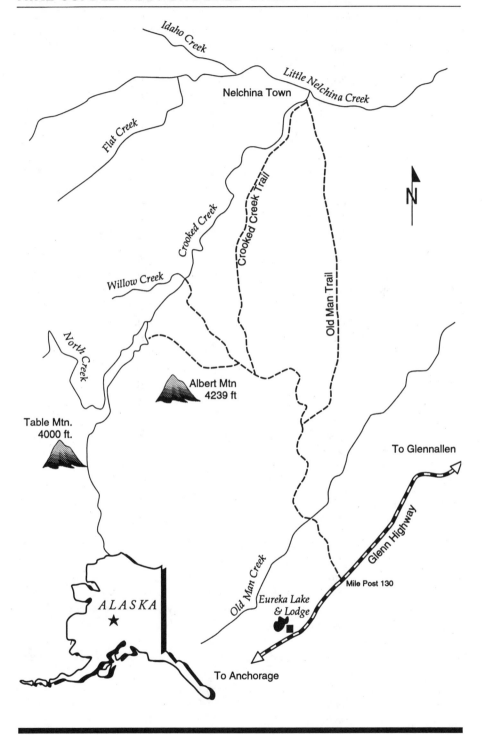

trails are modern remains of a golden age. Old Man and Crooked Creek are perfect trails into open high country with plenty of lakes and streams for fishing. High peaks and rolling hills can be seen for many miles in all directions. The best feature of these trails is the excellent chance to see many varieties of wildlife. A drawback to Old Man and Crooked Creek trails is that most of the old foot trails are used today by tractors, ORVs, and swamp buggys. Tundra has been disturbed and a deep, muddy track is the result. If hikers don't mind hiking under these conditions, or are willing to step off the trails and make their own way, these hikes are certainly worth the effort. Hiking into Nelchina on either Old Man or Crooked Creek Trails, and returning on the other, adds an interesting aspect to visiting this area.

HIKE 57: *PINOCHLE TRAIL*

General description: This trail, traveling from The Glenn Highway to Caribou Creek Trail, offers good possibilities for viewing lots of wildlife. It offers a wide variety of scenery: lakes, streams, mountains, timber, and tundra.
General location: 99.5 miles north of Anchorage on the Glenn Highway.
Trail begins: Mile 99.5 of Glenn Highway.
Trail ends: At the intersection of Caribou Creek Trail.
Maps: USGS Anchorage D2, D3.
Difficulty: Easy to moderate.
Length: sixteen miles.
Elevation: 1,100 to 3,500 feet
Special attractions: Scenery and access to Hicks Lake and Chickaloon-Knik-Nelchina Trail System
Best season: June through September
For more information: State of Alaska, Division of Parks and Recreation, HC32 Box 6706, Wasilla, Alaska 99687, (907) 745-3975
Finding the trailhead: The trailhead is located north of Anchorage on the Glenn Highway at Mile 99.4. The trail starts from the parking area on the north side of the highway. Directly southeast from the parking area is a magnificent view of the Matanuska Glacier and the Chugach Mountain Range.

The hike: Pinochle Trail, part of the historic Chickaloon-Knik-Nelchina Trail System, travels into vast, high, open country with splendid scenic views. It first moves through low, muddy marshland, then through a thick forest area, and slowly climbs into high rolling tundra. From the trail's high point it travels down steep hills into Hicks Creek Basin and follows the creek to Hicks Lake. On its way to connect with Caribou Creek Trail, it goes past a number of smaller lakes and travels along Divide Creek. The trail wanders through huge boulders in Divide Creek Floor and then works its way around these boulders where it meets Caribou Creek Trail.

Around the turn of century this trail became a major spur of the Chickaloon-Knik-Nelchina Trail System. It was used extensively for hauling supplies to gold mining camps in the Alfred Creek, Albert Creek, and Nelchina Creek area.

Lars Swenson prepares soup on a camp stove. In most Alaska National Parks open fires are not allowed.

HIKE 58: *PURINTON CREEK TRAIL*

General description: The beginning is a good trail for family outings. Purinton Creek Trail roams through low rolling hills with panoramic views of high rugged mountain peaks.

General location: North of Anchorage into the Talkeetna Mountains.

Trail begins: Glenn Highway Mile 89.

Trail ends: Headwaters of Boulder Creek.

Maps: USGS Anchorage D3, D4.

Difficulty: Easy to moderate.

Length: 1.3 miles to Chickaloon-Knik-Nelchina Trail, twenty-three miles to Chitna Pass.

Elevation: 1,000 to 4,700 feet.

Special attractions: The Puriton Creek Trail, (sometimes called Puritan Creek Trail) outstanding feature is its spectacular mountain vistas, wild flowers, and wildlife.

Best season: June through September.

For more information: State of Alaska Division of Parks and Recreation, HC32 Box 6706, Wasilla, Alaska 99687, (907) 745-3975.

Finding the trailhead: The trail begins from a parking area off the Glenn Highway, mile 89.2, at Purinton Creek. The trailhead sign reads Chickaloon-Knik-Nelchina Trail—Purinton Creek Entrance. Parking is on the north side of the Glenn Highway at the Purinton Creek Bridge. The State of Alaska Highway sign at the bridge reads, Puritan Creek.

The hike: Purinton Creek Trail links the Glenn Highway to the historic Chickaloon-Knik-Nelchina Trail System. The first eight miles gives hikers spectacular views of the Chugach Mountains to the south. The jagged peaks of Castle Mountain are to the west as the trail travels through the foot hills of Anthracite Ridge in Talkeetna Mountains. Cross Boulder Creek above the bluffs of Anthracite Ridge. In spring and early summer, Dall sheep are low on the hillsides birthing young. Near the trail I have been able to get close and observe their activities, take pictures, and without disturbing the sheep. The hills along the trail will almost always have sheep visible to hikers. Moose will often be seen. Boulder Creek begins at the eight-mile mark and the trail follows the drainage to about four miles below the Chitna Pass.

It is probably best to remain on the northwest side of Boulder Creek until you can safely cross where the creek becomes braided. The last 2.5 miles to the pass ascends gradually and makes for a pleasant hike.

HIKE 59: *SQUAW CREEK ACCESS TRAIL*

General description: Squaw Creek Access Trail accesses a system of easy to moderately hard hiking trails including Gunsight Mountain, Squaw Creek, and Belanger Pass Trails. These trails take hikers into the Alfred Creek and Nelchina area and are part of Chickaloon-Knik-Nelchina Trail System. The access trail goes through spruce timber toward Gunsight Mountain, into and above the timberline into good areas for seeing wild game. The trail is suitable for family hiking.
General location: Talkeetna Mountains north of Anchorage off the Glenn Highway.
Trail begins: Mile 117.6 of Glenn Highway.
Trail ends: Squaw Creek and trail system.

Squaw Creek Access Trail connects with a system of easy to moderately hard hiking trails.

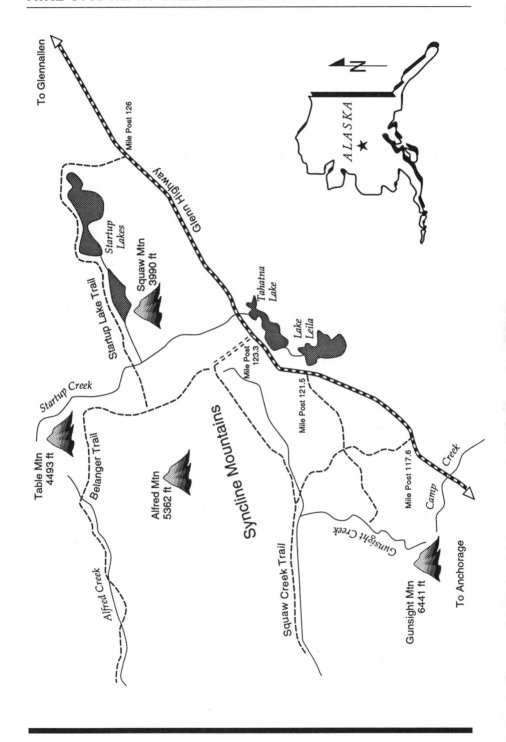

Maps: USGS Anchorage D1, D2.
Difficulty: Easy to Moderate.
Length: three miles.
Elevation: 3,000 to 4,000 feet.
Special attractions: Grayling fishing in Squaw Creek, scenery, flowers and animals.
Best season: June through September.
For more information: State of Alaska Division of Parks and Recreation, HC32 Box 6706, Wasilla, Alaska 99687, (907) 745-3975.
Finding the trailhead: There is a Chickaloon-Knik-Nelchina Trail System sign in a rest area on the north side of the Glenn Highway at mile 117.6.

The hike: Squaw Creek Access Trail is a three-mile trail giving hikers access to the historic Chickaloon-Knik-Nelchina Trail System via Squaw Creek Trail. There are moose, grizzly bear, and caribou in the area. By using Squaw Creek Access Trail it is possible to go to Squaw Creek Trail, on to Belanger Pass Trail, then up Belanger Pass Trail to Crooked Creek Trail and finally the town of Nelchina. Although the Squaw Creek Access Trail is in the trees most of the time, there is an excellent view of the high peaks of Sheep Mountain to the south, and Fortress Ridge to the west.

The trail is wide and level thanks to gold miners. There are still signs of old gold mine claim along the way. The vista from this trail has a natural balance of lakes, rivers, alpine forest and high mountain peaks, an abundance of wildlife, and fishing in Squaw Creek.

About .5 to .75 mile in, you will come to a fork in the trail. The trail to the left suddenly comes to a steep ravine with a small creek in the bottom. You can make it down and back up, but with a heavy pack it would probably be dangerous. The trail to the right takes you on a excellent lower trail which also crosses the creek and later joins the main trail to Squaw Creek.

Once while hiking, I met a young couple and asked how they liked the trail. They said they had hiked the easy trail to Squaw Creek and enjoyed the rich abundance of wild flowers. They had expected to see a fast moving creek of some size but were surprised to find the creek small and quiet. They had also hoped to see wildlife. I told them most wildlife bedded down during the day and were out feeding in early morning and late afternoon. I suggested they take a nap and hike the trail again in the early morning or late evening, bring binoculars, stop in open areas, and they would probably see fox, caribou, and moose.

PRINCE WILLIAM SOUND AND COPPER RIVER BASIN TRAILS

Climate and geography differ between Prince William Sound and Copper River Basin, but the areas are tied together by river systems and history. Fish traveling to their natal streams in Copper River Basin swim the length of Prince William Sound before entering their spawning water. Travelers to the Sound must pass through the basin. Both the Sound and Basin are outdoor playgrounds for visitors from outside and particularly residents from Fairbanks and Interior Alaska. The Largest National Park in America, Wrangell-St. Elias, is in the Basin and Sound. Hikes in these areas fall into two categories: meticulously maintained trails, and hikes without marked trails where hikers may roam at will, depending on their skill and physical condition.

Some hikes in the Basin and Sound do not have designated trailheads. Hikers need only chose their area of interest and begin hiking. Other hikes are from well identified trailheads and along well maintained trails. See individual trails for directions to finding each trailhead.

Valdez and Cordova are the principle areas for hiking in the Sound. Over the mountains from the Sound, Wrangell-St. Elias National Park and Preserve and environs attract backcountry walkers.

The Cordova area was first settled by Eyak Indians. The area received its name when Spanish explorer, Salvador Fidalgo called Orca Bay 'Bahia de Cordova' in 1790. Cordova's modern history began when copper was discovered in 1890, and a railroad was constructed to the mines in Kennicott. The railroad was considered an engineering feat in its time with two amazing bridges. One, the Million Dollar Bridge, spans the Copper River between Miles and Childs glaciers, fifty miles north of Cordova. The other, 600-foot-long, Kuskulana Bridge, is on the road from Chitna to McCarthy. Kuskulana Bridge was constructed during the cold winter of 1910, where outside temperature plummeted to fifty degrees below zero. The railroad died in 1938, when the copper mines closed. Today, Cordova is primarily a fishing town.

Valdez began when the United States began looking for an all-American route to the Klondike. Miners climbed up over Valdez Glacier and came down to Copper Center on the Klutina River. Later, when a route through Keystone Canyon, and over Thompson Pass, was discovered, a telegraph line was built to Eagle on the Yukon river.

Today the road from Valdez follows Lowe River and turns into Keystone Canyon at Mile 16. The original Goat Trail used by early explorers and miners can still be seen high on the mountain wall. Waterfalls plummet down rock cliffs, and, in winter, ice climbers from all over the world come here to climb the frozen water.

The Cordova area receives 200 inches of rain per year and trails are usually wet. The Sound is a rain forest climate. Expect rain and prepare for it. Waterproof boots are nearly always needed and good quality raingear is a must.

Bridal Veil Falls, one of the most popular attractions in the Prince William Sound area.

Most trails in the Sound were established, or at least maintained, for recreation purposes. Fishing and photography in addition to the joy of being in backcountry are the trails' main attractions.

Hiking in Wrangell-St. Elias National Park and Preserve is a singular experience. Even though the park is the nation's largest and easy to reach from Alaska's road system, it is also one of the most inaccessible for hikers. There are only two ways to approach the park by road: Edgerton Highway and Nebesna Road. Many hikers use air charter companies to take them above timberline and the beginning of their hike.

Three of my sons and I used our old Stinson Voyager Station Wagon, 1948 vintage airplane to get us to our trailhead on Nebesna Glacier. We carefully picked our landing spot on the glacier, one we had thoroughly investigated, and landed without incident. Upon landing we turned the plane into the prevailing wind and tied the old bird down with strong ropes, using mountaineers eighteen-inch ice augers for tiedowns. Satisfying ourselves that the plane was safe, we began our week-long trek to circle Mt. Gordon.

We were traveling light, with just enough food for our allotted time. Our packs, including all camping gear and food, weighed less than twenty-eight pounds each. Our diet consisted of trail mix and chea seed. We did not intend to have a fire. As a safety precaution we made an air drop of Military C rations off of a snow field at the base of the mountain.

We had a delightful trip, never spending a night in the same place twice. Each day we would pack up and go where our instincts directed and then pitch camp where night found us. Weather was typical. Periods of blue sky and sun mixed with times of wind, rain, and even snow.

When we reached our airdrop food cache we were ready for a change of menu. Even C rations sounded good, so good we decide to mix them all together in the only pan we had. In went wieners and beans, beef stew, spaghetti, and several other items peculiar to C rations. The concoction, under the circumstances, was edible, if not tasty, and it was hot. To this day when a conversation turns to hiking one of us will ask, "Do you guys remember Mt. Gordon Stew?"

When we returned to our airplane we received a surprise. During our absence the glacier had melted over eighteen inches. Our ice auger tiedowns were laying on top of the glacier. We do not know how long it took for the glacier to melt enough to free our anchors, but if the wind had come up it would have blown our transportation over the edge of the glacier where it would have rolled up into a little red ball at the bottom of a crevasse. We have yet to discover a safe way to tie an airplane down on a glacier for an extended time.

HIKE 60: *LIBERTY CREEK TRAIL*

General description: Liberty Creek Trail is close to Liberty Creek Campground. The campground is at the base of Liberty Creek Waterfall. The trail snakes among tall evergreen trees with no undergrowth. It is an easy climb on a well-used, defined trail. Hikers may go to the top of the falls or to a ridge where photographs may be taken of Copper River, Three Mile Lake, and a panorama of Copper Valley.

General location: Five miles north of Chitna

Trail begins: Mile 35 of Edgerton HIghway

Trail ends: The trail peters out in the timber at a ridge. There are game trails beyond if hikers desire to continue.

Maps: USGS Valdez C2, B2

Difficulty: Easy to difficult

Length: 2.5 miles

Elevation: 1,000 to 2,000 feet

Special attractions: Cascading waterfall and views of Copper River Valley.

Best season: June through September.

For more information: State of Alaska, Division of Parks and Recreation, Glennallen, Alaska 99588, (907) 822-5536

Finding the trailhead: Liberty Creek Campground is well marked but hikers must be alert to find the road to the trailhead. Traveling from the Richardson Highway toward Chitna look for a short dirt road turning off to the west just before you reach the campground. There is no trailhead in the camping area. From the dirt road you can park and walk to the trailhead in Liberty Creek Canyon.

The hike: Pleasant surprises await hikers at Liberty Creek. Liberty Creek Campground, in close proximity to Copper River subsistence- and personal-

From Liberty Creek Trail hikers can hike up a ridge for views of the Copper Valley.

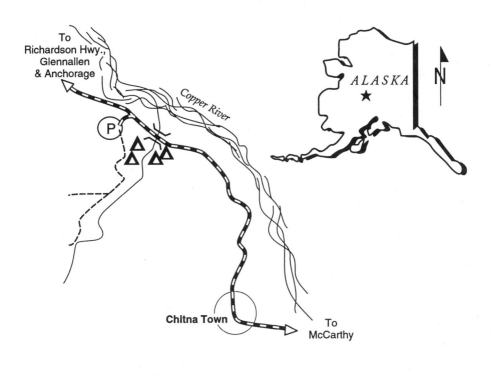

use fisheries, is used by travelers who desire an extra nice place to pitch a tent or park a motor home or camper. The campground surrounds a small clearwater creek at the base of a boiling, twenty-foot waterfall cascading among glacial rocks. Mist from tumbling water drifts across the creek and dampens plants growing along the banks. Rich green foliage creates a restful effect on campers lucky enough to find a vacant spot. Camping is on each side of the creek.

What a delight to find this short trail into a surreal forest setting. The grandeur and ease of this hike make it well worth taking to get a break from the long drive from Glennallen and Anchorage. There is very little undergrowth under tall, whispering trees. It is easy climbing on a popular, well-defined trail. Several meandering trails to the left go down to the top of the falls. The one to the right goes to the ridge where hikers can get a clear view of Copper River, Third Lake, and much of Copper Valley.

While hiking this trail, we discovered fresh bear scat and moose sign. We didn't want to surprise either one so we made lots of noise. Generally wild animals are timid and will run away. It is only when surprised that they are a problem. Use common sense and you won't have complications. We didn't.

HIKE 61: *MCKINLEY LAKE TRAIL*

General description: This trail offers a short, easy hike through a lush, moss-covered, mature, spruce and hemlock forest. Ideal for camping in a tent or Forest Service cabin, this trail goes through country loaded with wildlife and excellent salmon fishing.

General location: twenty-one miles east of Cordova

Trail begins: Mile 21 Copper River Highway

Trail ends: McKinley Lake Recreation Cabin

Maps: Cordova B4

Difficulty: Easy

Length: 2.1 miles

Elevation: 100 to 150 feet

Special attractions: Berry picking, cabin, fishing, winter sports

Best season: June through September

For more information: Chugach National Forest, Cordova Ranger District, 612 Second Street, Cordova, Alaska, (907) 424-7661

Finding the trailhead: Take the Copper River Highway from Cordova to signed, McKinley Lake trailhead at Mile 21.

The hike: Walking along a flat, wide, brush free footpath in a rain forest environment to excellent fishing and wildlife viewing is what McKinley Lake Trail is all about. Blueberries and salmon berries as well as abundant wildflowers add to the interest. Expected wildlife includes: brown bear, black bear, and beaver on the lake. Trumpeter swans, Canadian geese, and loons nesting on the lake are among waterfowl species. Harbor seals following salmon from the ocean to the lake may be seen chasing their dinner.

McKinley Lakes Trail. Photo by Chugach National Forest, Cordova Ranger Station

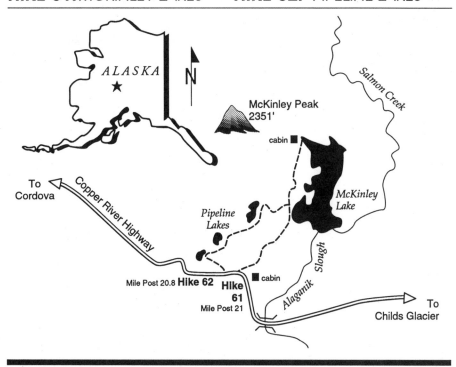

Fishing is the reason for the season. Silvers run in August and September and reds in late June and July. Cutthroat trout haunt McKinley Lake and its outlet stream, Alagnik Slough. Hikers may hunt for black bear, brown bear, and waterfowl in designated seasons. Review Alaska Department of Fish and Game hunting and fishing regulations.

The area receives a lot of rain and some areas may be muddy or have standing water. Proper raingear and good waterproof boots are a must. With appropriate equipment this trail is suitable for a family outing, a dayhike or extended stay at one of the two Forest Service cabins. One cabin is along the road near the trailhead. The other is at the far end of McKinley Lake. The cabin on McKInley Lake is insulated and both are suitable for winter use. Tent camping, in a good quality tent, can be near the lake and open country beyond. Water and dry wood is not always available.

As interesting as the main trail may be, curious hikers can take a side trip by walking .5 mile north of McKinley Lake to abandoned Lucky Strike Gold Quartz Mine for fishing in small ponds or traveling east to Mckinley Peak.

The Forest Service public recreation cabins on Mckinley Lake Trail may be reserved by mail or at any Chugach National Forest Service office as much as 179 days in advance of planned stay. Occupancy is by permit only for a cost of $20 per night per party. The cabin is available year-round. This is an excellent hike for family outing, day hiking, or a two day trip with tent camping at the lake or stay in one of the Mckinley Lake Trail cabins. As a courtesy to hikers staying at the cabin, please camp in other areas out of sight of the cabin.

HIKE 62: *PIPELINE LAKES TRAIL*

General description: A scenic hike along an old wooden water pipe
General location: twenty-one miles east of Cordova.
Trail begins: Mile 20.8 Copper River Highway.
Trail ends: Junction with McKinley Lake Trail.
Maps: Cordova B4.
Difficulty: Easy.
Length: 1.8 miles.
Elevation: fifty to 150 feet.
Special attractions:
Best season: June through September.
For more information: Chugach National Forest, Cordova Ranger District, 612 Second Street, Cordova, Alaska, (907) 424-7661
Finding the trailhead: Via Copper River Highway to signed, Pipeline Lakes trailhead at Mile 20.8.

The hike: The name, Pipeline Lakes Trail in Prince William Sound, conjures up thoughts of oil and Valdez. Cordova's Pipeline Trail has nothing to do with oil but follows an old, water pipeline. The nearly-level footpath is wet and crosses several large areas of muskeg where the old pipeline is occasionally visible. Wildflowers line the trail and dot the countryside.

Pipeline Trail offers a short, easy hike through wet muskeg to numerous fishing ponds. Photo by Chugach National Forest, Cordova Ranger Station

The trail offers a short, easy hike through wet muskeg to numerous ponds for excellent rainbow trout fishing. Some public information brochures list grayling in these ponds. Grayling were stocked several years ago but didn't do too well. Hiking and fishing in the area may be extended by continuing to the McKinley Lake Trail and using the Forest Service cabin at the north end of the lake. Tent camping is available near the lake and open country beyond. Fresh fish meals may be supplemented by the profusion of edible berries in the area.

Traveling south on McKinley Lake Trail leads back to the Copper River Highway. The parking area for Pipeline Lakes and Mckinley Lakes trailheads are .2 mile apart.

HIKE 63: *POWER CREEK TRAIL*

General description: Hiking into an area, rich in wildlife and berries, and first settled by Eyak Indians.
General location: End of Power Creek Road out of Cordova.
Trail begins: End of Power Creek Road.
Trail ends: Power Creek Basin.
Maps: Cordova C5.
Difficulty: Moderate to difficult.
Length: 2.5 miles.
Elevation: 100 to 450 feet.
Special attractions: Scenery, wildflowers, and berry picking.
Best season: June through September.
For more information: Chugach National Forest, Cordova Ranger District, 612 Second Street, Cordova, Alaska, (907) 424-7661.
Finding the trailhead: Follow Power Creek Road six miles to the trailhead at the end of the road.

The hike: One mile from the trailhead, Ohman Falls on power Creek is just off the main trail and the first stop on this picturesque hike. From the trailhead,

A steady .5-mile climb along the Power Creek Trail treats hikers to a magnificent view of the Power Creek Basin. Photo by Chugach National Forest, Cordova Ranger Stateion

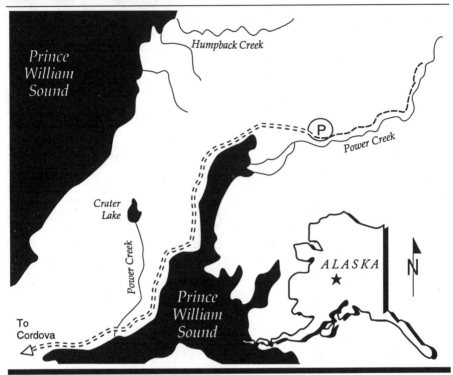

the wide, well maintained foot path parallels the boiling, whitewater of Power Creek. Power Creek drives through a narrow valley and is joined by numerous side streams, and waterfalls cascading from mountain slopes. A steady .5-mile climb, treats hikers to a magnificent view of Power Creek Basin.

A small, picturesque pond lies beside the trail as it enters the valley and continues for another 1.5 miles along Power Creek. The last mile treats hikers to views of high-mountain glaciers and wide open country. Walking west and climbing the saddle to the ridge line opens excellent views of glaciers, mountaintops, and Orca Inlet in Prince William Sound. Multi-day trips with good camping sites are possible in Power Creek Basin.

Crater Lake is five miles south on the ridge. The Chugach National Forest District is in the process of completing a trail to Crater Lake. Until the trail is complete don't attempt to hike the ridge without a topographic map and good orienteering skills. When wet, Prince William Sound is not a good place to be lost. With caution and planning the valley offers side trips to view glaciers, enjoy wildflowers, magnificent scenery, and abundant edible berries.

Bears come to the trail during berry season and should be treated with caution. Other Wildlife includes: Sitka black-tailed deer, mountain goats, ptarmigan, and spruce grouse. Hunting for black and brown bear, deer, mountain goats, ptarmigan, and grouse are in designated seasons. Become familiar with Alaska Department of Fish and Game hunting regulations before hunting.

HIKE 64: *SOLOMON GULCH TRAIL*

General description: Solomon Gulch Trail extends 1.3 miles into the valley of eight-mile-long Solomon Creek. At the upper end of the trail is Solomon Lake which is created by a dam measuring 112 feet high. An earlier twenty-two-foot dam now lies submerged in Solomon Lake. The current dam, completed in 1981, is the source of 80% of Valdez's electric power.

General location: Five miles from Valdez, west along Dayville Road.

Trail begins: 150 yards northeast of the fish hatchery on Dayville Road.

Trail ends: On the shore of the lake at the top of the dam on Solomon Creek.

Maps: USGS Valdez A5, A6, A7.

Difficulty: Easy to difficult.

Length: Three miles.

Elevation: Sea level to 700 feet.

Special attractions: Cascading waterfall and views of Port of Valdez and Valdez Bay.

Best season: June through September.

For more information: Valdez Convention and Visitors Bureau. P.O. Box 1603 Valdez, Alaska 99686 (907) 835-2984.

Finding the trailhead: Drive about seven miles from Valdez, turn onto the Dayville road. About four miles along the road is the Fish Hatchery. Solomon Gulch Trailhead is 150 yards northeast. It is located directly behind the power plant.

The hike: Solomon Lake area and surrounding mountains were once rich in gold deposits. To take advantage of this mineral wealth, a number of mines were constructed. Midas Mine, located at the head of the valley, was connected to the beach by a wagon trail. In addition to housing and kitchen buildings, storage sheds and warehouses, and maintainance shops, the mine was equipped with an aerial tram five miles long. The tram was the longest tram in the world in its day, carrying ore from the mine in the upper valley to the camp at tidewater. Here the ore was loaded on ships and taken to a smelter in Tacoma,

View of Valdez arm and the city of Valdez from the Solomon Gulch trail.

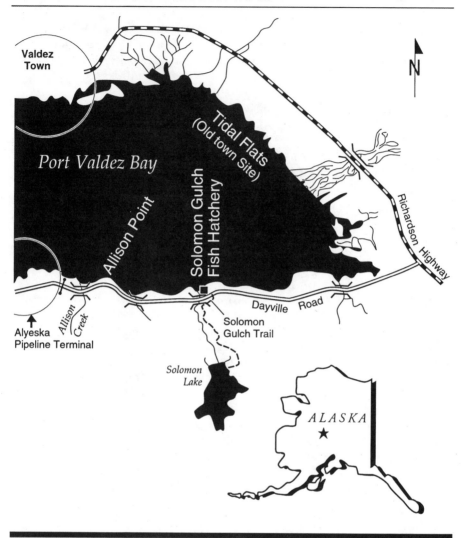

Washington. In 1920 the mine closed.

In 1983, Solomon Gulch Trail was created and provided a close look at the lake, dam, and aqueducts as well as a scenic view of the Port of Valdez, Valdez Bay, and the city beyond. The lake's elevation is 690 feet above sea level.

The trail is well defined and begins 150 yards northeast of the fish hatchery on Dayville Road. The hike, except for three steep, lengthy inclines, is one most hikers will enjoy. The first steep incline starts a short distance from the road and has a flight of steep stairs to aid ascent. Sixty stairs have a vertical rise of twelve inches each. Banisters, made from 2 X 4's, protect hikers and give them a hand hold to assist their climb. The second set of stairs, consisting of forty stairs, isn't as steep.

The trail levels out for a short distance and is followed by another steep climb. This rise has no stairs, but there is a hand rope to hold while you climb. The rope makes it easier going up and comfortable coming down. Once you reach the top of this rise it is smooth sailing to the lake.

Although this hike is steep in the beginning, there are numerous places to rest along the way. When you get on top, there are three different places where you can see Valdez Arm and Valdez Bay for taking pictures. About half-way to the lake the trail breaks out of timber above the power plant. Here hikers have a beautiful view of Valdez Arm and the small boat harbor. The day I took the hike there was a state ferry departing the terminal. Blue ocean water and deep aqua sky was divided by snow capped mountains. An oil tanker was leaving Alyeska Terminal. The combined effect of sky, boats, water, and mountains created a picture fit for a movie.

Looking in the opposite direction of Valdez you can see the dam and big water pipes coming out of it. As you walk toward the dam there is a slight decline. At the bottom of the decline there is a sign directing hikers to a small set of stairs. If you're superstitious don't go this way, but take the trail, because there are thirteen stairs. When you get to the bottom of the stairs you will notice what looks like a road going right and left. It is not a road but you are standing on top of the Alyeska Oil Pipeline, mile 798, just two miles from the terminal.

If you brought a picnic lunch it will taste extra good as you eat and contemplate what the miners of the past did in this area before the dam backed up the creek and covered up the mines.

On my way out, I found I could hang on the rope in the steep places, and take giant steps all the way to the stairs. I felt like a real mountain climber for a moment. I was carrying an aluminum frame pack. When I started to descend the flight of sixty stairs they were so steep my back pack hit the stairs behind me and had a tendency to pitch me forward. For someone shorter it could be dangerous so be careful.

A typical family, in no rush, should allow three hours for a leisurely hike on this trail. Pack a picnic lunch and have a little fun while you enjoy Valdez.

HIKE 65: *SUMMIT LAKE TRAIL*

General description: Summit Lake Trail is not a defined trail, but an area of great beauty, high alpine meadows, wildflowers, marmots, and ptarmigan. The panorama of this area is unique. Hikers can see down into Keystone Canyon, with the Lowe River in the bottom. Worthington Glacier may be seen at mile 27. To accommodate hikers who desire to remain in the area, there are several campsites around Summit Lake and in Blueberry Lake Campground.
General location: Top of Thompson Pass thirty-five miles from Valdez on the Richardson Highway
Trail begins: Road to the north into a campground
Trail ends: Summit Lake and surrounding country
Maps: USGS Valdez A5, A6, A7
Difficulty: Easy

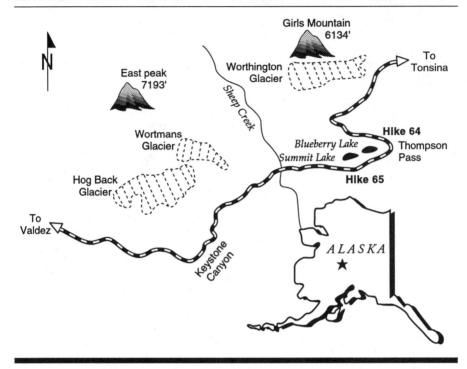

Length: As long as you want to hike in wide open, top-of-the-mountains country.
Elevation: 2,800 feet
Special attractions: Vistas, glaciers, small animals, camping
Best season: June through September
For more information: Chugach National Forest, Cordova Ranger District, PO Box 280, Cordova, Alaska 99574 (907) 424-7661
Finding the trailhead: Summit Lake Trail begins in the top of Thompson Pass wherever a hiker wants to begin. Just park your car at a designated pullout, or any other place you can safely park, and begin hiking.

The hike: At the top of Thompson pass is a nest of lakes easily accessed from the highway. One of the lakes is Summit Lake. The vistas are endless, the scenery grand. Hiking in this area can be be done anywhere, through valleys, canyons, and over peaks. Rapidily changing weather patterns can be watched; the feeling of being on top of a beautiful world may be enjoyed. Summit Lake provides camping sites for late afternoon barbecues and restful nights. From Summit you can hike to Blueberry Lake for good trout fishing. Worthington Glacier, the Hogback, and Wortmans glacier are within hiking distance. Hike where you want, fish in Blueberry Lake, photograph the vistas, and take close-ups of the tundra plants and animals.

HIKE 66: *THOMPSON PASS TRAIL*

General description: Thompson Pass Trail is not a defined trail, but an area of great beauty, high alpine meadows, wildflowers, marmots, and ptarmigan. Thompson Pass, the highest point on the Richardson Highway, is 2,800 feet above sea level. The panorama of this area is unique. Hikers can see down into the Keystone Canyon, with the Lowe River in the bottom, and hike to Worthington Glacier. To accommodate hikers who desire to remain in the area, there are several campsites in Blueberry Lake Campground at the top of the pass.

General location: Thompson Pass, thirty-five miles from Valdez on the Richardson Highway.

Trail begins: Anywhere a hiker wants to start hiking in Thompson Pass.

Trail ends: When a hiker gets tired and returns to the highway.

Maps: USGS Valdez A5, A6, A7.

Difficulty: Easy to moderate.

Length: Length may vary from just a few feet from the highway, for a quick photo, to an overnight, or extended hike.

Elevation: 2,800 feet.

Special attractions: High alpine meadows, glaciers, and wildflowers.

Best season: June through early September. Late August and early September is best for a variety of colors.

For more information: Chugach National Forest, Cordova Ranger District, 612 Second Street, Cordova, Alaska, (907) 424-7661.

Finding the trailhead: Thompson Pass Trail begins in many spots at the top of Thompson Pass and wherever a hiker wants to begin. Just park your car at a designated pullout, or safe parking place, and begin hiking.

The hike: Traveling to the area from Valdez you experience a long steep grade almost immediately after leaving Keystone Canyon. If entering the pass from the other direction the grade is not as pronounced. Regardless of which direction hikers drive to Thompson Pass, they are sure to be awed by the stunning scenery surrounding them as the highway moves from forest to high meadow.

Blueberry Lake, resting at the top of Thompson Pass, is the kind of area hikers may enjoy for just a few minutes or stay for days. Hike where you want, fish in Blueberry Lake, photograph the vistas, and take close-ups of tundra plants and animals.

There are many parking areas in the pass along the highway and in Blueberry Lake Campground. Hikers need only chose one, park their vehicle, and hike wherever their senses direct. There are a few animal trails to follow but most people just go where they desire, letting the last step dictate the next. The entire area beckons and invites the hiker to see this spot first. Come over here, smell this flower, hear the marmot whistle, see flights of ptarmigan feeding in the brush, tenderly touch the fragile petals of a forget-me-not, or feel the dense cold of million-year-old glacier ice.

I have been to the pass many times, in all seasons, and have never seen the same scene. Weather in the pass constantly changes—altering cloud forma-

Fall view of the Alaska Range. The glacier is fifteen miles away.

tions crush against distant peaks. Other times, clouds have been beneath me, obliterating any view of the surrounding territory, leaving me feeling like I was awash on a beautiful rocky island in the top of Thompson Pass. Then, there have been days of blue sky and sunshine, when my view of the world was only limited by obstructions of faraway mountains.

When you go, wander where you will, see your own sights. Perhaps you are the only human being to have stood where you are standing and to have seen what you are seeing, to hear what you are listening, or to smell a wisp of fragrances you smell. At least, in Thompson Pass, you will feel like it.

HIKE 67: *WRANGELL-ST. ELIAS NATIONAL PARK*

General description: Hiking in Wrangell-St. Elias National Park and Preserve is like entering a time warp. Unbelievably, there are no maintained trails. Hikers make their own track and mark their own time. If ever the urge strikes to test one's mettle with the elements, Wrangell-St. Elias National Park and Preserve is the proving ground.

General location: 200 miles north east of Anchorage

Trail begins: There are no designated trailheads in the park

Trail ends: All hikes end when a predetermined destination is reached or the hiker runs out of energy or time.

Maps: Various

Difficulty: Easy to difficult

Length: Countless miles

Elevation: 200 to 18,008 feet

Special attractions: Flora, fauna, rivers, scenery, mountains, and glaciers in North America's largest National Park

Best season: May through October

For more information: Superintendent, Wrangell-St. Elias National Park and Preserve, P.O. Box 29, Glennallen, Alaska 99588 (907) 822-5234

Finding the trailhead: There are no marked and maintained hikes in Wrangell-St. Elias National Park and Preserve. The area may be accessed by road from Chitna to McCarthy and from Slana on the Tok cutoff to Nabesna, and by air from Glennallen, Yakutat, or Gulkana.

The hike: Wrangell St. Elias gives new meaning to the word incredible. Number and scale of everything is enormous. The park includes nine of the highest peaks in the United States. Here, Wrangell-St Elias and Chugach mountain ranges converge with a great collection of peaks over 16,000 feet in elevation, including 18,008 foot, Mt. St. Elias, the second highest peak in the United States. Its major peaks: Drum, Blackburn, Sanford, and Wrangell, can be seen from nearby highways. Across the Yukon border in Kluane Park, Mt. Logan, second only to Mt. McKinley in North American Summits, ascends to a height of 19,850 feet. This is North America's mountain kingdom. There are so many high mountains that the urge to learn their names is lost, replaced by the desire to just settle back and appreciate their size, beauty, and ruggedness.

The park and preserve contains North America's largest assemblage of glaciers. One, the Malaspina, is larger than the State of Rhode Island. Following any of the many braided rivers and streams to their source will inevitably end at a receding glacier, an advancing glacier, or a tidewater glacier.

Peaks upon peaks. Glaciers after glaciers. The total acreage of Wrangell-St. Elias National Park and Preserve makes it the largest United States National Park, the size of six Yellowstones.

Beyond all that, it contains a representative sampling of Alaska's wildlife and old mining sites. The park and preserve is characterized by rugged mountains, remote valleys, wild rivers, and exemplary populations of wildlife. It also embraces coastal beaches on the Gulf of Alaska.

The area abounds in opportunities for wilderness backpacking and mountain climbing. Hike into these mountains and see geology in the making. Amid the splendid isolation comes a feeling of discovery, a feeling of the first person to see such sights.

There are no maintained hiking trails in the park. Yes, no marked hiking trails in the nations largest park. Long before the Park Service took possession Indians, miners, trappers, explorers, and other backcountry travelers crisscrossed the area in search of furs, mineral, trade routes, and isolation. Their trails, for the most part, have been lost or shortly will die in a tangle of new trees and underbrush.

Resurrected from dying trails is living opportunity for exploration. A chance to discover anew the land once walked by ancients. Every step taken on a backcountry walk in Wrangell-St. Elias National Park and Preserve may be considered as the first human to tread its land. Even Park Service Rangers and local residents may not be familiar with particulars of a planned route.

View of the Worthington Glacier, the closest glacier to the road system.

Mostly, hikers in the park are on their own. By all means check with Park Service Rangers about weather conditions, reasonableness of trying to reach certain points, and difficulties of dealing with weather and terrain, but be prepared to go it on your own. For safety's sake leave an expected route and completion time with someone.

Hiking in the park is one trip where a hiker begins to relate with Daniel Boone and Lewis and Clark. Backcountry park hikers must be self-sufficient, and prepared for wilderness, real wilderness! Walking across spruce muskeg with a pack can take much more time and energy than expected. From a distance the landscape may look like scrub lands, but place a foot in it and you quickly find out the land tests your endurance as you hop from tussock to tussock and try to avoid hidden pools of water. You can be knee deep in water or flat on your back before you know it.

Hikers must be familiar with safe techniques for crossing rivers and streams. Many are impassable, even for experts. Others can quickly change from trickling creeks to raging torrents. Only those with courage and backcountry expertise should attempt long hikes into the park. Be extraordinarily careful in this vast region. Gain proper survival gear and skills before packing up and heading into the backcountry of this, the nations largest plot of unexplored territory.

SOUTHEAST TRAILS

Southeast Alaska is a land of lakes, rivers, glaciers, mountains, waterways, islands, straits, narrows, and channels. It is mostly a marine environment, heavily forested with stately Sitka spruce, hemlock, and cedar trees. Wildlife unique to the area include Sitka blacktail deer, brown and black bears, mountain goats, and numerous small fur bearing animals. Along the inland waterways orca and humpback whales may be seen. Southeast is bald eagle capitol of America.

Miles of hiking trails provide beach access to lakes and streams, upland bird and wildlife viewing, and countless opportunities to see spectacular glaciers, fiords, islands, and scenery.

Average precipitation varies from 154 inches per year in Ketchikan to twenty-six inches per year in Skagway. Downtown Juneau averages ninety-seven inches per year and only fifty-four inches at the airport. Lush moss-covered rain forest cover the land doted by ice-blue glaciers. Summer temperatures average 55° to 60° with clear, warm days reaching 75° to 80°.

HIKE 68: *DEER MOUNTAIN/JOHN MOUNTAIN*

General description: A hike to scenic overviews of the greater Ketchikan area.
General location: Ketchikan
Trail begins: Junction of Granite Basin and Ketchikan City Dump Roads
Trail ends: Beaver Falls Fish Hatchery at the end of Tongass Road
Maps: Ketchikan B5
Difficulty: Difficult
Length: 9.9 miles
Elevation: 0 to 3000 feet

On the trail near Waterfall Resort. Boardwalks make hiking through swampy areas possible.

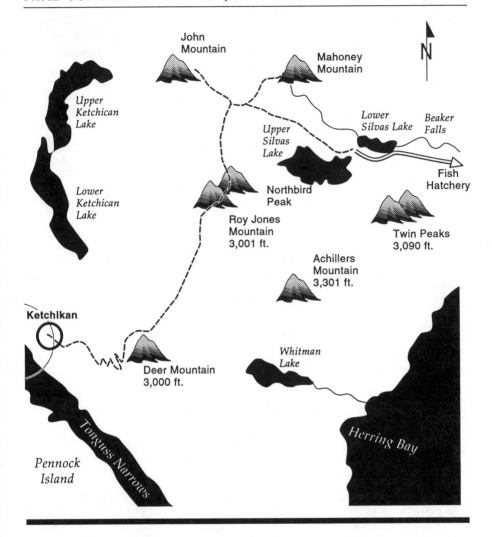

Special attractions: There are dramatic views from the summit. Alpine vegetation may be observed in July and August.

Best season: June through September

For more information: U.S. Department Forest Service, Tongass National Forest, 3031 Tongass Avenue Ketchikan, Alaska 99901 (907) 225-2148

Finding the trailhead: The closest trailhead is located in a large parking lot at the junction of Granite Basin and Ketchikan City Dump Roads. The other trailhead is twelve miles south of town at the end of Tongass Road. Parking is outside Beaver Falls Fish Hatchery and the trail begins to the immediate left just past the fish hatchery.

The hike: Deer Mountain Trail, a National Recreation Trail, begins on boardwalk across flat muskeg. There are wooden steps as it begins the climb up the mountain. Beyond the wooden steps the trail is unsurfaced and steep to the summit. Stay on the trail and do not try to short cut the switchbacks. Spectacular scenic overlooks of Ketchikan and Tongass Narrows with a panorama of the entire Ketchikan area make the climb worthwhile.

Only experienced hikers should continue past the summit. An insulated A-frame shelter is available for hikers just below the North side of the summit. A permit is required. A small backpacking stove will heat the structure. The trail on the ridge can be dangerous during poor visibility and is not well marked as it approaches Upper Silvis Lakes. The trail ends at Lower Silvis Lake and follows a dirt road two miles to Beaver Falls Fish Hatchery and an alternate trailhead. This is the preferred route but the trail my be hiked beginning at Beaver Falls trailhead and ending near the city dump.

Southeast Alaska is wet. The rain forest is correctly named, and hikers must be prepared for rain. Wet weather should not discourage hikers but only prompt them to properly prepare, both with correct equipment and positive attitude. Residents of the area expect rain and make fun about weather. They claim Ketchikan has the world's largest barometer, Deer Mountain. If you can't see the mountain, it is raining. If you can see it, it's going to rain.

HIKE 69: *EAST GLACIER LOOP*

General description: A hike into the wonderland of glaciers and old gold mining activity.
General location: Downtown Juneau behind the Visitors center
Trail begins: On stairs behind Mendenhall Glacier Visitor Center.
Trail ends: Junction with Mendenhall "Trail of the Glacier"
Maps: USGS Juneau B2
Difficulty: Moderate to difficult
Length: 3.5 miles
Elevation: Sea level to 400 feet
Special attractions: Woodland song birds including thrushes, warblers and wrens. Old mining sites and glacier views.
Best season: June through September
For more information: Tongass National Forest, Juneau Ranger District, 8465 Old Dairy Road, Juneau, Alaska, 99801 (907) 586-8800
Finding the trailhead: A self-guided, interpretive walk begins on the stairs behind Mendenhall Glacier Visitor Center. The East Glacier Trail begins to the left just past a small kettle pond near sign #6.

The hike: The lower portion of the trail, bordered by very dense willow, alder, and cottonwood, is below the glacier trimline. East Glacier Trail provides excellent views of the glacier from a safe distance. Never approach the glacier's face. It is extremely dangerous. A short side trail, beginning 1.3 miles from the trailhead, leads to the A-J Waterfall. Water still passes through the old tunnel from the A-J waterfall.

Rain sign in Ketchikan, which has more rain than any other part of the state.

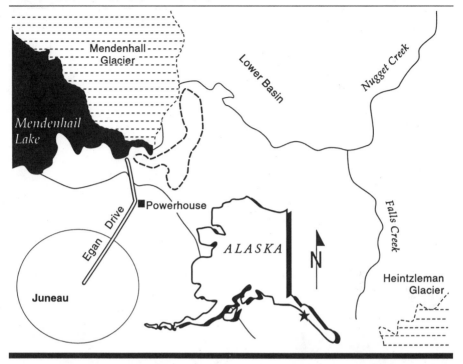

The next section of trail parallels Nugget Creek and enters a dense moss-covered forest above the glacier trimline. Nugget Creek dam is visible here. The dam on Nugget Creek was built by the Treadwell Company from 1911 to 1914 as a source of electricity for the mines on Douglas Island. The Alaska-Juneau Industries later bought and operated the power plant seasonally until 1943. A 600-foot tunnel and 6,000-foot flume carried water to the powerhouse. Remains of an old wooden flume and a rail tram are at the upper portion of the trail. The remains of the Nugget Creek project are cultural artifacts and should not be disturbed.

Via a series of switchbacks, the trail loops back to the self-guided interpretive walk. Planks and steps on the upper section of the trail were build by the Youth Conservation Corps in 1977.

HIKE 70: *MT. JUNEAU TRAIL*

General description: Difficult trail to the top of Mt Juneau
General location: Mountain to the north of Juneau.
Trail begins: At the end of Basin Road
Trail ends: Summit of Mt. Juneau
Maps: USGS Juneau B2
Difficulty: Difficult

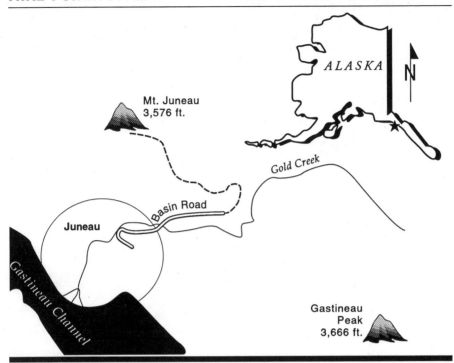

Length: Two miles
Elevation: Sea level to 3,000 feet
Special attractions: Hoary marmots, spruce grouse, salmon berries, and alpine wildflowers including monkshood, white heather, and monkey flowers appear in wild abundance on this trail. Bears can be seen in the upper meadows
Best season: June through September
For more information: Department of Natural Resources, Division of Parks and Recreation, 400 Willoughby Avenue, Juneau, Alaska 99801 (907) 465-4563
Finding the trailhead: Begin on Perseverance Trail at the end of Basin Road. The Mt. Juneau trailhead is located to the left about one mile from the beginning of Perseverance Trail.

The hike: At first the trail winds back and forth through dense brush. At the second forested area, a short path to the left opens to spectacular views of the city of Juneau. The next section of the hike traverses a steep slope with cascading falls. After the final patch of trees, the climb is extremely steep to the summit. During periods of fair weather, a hiker experienced in backcountry travel may enjoy walking over the ridge toward Granite Basin. Take the descent slowly and follow the trail.

The name "Juneau Mountain" was first used in the mining records by Pierre "French Pete" Erussard when he located mining claims on the mountain in 1888. Many lives have been lost on this mountain because of carelessness. Do not stray from the trail or attempt to climb Mt. Juneau by any unestablished route. Avalanche danger may persist until late spring, and large snowbanks may be present on the steep sections of the trail. An ice axe could be useful early in the summer season.

HIKE 71: *MT. ROBERTS TRAIL*

General description: A trail accessible from downtown Juneau
General location: In the mountains above Juneau
Trail begins: Wooden stairway at the end of Sixth Avenue
Trail ends: Mt. Roberts overlook
Maps: USGS Juneau B2
Difficulty: Easy to moderate
Length: 2.5 to 4.5 miles
Elevation: Sea level to 3,819 feet
Special attractions: Bears marmots, spruce grouse, forest birds, and numerous wildflowers from rain forest to alpine types
Best season: June through September
For more information: Department of Natural Resources, Division of Parks and Recreation, 400 Willoughby Avenue, Juneau, Alaska 99801 (907) 465-4563
Finding the trailhead: The trail begins up a wooden stairway at the end of Sixth Street above downtown Juneau

The hike: Roberts Trail was once named "Father Brown's Trail" after a Jesuit priest who constructed the trail with a group of volunteers in 1908 and erected

Wild raspberries growing out of stumps along the Mt. Roberts Trail.

143

a large wooden cross 2.5 miles up the trail. A replica of the cross still stands.

Although this trail is not as difficult as the Mt. Juneau Trail, it is a steep climb toward the end. The trail starts around the north side of Gastineau Peak through a shaded forest and makes numerous switchbacks until it breaks into a alpine terrain just before the large wooden cross. The rest of the trail is above timberline and is very steep. There are excellent views of Gastineau Channel, Juneau, and Douglas. After reaching the ridge, the trail continues to the right and climbs up another, narrower ridge to Gastineau Peak. The trail appears to end there, but those who are still energetic can continue on to Roberts Peak through the low alpine vegetation. Do not try to descend through the many side basins as they are very steep and dangerous. The only good route down, other than returning on the trail, is to hike to Sheep Mountain and follow the Sheep Creek Trail down. Check maps carefully.

HIKE 72: *POINT BRIDGET TRAIL*

General description: This beautiful 2,850-acre state park, located forty miles north of Juneau, offers meadows of wildflowers, forested mountains, cliffs, spectacular views, rocky beaches, and the sea. In the winter the meadows and open forest allow excellent skiing and snowshoeing opportunities.
General location: Forty miles north of Juneau
Trail begins: Mile 39 of the Glacier Highway
Trail ends: Point Bridget
Maps: Juneau C3, Juneau C3 NW
Difficulty: Easy to moderate
Length: Seven miles
Elevation: 100 to 800 feet
Special attractions: Whale watching, wildlife viewing, and an unique combination of intertidal and muskeg wildflowers.
Best season: June through September—open all year
For more information: Department of Natural Resources, Division of Parks and Recreation, 400 Willoughby Avenue, Juneau, Alaska 99801 (907) 465-4563
Finding the trailhead: Point Bridget trailhead is on the left side of the Glacier Highway one mile past the North Bridget Cove sign.

The hike: The beginning of maintained Point Bridget Trail treats hikers to a host of interesting plants as it passes through rain forest muskeg. Included are violets, shore pines, sphagnum moss, and Labrador tea. Sundews with their leaves covered with a sticky substance for trapping insects are found. Sparrows, swallows, and woodpeckers frequent the area. In fall, tiny brightly colored leaves carpet the muskeg.

Approximately .5 mile from the trailhead the trail opens to Upper Cowee Meadow and then continues in the woods at the edge of the meadow. Vancouver Canada Geese can frequently be seen in and along the meadow's sloughs. They live year round in Southeast Alaska with more than 700 wintering in the Juneau area. Center stage in the middle of the meadow is a very large beaver

HIKE 72: *POINT BRIDGET TRAIL*

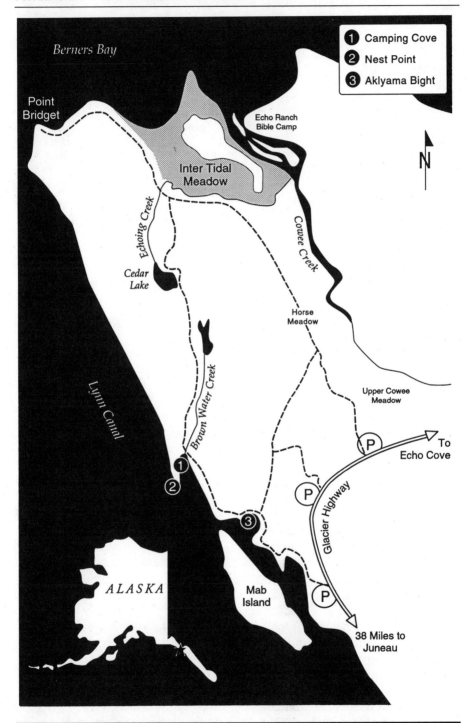

Berners Bay

Point Bridget

1 Camping Cove
2 Nest Point
3 Aklyama Bight

N

Echo Ranch Bible Camp

Inter Tidal Meadow

Echoing Creek

Cowee Creek

Cedar Lake

Horse Meadow

Lynn Canal

Brown Water Creek

Upper Cowee Meadow

P

To Echo Cove

P

Glacier Highway

P

ALASKA

Mab Island

38 Miles to Juneau

Getting a drink from a small stream cascading down a hill on the Point Bridget Trail.

dam and lodge. Black bears visit the meadow feeding on sedges, horsetail, and skunk cabbage roots. When pink and chum salmon are spawning in Cowee Creek, bears leave the meadow to fish the stream.

Horse Meadow, beyond Upper Cowee Meadow, is the setting for a spectacular wildflower show. Alaska cotton, black lilies, and fragrant bog orchids dot acres of shooting stars and buttercups in mid-May, followed in a few weeks by lupine, iris, and wild geranium, and then fireweed completes the exhibition.

Bald eagles live along the edges of the meadows where, from late June to October, they fish in Cowee Creek for spawning salmon. Dozens may be seen at one time perching in the trees along the edge of the meadows above the trail.

High tide floods the lower part intertidal meadow twice daily. Hiking out in the meadow on an incoming tide may require detours around flooded sloughs. Goose tongue, with its rosette of long tapered leaves coming from the base, and grass-of-parnassus have adapted to salt water and may be seen in the meadow.

Milky-colored Cowee Creek, paralleling the meadows, is partially fed by melting glaciers. Deep, swift, milky-colored water make it impossible to see the bottom and unsafe to cross. Heavy rain and hot weather speeds the melting of glaciers and alters the level of the tidal influenced creek. In early spring and winter, when glaciers do not melt, the water is beautifully clear.

Black lilies, buttercups, and wild geraniums cover the berm above Berners Bay. Directly across Berners Bay, a long peninsula juts out into the bay and to the right and further north is Lion's Head Mountain. Lynn Canal and Chilkat Mountain are to the west.

Walking on rocky beaches in this part of the park is difficult, but possible except during extremely high tide. An interesting spectacle occurs in spring when thousands of white winged and surf scooters swim wing to wing in one great raft. They feed by diving in orchestrated unison to the bottom for sea life. One of their favorite foods is blue mussels which they swallow whole. Once their prey is captured they surface and become a packed mass again.

Sea lions and harbor seals are frequently seen frolicking near the shore. In late April though September humpback whales spouting offshore while feeds on herring, smelt, and krill around Point Bridget. Adult humpback can be be forty-five to fifty feet long and possibly live as long as twenty-five years.

Old growth rain forest along this section of the trail contains old, large, beautiful Sitka spruce trees. Winding from the beach and back into the forest the trail goes through high bush cranberries, devil's club, crab apples, and whole hillsides of lichen. Beautiful wildflowers complete the panoramic view of Lynn canal and the Chilkat Mountains at trails end at Point Bridget.

HIKE 73: *SHEEP CREEK TRAIL*

General description: Sheep Creek Trail is representative of many Southeast Alaska hikes. It traverses steep hills, valleys, and alpine slopes and meadows and allows hikers typical Southeast Alaska scenic views.
General location: Juneau
Trail begins: Mile 4 of Thane Road south of Juneau
Trail ends: Bishop's Point
Maps: Juneau B1
Difficulty: Moderate to difficult
Length: Three miles
Elevation: Sea level to 4,050 feet
Special attractions: Historic mining remains, scenery
Best season: June through September
For more information: Department of Natural Resources, Division of Parks and Recreation, 400 Willoughby Avenue, Juneau, Alaska 99801 (907) 465-4563
Finding the trailhead: The marked trailhead is off Thane Road, four miles south of downtown Juneau. It begins at a stairway near the intersection of Thane Road and a gravel spur road to the left leads to a substation of the Snettisham Power plant.

The hike: Miners, Joe Juneau and Richard Harris, knew their gold but not their animals. They named Sheep Creek after incorrectly identifying mountain goats clinging to the cliffs. The trail, beginning in a moss-covered forest, rises abruptly, and then drops into sheltered Sheep Creek Valley. Relatively level through the valley it then follows switchbacks up a forested hillside until it reaches the alpine zone. Above timberline the trail may be difficult to follow. If the trail is lost, simply follow the power line. Hikers can follow the ridge to Sheep Mountain, Mt. Roberts, Gastineau Peak, and then return to Juneau on the Mt. Roberts Trail. If this route is taken carry an ice axe, because snow persists on the ridge throughout summer.

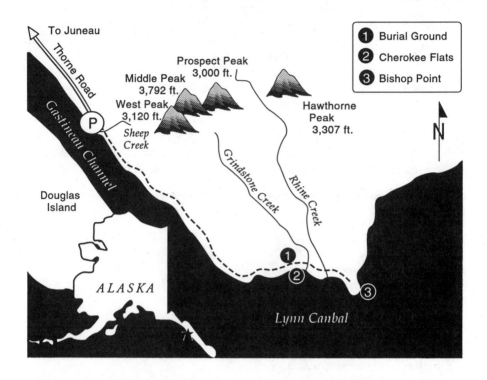

To Juneau

Thorne Road

Gastineau Channel

Prospect Peak
3,000 ft.

Middle Peak
3,792 ft.

West Peak
3,120 ft.

Sheep Creek

Hawthorne Peak
3,307 ft.

Douglas Island

Grindstone Creek

Rhine Creek

ALASKA

1 Burial Ground
2 Cherokee Flats
3 Bishop Point

N

Lynn Canbal

TURNAGAIN ARM TRAILS

Turnagain Arm was named by Captain James Cook in 1778. He thought the arm was his hoped for Northwest Passage but had to turn again when he found the valley's end. Two hundred years after Captain Cook turned again, hikers are discovering things the English captain was not able to see from the deck of the Endeavor. Trails in the arm, once used as trade and supply routes, are utilized today by modern explorers and hiking adventurers.

Turnagain trails are accessed from the Seward Highway from Potter to Portage Glacier, forty-nine miles south of Anchorage. There are many trailheads along Turnagain Arm accessible from the Seward Highway. Trailheads are found next to the highway, at the end of gravel roads, and even near a railroad tunnel. All but one Turnagain Arm trail is accessible by automobile. See individual trails for directions to finding each trailhead.

Turnagain Arm has claim to America's greatest tide differentials, with a range over thirty-seven feet. It is frequently visited by tidal bores, the leading wave of an incoming tide traveling in excess of twelve miles per hour. The arm, dug by glaciers, is being refilled by silt carried by streams originating from melting of the arm's retreating rivers of ice. At low tide, mud flats are exposed,

The Alaska Railroad permits hikers and homesteaders to get off at almost any spot on the tracks.

leaving the arm with just a river flowing the thirty miles to Cook Inlet. As the tide changes direction and rushes in, the drying mud of the narrow arm is covered with water. Rapidily-moving tides flush the arm twice a day. Frequent high winds and shallow, dangerous water prohibit small boats in the arm.

Portage Valley, before Portage Lake was formed by the receding glacier, was a twelve-mile portage between Prince William Sound and Turnagain Arm. It served as a trade route connecting two cultures: Chugach Eskimos of the Sound and Cook Inlet Tanaina Athabascan Indians. As late as 1896, 400 gold seekers crossed Portage Pass on foot to Turnagain's Hope and Sunrise mining regions.

Today's traveler, is very likely an escapee from urban Alaska or a visitor from Outside. Where once native cultures were united on the trail, now peoples from many lands and languages hike, camp, fish, and photograph Portage Valley and Turnagain Arm. There are trails designed to educate for an hour or recreate for a week. Turnagain Arm is one place a hiker may be in absolute wilderness and still hear the sound of cars on a highway or the whistle of a train.

My first Alaska hike, nearly three decades ago, was along Turnagain Arm. It was before trailhead markers, brushed out trails, and polypropylene. Three of my children and myself hiked for a couple of hours into an unknown valley, camped on an unnamed stream, and drank clear, cold water without fear of contracting Beaver Fever. A fire was built and dinner was cooked. Freeze dried was yet to be invented, so we roasted meat on a stick over the flame and baked potatoes, wrapped in mud, under the coals. We were to purchase our first down sleeping bag ten years hence, but mom's homemade camping quilts protected us from the night's chill. Thermarest was a long way in the future. Our mattress was a ground cloth spread over spruce boughs. The tent was a makeshift enclosure, constructed by throwing a canvas over the lower branches of a large spruce tree, selected because of its rain shedding qualities.

We were in wilderness Alaska with, what we consider by today's camping and hiking standards, minimum equipment. One of us quoted a couple of verses from Robert Service's 'Spell of the Yukon' as the fire died, and we slipped into our robes beneath the spruce. We were far enough from the Seward Highway that we could not hear cars and trucks passing through the night. Sometime after the kid's eight-hour hibernation was in full effect, an Alaska Railroad freight train ambled along the tracks on its way to the rail yard in Anchorage. As the train passed the bottom of our valley, the engineer pulled the whistle cord and the moanful sound carried to our spruce tree camp. Even now, when I hear a train in the night, it reminds me of my first camp on the trail in Alaska on Turnagain Arm.

HIKE 74: *BIRD CREEK TRAIL*

General description: Bird Creek hike has long been the spring practice and tune up trail. It is easy enough for novice but hardy enough to stretch experienced muscles. The trail takes hikers into the hills along Turnagain Arm
General location: Along the Turnagain Arm hills about Mile 102 Seward Highway
Trail begins: Mile 100 Seward Highway
Trail ends: In Bird Creek and Penguin Creek Valleys
Maps: USGS Anchorage A7, USGS Seward D7
Difficulty: Easy to moderate
Length: six miles
Elevation: 50 to 4,650 feet
Special attractions: Vistas of Turnagain Arm with opportunities to see eagles, whales, glaciers, flowers, bore tides, and mountain goats.
Best season: April through October
For more information: Chugach National Forest, Glacier Ranger District, P.O. Box 129, Monarch Mine Road, Girdwood, Alaska 99587 (907) 783-3242
Finding the trailhead: Drive twenty-eight miles south of Anchorage on the Seward Highway to Mile 100. Turn north into parking area and begin hiking.

The hike: Bird Creek Trail begins in a birch forest and climbs into an alpine area above Turnagain Arm. It is one of the first hikes open to sufferers of cabin fever. Warm, early spring Chinook winds blowing from Prince William Sound, over Portage Pass into Turnagain Arm melt snow and dries the trail along the southern exposed hills. The southern exposure brings early flowers to an area surrounded by snow. Spring hikers often find an open spot exposed to the sun, and attempt to obtain a pre-season tan by spreading a space blanket and basking in the season's first rays.

A good spring tune-up hike would be to follow the trail as it climbs through a birch forest to meet the powerline/pipeline access road. The road goes .25 mile to the ridge crest. Leaving brush behind, the path then continues up the steep ridge to elevation 3,505 feet. From this, the first high, open point on the trail, hikers receive a sweeping view of Turnagain Arm and Bird and Penguin Valleys. The short vertical rise makes it a good hike to stretch lazy, unused muscles. Ptarmigan, the State Bird, and Dall sheep visit the ridge, and bald eagles may be seen riding the winds as they hunt for hooligan coming in on the tide.

The next four miles goes to a saddle at elevation 4,650. Looking north hikers get a view of the headwaters of Ship Creek. The ridge continues to 4,960 feet but most hikers are content to turn again at this point.

A few years ago, before the trail was clearly marked, we bucked our way to the saddle between Bird and Ship creeks. It was a fall hike. The trail was dry and free of snow. Arriving at the saddle at midday, we stopped for lunch. As we ate, we imagined we were the area's first visitors. It seemed we had stepped back in time and were discovering Alaska. It was wonderful to survey the valleys and to see sheep on the mountain tops. Perhaps the first man to have done so. We were alone in a time-locked land and the feeling was grand.

As we proceeded over the saddle into Ship Creek Valley, we were immediately brought out of our time warp into the 20th century. There on the hillside was the remains of earlier hikers' lunch. They had packed in Government Issue C rations and had scattered the cans over a large area. We picked up their mess, but our hike had been desecrated. The experience forcibly drove home the need to pack out what is packed in.

Turnagain Arm has claim to America's greatest tide differential, with a range of over thirty-seven feet.

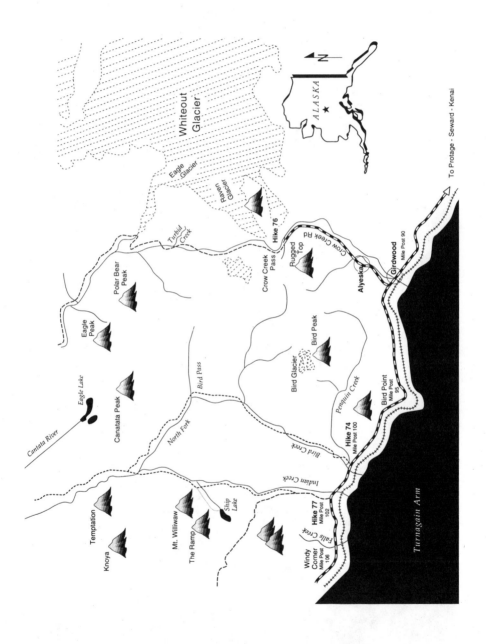

HIKE 75: *BYRON GLACIER TRAIL*

General description: An easy, scenic hike in a glacial area with a variety of things to do and see for adults and children. An easy walk for all ages, the trail gives a close-up view of glaciers and rugged mountains. Elusive iceworms may be encountered on Byron Glacier during summer twilight hours.

General location: Portage Glacier Ice Field, forty-nine miles south of Anchorage.

Trail begins: End of Portage Road

Trail ends: Snowfields below Byron Glacier

Maps: USGS Seward D5

HIKE 75: *BYRON GLACIER TRAIL*

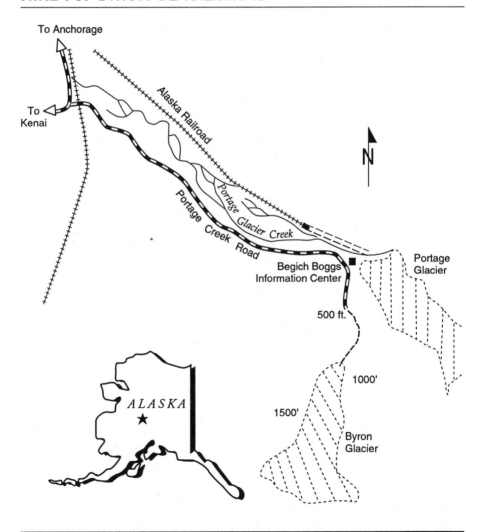

Difficulty: Easy
Length: .8 mile
Elevation: 150 to 250 feet
Special attractions: Scenery and glaciers
Best season: June through September
For more information: Chugach National Forest, Glacier Ranger District, P.O. Box 129, Monarch Mine Road, Girdwood, Alaska 99587 (907) 783-3242
Finding the trailhead: Forty-nine miles south of Anchorage at Mile 79, Seward Highway turn north onto Portage Valley Road to Begich, Boggs Visitor Center. Portage Valley Road travel six miles to the visitor center. Go past the center to trailhead parking.

The hike: The trail follows Byron Creek, a cascading, whitewater, glacial stream. The flat, well maintained trail begins in an alder/cottonwood forest with lush fern undergrowth. A wide, cleared footpath leads hikers the first half of the trail to Byron Glacier viewpoint. Beyond the viewpoint the trail becomes rocky and crosses small streams.

Remains of winter's avalanches along the trail invite hikers to stop for a friendly snowball fight. Nearer and below Byron Glacier the trail winds through big boulders and along terminal moraines. Looking north from the trail, Portage Lake and Valley can be seen.

Wildlife in the area includes, eagles, moose, marmots, black and brown bear, and numerous birds and migrating waterfowl. During summer twilight hours, iceworms are commonly found on snowfields near the glacier at the end of the trail. New hikers to Alaska put iceworm searching in the same category as snipe hunting. Iceworms are real and Forest Service interpreters at Begich, Boggs Visitor Center lead visitors on iceworm safaris.

Climbing on snow over Byron Creek is discouraged. The valley has frequent avalanches and winter hikes are not recommended. Experienced, properly equipped mountaineers may climb on the glacier. Others should stay off. Be prepared for rapid weather changes.

HIKE 76: *CROW PASS TRAIL*

General description: A steep climb into a glacial mining district, the trail offers a majestic mountain wilderness day-hike or an extended multi-day trip. Variety is the highlight of picturesque, Crow Creek Pass Trail.
General location: South side of Chugach Mountains near Alyeska
Trail begins: Mile seven Crow Creek Road
Trail ends: Raven Glacier in Crow Pass
Maps: USGS Anchorage A6, A7
Difficulty: Moderate to difficult
Length: four miles
Elevation: 100 to 3,500 feet
Special attractions: Scenery, wildflowers, wildlife viewing
Best season: June through October

For more information: Chugach National Forest, Glacier Ranger District, P.O. Box 129, Monarch Mine Road, Girdwood, Alaska 99587 (907) 783-3242
Finding the trailhead: The road to Alyeska, thirty-eight miles south of Anchorage, is at Mile ninety, Seward Highway. Turn north on Alyeska Road and go two miles and turn off to the left onto, graveled, Crow Creek Road. The trailhead is seven miles beyond at the end of Crow Creek Road.

The hike: Well maintained, Crow Creek Trail is part of the Iditarod National Historic Trail which was used for shipping mail and supplies between Turnagain and Knik Arms of Cook Inlet. From the trailhead it is a steady uphill climb with steep sections and switchbacks. At mile 1.7 are ruins of Girdwood Mine, a hard rock gold mine operating from 1906 to 1948. Go .25 mile beyond the ruins for a side-trip to Crow Creek Cascades which is west of the main trail.

There is a Forest Service public recreation cabin at mile three for use by hikers, and may be reserved by mail or at any Chugach National Forest Service office as much as 179 days in advance of planned stay. Occupancy is by permit only for a cost of $20 per night per party. As a courtesy to hikers staying at the cabin, please camp in other areas out of sight of the cabin.

Beyond the cabin is Crystal Lake where the trail continues on to Crow Pass and Raven Glacier and where other glaciers may be seen. Dall sheep and mountain goats may be seen on rocky cliffs. Ptarmigan and brown and black bear are in the area. Experienced climbers who want a challenge climb the glaciers and peaks around the pass.

Turnagain Arm hikers will often have the opportunity to photograph Dall Sheep.

HIKE 77: *INDIAN VALLEY TO ARCTIC VALLEY*

General description: Indian Valley Trail takes hikers along Indian Creek and through a combination of forests and meadows in the Chugach Range to alpine tundra and tiny high mountain lakes. This trail is ideal for a short hike or a two-day stay.

General location: In the Chugach Mountains east of Anchorage

Trail begins: Indian Creek Road

Trail ends: Indian Creek Pass or Arctic Valley

Maps: USGS Anchorage A7, B7, A8

Difficulty: Moderate to difficult

Length: Six miles from Indian Valley trailhead to Indian Pass. Fifteen miles from Indian Pass to Arctic Valley trailhead. Twenty-one miles from Indian Valley trailhead to Arctic Valley trailhead.

Elevation: 250 to 2,350 feet northbound and 1,950 to 2,350 feet southbound

Special attractions: Wilderness, wildlife, and camping

Best season: June through September

For more information: Chugach National Forest, Glacier Ranger District, P.O. Box 129, Monarch Mine Road, Girdwood, Alaska 99587 (907) 783-3242

Finding the trailhead: Indian Creek Road turns north off the Seward Highway at Mile 103.1 in the community of Indian. Indian Creek Road is an unpaved gravel road beginning just west of Indian Creek, twenty-five miles south of Anchorage. Travel on Indian Creek Road for .5 mile and take the right fork Continue .8 mile, turn left at the pump station, and then to the road's end. Park in area provided and begin hiking. The Ship Creek trailhead is at Mile 6.5, Arctic Valley Road. There is a turnout sign in the parking area.

The hike: Mushers drove their dogs in the early 1900s from Indian to Ship Creek, now known as Anchorage. They went over Indian Creek Pass, a part of the Iditarod National Historic Trail, from Seward to interior gold fields. Crow Pass Trail and Indian Pass Trail were alternately used.

The trail follows through conifer trees and across meadows created by winter avalanches. The trail to the pass is gentle with few steep places. It can be wet and may be overgrown in places in late summer. The pass, an old moraine, is surrounded by side valleys dotted with small lakes and covered with high alpine tundra. It is vegetated by scrub hemlock and crow berries. Ship Lake is across Indian Pass and 3.5 miles up the South Fork of Ship Creek. There are few flat areas in the pass for camping but enough to make it a desirable place to overnight. Water is available but campfires are not permitted, so bring a stove.

The trail to Indian Pass is lined with fiddlehead ferns. The plant gets its name from the shape of the sprout as it begins to grow in spring. It grows rapidly and accounts for much of the foliage that hides trails in the latter part of summer. When fiddlehead ferns sprout in spring they are edible and not bad tasting if boiled in salted water. We decided to try our luck at survival camping one spring hike up Indian Valley and boiled up a batch. With the addition of a piece of steak cut up and cooked on a stick over the fire, we survived the outing and lived to return to McDonalds for breakfast.

The section of the trail from the trailhead to the pass is cleared and well marked. From the pass to Arctic Valley it is brushy, boggy, and occasionally difficult to follow. Two full days are recommended if taking the trail the entire twenty-one miles from Indian Valley to Arctic Valley. Alpine sections of the trail are well marked with yellow poles. Areas of brush and bogs in the lower end are unmarked. Traces of the old Iditarod Trail can still be seen. Ruins of a roadhouse are on the west side of Ship Creek.

Northbound hikers will have no problem finding the clearly marked ford across Ship Creek about .5 mile north of the North Fork confluence. If hiking southbound be sure and ford at this site and follow the marked route to the pass. Careless hikers have missed the marked ford and taken a wrong turn to the North Fork.

HIKE 78: *MORAINE NATURE TRAIL*

General description: A short, easy, handicap accessible, hike in the Portage Glacier area giving better views of Portage Glacier, Lake, and Portage than from the visitor center.

Many hikers carry a gold pan, although hikers should be careful not to pan on private claims.

HIKE 78: *MORAINE NATURE TRAIL*
HIKE 80: *WILLIWAW NATURE TRAIL*

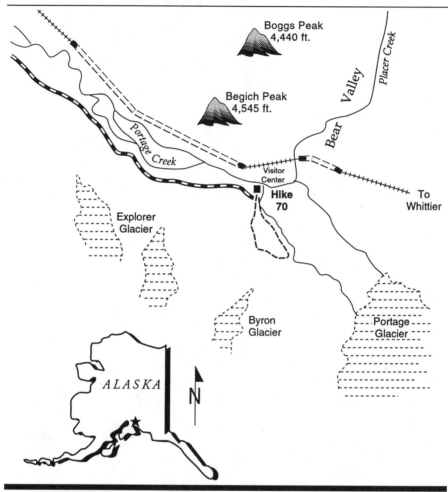

General location: Portage Glacier, forty miles south of Anchorage.
Trail begins: Just south of Begich, Boggs Visitor Center.
Trail ends: Trail loops back to the trailhead.
Maps: USGS Seward D5.
Difficulty: Easy.
Length: .15 miles.
Elevation: 150 to 175 feet.
Special attractions: Improving knowledge of Portage Glacier and its surrounding flora and fauna.
Best season: May through October.
For more information: Chugach National Forest, Glacier Ranger District, P.O. Box 129, Monarch Mine Road, Girdwood, Alaska 99587 (907) 783-3242.
Finding the trailhead: Forty-nine miles south of Anchorage at Mile 79, Seward

Highway, turn north onto Portage Valley Road to Begich, Boggs Visitor Center. Portage Valley Road travel six miles to the visitor center. The trailhead is just south of the center.

The hike: When a glacier retreats, glacial rubble called a moraine is left. This trail climbs the remains left by Portage Glacier as it melted and retreated. This newly constructed trail is well surfaced and marked with interpretive signs. The signs help visitors understand the process of glacial advance and recession and the effect climate and glaciers have on plants growing in the area. Wild flowers decorate the trail in summer. Birds stop to rest and feed in Portage Valley in their spring and fall migratory flights. The trail has minimal change in elevation but a viewing platform for bird watching is at the trail's highest point. Moose, eagles, and black and brown bear live in Portage Valley. Visitor center displays enhance and explain what is observed on the trail.

During summer, hugh icebergs float in Portage Lake. Eighty percent of an iceberg's volume is underwater. In spring, before the tourist season brings visitors and rangers, local picnickers and adventurers paddle canoes and kayaks to the icebergs. Ignoring warning signs, they get out of their craft and climb on icebergs. Because of delicate balance of the ice above and below water level the added weight causes the iceberg to roll over. Several people have been killed in past years. Always follow safety rules and pay attention to signs posted for hiker's protection.

HIKE 79: *PORTAGE PASS*

General description: A challenging hike to unsurpassed scenery above Portage Glacier.
General location: Portage Glacier, forty-nine miles south of Anchorage.
Trail begins: Train tunnel exit at Whittier.
Trail ends: Un-named ledge overlooking Portage Glacier.
Maps: USGS Seward D5.
Difficulty: Moderate to difficult.
Length: four miles.
Elevation: 100 to 1,200 feet.
Special attractions: Glacier, scenery, vistas, wildlife viewing.
Best season: July through September.
For more information: Chugach National Forest, Glacier Ranger District, P.O. Box 129, Monarch Mine Road, Girdwood, Alaska 99587 (907) 783-3242.
Finding the trailhead: Hikers can take the Alaska Railroad train from Portage to Whittier. By informing the conductor in advance, the train will stop after it exits the tunnel on the Prince William Sound side of the Chugach Mountains at Whittier. The train continues 1.5 miles further to town. Hikers can walk to the trailhead from Whittier but must add 1.5 miles to the hike. After waving good-bye to the conductor, take the gravel road paralleling the tracks to the tank farm near the tunnel. Take the only road going left across the tracks. This is the start of the trail.

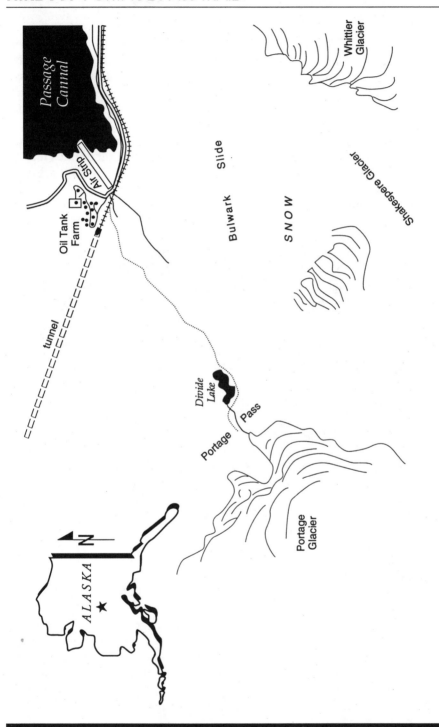

The hike: Hundreds of years ago, before Portage Lake was formed, Indians, Eskimos, Russians, and miners used the trail as a trading route, crossing Portage Glacier from the pass. Today, the trail starts in low brush, then trees, and is in open tundra by the time it reaches the pass. The first part is a route more than a trail as it goes up the steep hills. Weak-hearted hikers will want to stop, and it is about now they need to be reminded it is less than a mile to the easier part, and the end will be worth the effort. There may be bear in the brush along the trail, but bushwhacking and loud cursing of the route will probably scare them away.

Whittier is one of the three entry ports to Prince William Sound.

Divide Lake is the first destination past the pass as the route goes down a steep but easy hill on the old roadbed to Portage Pass Viewpoint. Go to the lake and travel around the left side and head down the slope to the glacier. Hikers may stop here but for the full reward continue walking up the outlet stream, climb the cliffs on the opposite side of the stream by going through a rocky chute to a bench of bedrock, and to a ledge above the glacier. Persistent bushwhackers/hikers are rewarded with scenic vistas of Portage Glacier and Lake. Swans, ducks, geese, Arctic terns, and sandhill cranes, use Portage Pass as a major migration route.

Portage Pass can be a wind funnel, so be prepared for rapid weather changes. Whittier, with 175 inches of rain, has Alaska's second highest annual precipitation. Although low in elevation, the pass may still have snow through June. Avalanche hazards make this trip dangerous in winter and spring.

HIKE 80: *WILLIWAW NATURE TRAIL*

General description: Easy, interesting short nature hike among representative flora and along a stream of Portage Valley
General location: Williwaw Campground two miles west of Begich, Boggs Visitor Center at Portage Glacier
Trail begins: Between site 5 and 6 of the Williwaw Campground
Trail ends: Loops back to the trailhead
Maps: USGS Seward D5
Difficulty: Easy
Length: .5 mile
Elevation: 100 to 150 feet
Special attractions: Spawning salmon, scenery, glaciers, flowers, and small animals.
Best season: June through September
For more information: Chugach National Forest, Glacier Ranger District, P.O. Box 129, Monarch Mine Road, Girdwood, Alaska 99587 (907) 783-3242
Finding the trailhead: At Mile 79, Seward Highway, forty-nine miles south of Anchorage, turn onto Portage Valley Road. Travel four miles to Williwaw Campground. Trailhead begins between campsites 5 and 6.

The hike: Although the hike begins in Williwaw Campground, hikers should visit Begich, Boggs Visitor Center at Portage Glacier before taking this easy half mile trail. Numbered posts are set along the trail. A helpful trail guide is available at the visitor center. The numbered trail posts correspond to information in the guidebook to assist hikers understand and enjoy vegetation and natural features of the trail and Portage Valley.

Spawning salmon are part of the attraction of Williwaw Nature Trail and a viewing platform is near the entrance of Williwaw Campground. Spawning salmon may be seen from mid-August through September. The flat, loop trail is a wide, well surfaced path entering an area that is representative of Portage Valley flora. The first section, to a thirty-foot span bridge, is wide enough for handicapped access. Beyond the bridge, trail condition is narrow and wet part

A hiker bites into a piece of ice at Portage Glacier.

of the time. Even if your feet get damp the interesting things discovered on this short hike make it worth it. Wildflowers grow along the trail and edible berries abound in late summer. Beyond the bridge are many spur trails, a waterfall, and a cascading creek. Wildlife in Portage Valley include moose, eagles, black and brown bear, and migratory birds in spring and fall.

Additional glacier information and data about Portage Valley may be obtained by visiting the Begich, Boggs Visitor Center. Portage Glacier icebergs float close to the viewing platform of the Center. Portage Valley is subject to high winds and driving rain. Be prepared for rapid weather changes.

HIKE 81: *WINNER CREEK TRAIL*

General description: An easy, four-hour hike above the ski slopes of Alyeska, and a good overnight hike or multi-day trip.
General location: The ski slopes of Alyeska, thirty-five miles south of Anchorage.
Trail begins: Alyeska Ski Resort parking lot.
Trail ends: Headwaters of Winner Creek.
Maps: USGS Seward D6.
Difficulty: Moderate to difficult.
Length: Nine miles of hiking trails.
Elevation: 100 to 2,820 feet.
Special attractions: Scenery, berry picking, vistas.
Best season: June through September.

HIKE 81: *WINNER CREEK TRAIL*

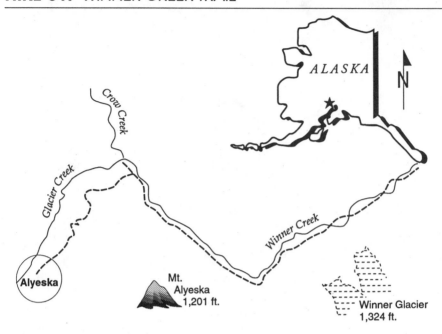

For more information: Chugach National Forest, Glacier Ranger District, P.O. Box 129, Monarch Mine Road, Girdwood, Alaska 99587 (907) 783-3242.
Finding the trailhead: Turn north onto Alyeska Road at Mile 90, Seward Highway. Drive three miles to Alyeska Resort's parking lot. The trail begins on the ski slopes, past the north end of the Nugget Inn and the upper condominiums, just beyond the rope tow.

The hike: Winner Creek Trail follows a portion of the old Iditarod Trail, established in 1910, that went from Seward over Crow Pass to the gold fields. Easy going best describes the first 2.5 miles. The trail starts in spruce, hemlock, and cottonwood, and continues through alders, meadows, and willow patches. Blueberry picking in season is possible on lower portions of the trail. Soggy spots in the first section are covered by wooden planking. Beyond the planking the trail steepens and it may be necessary to occasionally wade the stream to avoid brush. Once out of low brush at about 1,500 feet, hiking is easier.

At about 3.5 miles the trail divides. The right fork continues on to Upper Winner Creek. The left fork terminates after one mile at Winner Creek Gorge. The gorge is formed where Winner Creek is forced through a small cleft in the rocks, creating a series of small waterfalls and cascades. It is worth the short diversion to see the picturesque falls.

Good camping sites and water are available along the trail to Upper Winner Creek. Watch for bear and moose.

WHITE MOUNTAIN WINTER TRAILS

This is winter, wilderness Alaska right out of the pages of Jack London and Robert Service. These hikes are not for the unprepared. A minor incident on one of these trails may end in major tragedy. For the prepared and informed these trails lead to high adventure.

Five public recreation cabins are available to give succor to trail-weary travelers of the 175 miles of winter hiking trails. Make reservations up to thirty days in advance. For $15 per night, which goes to a cabin maintenance program, the cabins are furnished with an axe, bow saw, wood stove, coleman lantern, and cook stove, and outhouse. Hikers supply the white gas and toilet paper. There will probably be dry wood cut and stored so a fire can be started immediately upon arrival. Please replace wood, and a little extra, and have it ready for a quick fire in case the next visitor is in an emergency.

Many of the trails within the park are flagged and easy to follow, but carry a map, compass, and other written material designed to help to find and follow the trail. The Bureau of Land Management, governing agency for White Mountain National Recreation Area, is anxious to serve the hiking public. Writing or calling will produce all the information required to have a safe and enjoyable time. The three most important rules of winter hiking in Alaska are: be prepared, be prepared, and be prepared.

My experience on the winter trail has given me many unusual memories. Once, at fifty-nine degrees below zero, I had to preheat white gas with a small fire before it would vaporize enough to burn in the Coleman stove and lantern. Cooking breakfast was a problem in sub-zero weather one morning, when frozen raw eggs had to be peeled before they could be put in the frying pan. Pancakes cooked over an open fire were burned on the outside and nearly raw in the middle. The fire could only give enough heat to cook the batter next to the pan. The outside temperature was so cold it kept the top and middle from enough heat to change the batter to a pancake.

I have seen breath vaporize and freeze on a beard causing whiskers to break when touched. At sixty degrees below, spit turns to ice before it hits the snow, any exposed flesh will freeze within thirty seconds, and extreme cold air entering lungs can cause damage. When ice fishing, fish are flash frozen when pulled from the ice hole.

Unexplained phenomenons occur in cold, clear air. Once I saw a large, Chicago-like city, complete with high rises and skyscrapers. It wasn't a cloud formation but the refracted image of the city projected against the deep blue southern sky. Another time, standing on level ground at night, I was able to see taxiway lights of an airport over thirty-five miles away.

Yes, as Robert Service wrote, "there are strange things done in the midnight sun." For the adventurous and well prepared, a winter hike into White Mountain National Recreation Area at top of the world, will find, "Arctic trails have their secret tales," and the strangest sights of the Northern Lights may well be the ones the Great Land reserves for you.

HIKE 82: *COLORADO CREEK TRAIL*

General description: A hiker's challenge into the scenic valley of the 1977 great burn and the valley of the Tolvona River.
General location: Tolvona River system just south of Livengood on the Elliot Highway.
Trail begins: Mile 57 Elliot Highway
Trail ends: Beaver Creek
Maps: USGS Livengood B2, B3, C2, C3
Difficulty: Moderate
Length: Twenty-three miles
Elevation: 612 to 1,625 feet
Special attractions: Scenery and winter hiking recreation
Best season: Winter
For more information: United State Department of the Interior, Bureau of Land Management, Steese/White Mountain District Office, 1150 University Avenue Fairbanks, Alaska 99709 (907) 474-2366. For current recorded trail condition information call (907) 474-2372.
Finding the trailhead: The trail originates in the parking lot at Mile Post 57 of the Elliott Highway. The trail begins where the highway crosses the Tolvona River. To get to the trailhead, cross the highway and turn right fifty yards beyond the bridge. Hikers may cross the highway by walking across the road or by going under the bridge.

The hike: Before beginning Colorado Creek Trail hikers should be sure they are well prepared. Winter hiking demands more energy than summer treks. Always keep the half-way point to the next shelter in mind, and make wise decisions, press on, or return to the trailhead in the face of fatigue or bad weather. The first cabin is fifteen miles from the trailhead.

Colorado Creek Trail begins at the Tolovana River Bridge on the Elliott Highway and follows Duncan Creek drainage eastward approximately 13.5 miles to the boundary of the White Mountain National Recreation Area. This part of the trail goes through areas of open meadows, mixed with spruce and birch trees. From the trailhead altitude of 612 feet, the trail climbs slowly to where it breaks out on top of the ridgeline at 1,625 feet. The ridge overlooks a large, old burn, open meadow area and Beaver Creek drainage with White Mountains visible in the distance. A half mile from the ridge there is a trail junction: the left trail continues on to Beaver Creek, nine miles away, and the right trail goes to Colorado Creek Trail cabin .5 mile from the junction.

Colorado Creek Trail cabin is located along the west side of a small lake draining into Colorado Creek. This twelve-foot by sixteen-foot log cabin has bunk beds and a loft that can sleep four to five people comfortably. Hikers should evaluate the time of day, weather conditions, and their own physical abilities before moving past Colorado Creek Cabin. The next cabin, Wolf Run Cabin, is nine miles away.

From the trail junction, Colorado Creek Trail continues toward Beaver Creek. It goes through an old burn area, then through forested sections of

HIKE 82: *COLORADO CREEK* HIKE 83: *LOWER CREEK*
HIKE 84: *SUMMIT TRAIL* HIKE 86: *WINDY CREEK*
HIKE 85: *WICKERSHAM CREEK*

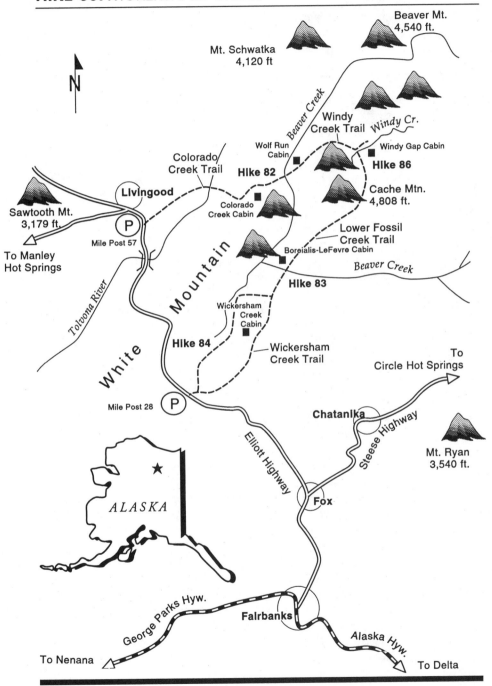

Beaver Mt.
4,540 ft.

Mt. Schwatka
4,120 ft

N

Beaver Creek

Windy
Creek Trail

Windy Cr.

Wolf Run
Cabin

Windy Gap Cabin

Colorado
Creek Trail

Hike 82

Hike 86

Livingood

Colorado
Creek Cabin

Cache Mtn.
4,808 ft.

Sawtooth Mt.
3,179 ft.

P

Lower Fossil
Creek Trail

Mile Post 57

Borealis-LeFevre Cabin

To Manley
Hot Springs

Beaver Creek

Mountain

Hike 83

Tolvona River

Wickersham
Creek
Cabin

To
Circle Hot Springs

Hike 84

Wickersham
Creek Trail

White

Mile Post 28

P

Chatanika

Steese Highway

Mt. Ryan
3,540 ft.

ALASKA

Elliott Highway

★

Fox

George Parks Hwy.

Fairbanks

Alaska Hwy.

To Nenana

To Delta

spruce, occasionally breaking into open meadows which provide good views of White Mountain Range. In the forested areas, the cut trail is visible and marked, but a storm or frequent high winds may drift snow across the open sections of trail, making it difficult to follow. This holds true for the last two miles before Beaver Creek, as the trail passes through an open meadow that has frequent high winds. Once across the meadow, the trail drops to Beaver Creek and heads south. After traveling along Beaver Creek for about .5 mile, the Windy Creek trail marker sign is visible on the left bank.

HIKE 83: *LOWER FOSSIL CREEK TRAIL*

General description: Lower Fossil Creek Trail is the farthest section from the trailhead of the looping White Mountains Winter Trails.
General location: Near the center of White Mountains National Recreation Area.
Trail begins: Wickersham Creek Trail, mile 20 Beaver Creek
Trail ends: Windy Creek Trail
Maps: USGS Livengood Bi, B2, C1
Difficulty: Moderate to difficult
Length: twenty-three miles
Elevation: 1,280 to 1,750 feet
Special attractions: Scenery and animals
Best season: Winter
For more information: United State Department of the Interior, Bureau of Land Management, Steese/White Mountain District Office, 1150 University Avenue Fairbanks, Alaska 99709 (907) 474-2366. For current recorded trail condition information call (907) 474-2372.
Finding the trailhead: The Lower Fossil Creek Trail begins at Beaver Creek and connects Windy Creek Trail with Wickersham Creek Trail.

The hike: Before beginning The Lower Fossil Creek Trail hikers should take note that there are no shelters or cabins on the trail. It is twenty-three miles to Windy Gap cabin.

The trail heads north across a lake and into spruce forests for the first four miles. In 1987, there was a large, naturally occurring wild fire in this area. The trail passes through this burn area for two miles before crossing a lake for one mile. Use caution when traveling on these frozen lakes. Watch for overflow and open water! After crossing the lake, the trail follows the lake outlet and drops for two miles toward Fossil Creek. Here the trail passes through another burned area for about four miles before dropping onto Fossil Creek. The trail follows Fossil Creek for about .5 mile, then heads back into unburned spruce forests for about one mile before dropping back onto Fossil Creek for another .5 mile. It then climbs and parallels Fossil Creek for about 2.5 miles. The trail returns to the creek for 5.5 miles to the Windy Gap Cabin. Another .25 mile past the cabin is the Windy Creek Trail junction, which leads 8.5 miles to the Wolf Run Trail shelter and connects with the Colorado Creek trail to the Elliott Highway.

HIKE 84: SUMMIT TRAIL

General description: A summer hike into an area usually hiked in winter. Excellent area for summer-scenery, birds, flowers, alpine forests, and view of northern mountains.

General location: White Mountains National Recreation Area

Trail begins: Mile 28 Elliot Highway

Trail ends: Beaver Creek at Borialis-LeFevre Cabin

Maps: Livengood A3, B2, B3

Difficulty: Easy to moderate

Length: Twenty miles

Elevation: 425 to 3,100 feet.

Special attractions: Scenery, birds, flowers, alpine forests

Best season: June through September.

For more information: United State Department of the Interior, Bureau of Land management, Alaska 99709 (907) 474-2366. For current recorded trail condition information call (907) 474-2372.

Finding the trailhead: White Mountains Summit Trail begins at Mile Post 28 of the Ellitott Highway near Wickersham Dome.

The hike: This is a developed trail with boardwalks over the wettest areas. The trail follows the ridge line northward, passing through treeless alpine tundra at higher elevations and dropping into spruce forests in the saddles. There is not much water along this trail until Beaver Creek. It is advisable to carry water with you.

From the trailhead's 2,200-foot altitude, the trail gently climbs and descends past Wickersham Dome for the first seven miles. It drops into spruce forests for the next two miles before climbing toward its highest point at about 3,100 feet near mile ten. The trail then descends for two miles to 2,150 feet and then climbs back to 2,505 feet in one mile. From here it is a steady descent for four miles through spruce forests with views of the Beaver Creek drainage. The last three miles drop steeply from 2,408 feet to about 1,325 feet at Beaver Creek. The last two miles to Beaver Creek are along the Wickersham Creek Trail.

Crossing Beaver Creek to get to the Borialis-Lefevre Cabin can be dangerous at high water. Use caution. Try either upstream or further downstream from where the trail meets the creek to find the shallowest spot. Loosen pack straps and waist belt when crossing. A pole to lean on will also help keep balance in this swift, cold water creek.

Borialis-LeFevre Cabin is located at the eastern side of a large meadow. This twelve-foot by sixteen-foot log cabin has bunk beds and a loft, that can sleep four to five people comfortably. There is a wood stove for heat, a colemen cook stove and lantern, a table and benches, an axe and an outhouse. This cabin must be reserved in advance. The cost is $20 per night. Users should bring their own pressure appliance fuel to use in the stove and lantern.

HIKE 85: *WICKERSHAM CREEK TRAIL*

General description: Wickersham Creek Trail accesses Wickersham Dome for outstanding views of White Mountains and the Alaska Range.
General location: White Mountains National Recreation Area
Trail begins: Elliot Highway Mile Post 28
Trail ends: Borialis-LeFevre Cabin
Maps: USGS Livengood A2, A3, B2
Difficulty: Easy to moderate
Length: Twenty miles
Elevation: 1,220 to 2,200 feet
Special attractions: Views of White Mountains and Alaska Range
Best season: Winter
For more information: United State Department of the Interior, Bureau of Land Management, Steese/White Mountain District Office, 1150 University Avenue Fairbanks, Alaska 99709 (907) 474-2366. For current recorded trail condition information call (907) 474-2372.
Finding the trailhead: The marked trailhead, at Mile Post 28 of the Elliott Highway, begins in the south west corner of White Mountains National Recreation Area.

The hike: The Wickersham Creek Trail begins near Wickersham Dome on the Elliot Highway and follows a forested ridgeline eastward for five miles past a 2,545-foot-high rocky peak. This rocky peak offers good views of the Alaska Range and the White Mountains. Wickersham Creek Trail drops steeply for 2.5 miles before it crosses Wickersham Creek. The trail goes through wooded

Hooked up and ready to go do mushing. The Iditrod route follows the old dog sled trail from Seward to Nome.

areas of black spruce and meadows for another three miles before reaching the Wickersham Creek Trail Shelter.

The small, Wickersham Creek Trail Shelter is 11.2 miles from the trailhead. It can sleep two people in bunk beds. The shelter is on a first come first serve basis and cannot be reserved. It is nine miles from Wickersham Creek Trail Shelter to Borialis-LeFevre Cabin. Hikers should evaluate the time of day, weather conditions, and their own physical abilities before moving past the shelter.

From the trail shelter, the trail gently descends for four miles through spruce forests. In these forested areas, the cut trail is visible and marked. There are also several sections of trail that usually have overflow ice across them. Use caution when crossing these icy sections, as the ice slopes downward. These areas can be traversed by taking your time. The trail then climbs for the next three mile before breaking into open forest and views of the White Mountains, Big Bend, and Beaver Creek. The trail drops steeply for two miles, crossing several sloughs before meeting Beaver Creek. The Borialis-LeFevre Cabin is visible through the trees on the north side of Beaver Creek. Cross Beaver Creek and follow Lower Fossil Creek Trail left, around the bluff to access the cabin. Lower Fossil creek Trail continues northward, past Borialis-LeFevre Cabin, for twenty-three miles to Windy Gap Cabin.

HIKE 86: *WINDY CREEK TRAIL*

General description: A winter hike along a plateau overlooking Fossil Creek drainage and the spectacular White Mountains, Limestone Gulch, and Windy Arch.

General location: White Mountains National Recreation Area

Trail begins: Colorado Creek Trail, mile 23 at Beaver Creek

Trail ends: Fossil Creek at Windy Gap cabin

Maps: Livengood C1, C2

Difficulty: Moderate to difficult

Length: Ten miles

Elevation: 1,000 to 2,408 feet

Special attractions: Winter recreation hiking

Best season: Winter

For more information: United State Department of the Interior, Bureau of Land Management, Steese/White Mountain District Office, 1150 University Avenue Fairbanks, Alaska 99709 (907) 474-2366. For current recorded trail condition information call (907) 474-2372.

Finding the trailhead: The Windy Creek Trail begins at Beaver Creek, about .5 mile south (up-stream) from the end of Colorado Creek Trail.

The hike: From Beaver Creek, the trail goes through a wooded area before breaking out onto a large open meadow. The trail follows this meadow along its northern edge before reentering the forest and crossing Windy Creek.

Wolf Run Cabin is about 1.5 miles from Beaver Creek and is visible on the hillside north of the trail. This 10 foot by 12 foot log cabin has bunk beds that can sleep six people comfortably. Past the cabin, the trail parallels Windy Creek on the north side and follows the creek drainage up the valley. It winds through black spruce forests and open meadows while gently climbing for the next five miles. Over the next two miles the trail climbs steeply through Windy Gap and emerges on top of a plateau overlooking the Fossil Creek drainage and the spectacular White Mountains, Limestone Gulch and Windy Arch. From here, the trail descends into the forest and drops steeply for one mile to Fossil Creek and ends at Windy Gap cabin. Windy Gap cabin is located at the foot of the White Mountains on the east side of Fossil Creek.

FINAL FOUR

These trails are not for everyone. These are difficult trails for experienced hikers. They are long, strenuous, intimidating. Hiking the Final Four is an exposure to wet, cold, long, windy, and exhausting conditions with many obstacle to overcome.

The Final Four are for the few and the brave. They are for the few willing to pay the price; brave hikers of courage accepting the challenge to climb Mt. McKinley, North America's tallest peak, to trudge the Golden Stairs of Chilkoot Pass, to winter walk the Iditarod's 1,000 mile wilderness, or trek the Dalton Highway's edge from the Yukon to the Arctic. The Final Four require rigorous training, dedicated practice, special equipment, and support services.

Other hikes in the Hiking Guide to Alaska can be accomplished by the average person in an afternoon, a day, on a weekend, or the time frame of a vacation. The Final Four require planning, preparation, training, conditioning, and even some expense. Not many of us are brave enough to challenge the Final Four, but after reading about them I'll wager you'll think about it, you may even write for more information, and a few may give it a try.

Surveys show the vast majority of the United States population desires to come to Alaska, yet fewer than two percent will ever take the plunge and brave the trip. Most are convinced it costs too much, it's always cold, dark, and frozen, and it's too far away and unaccessible. They are the timid majority. The others, people like you, will budget their money, set aside the time, and brave it. The Final Four is for everyone who ever dreamed about looking down on the world from 20,300 feet, whose secret desire is to cross the Yukon River and find the Arctic Circle, or fantasy is following the trail of 98.

The Final Four is for the brave few; perhaps you.

HIKE 87: *CHILKOOT PASS TRAIL*

General description: A well-maintained National Parks hike chiseled into historic gold rush country. This trail is not for everyone. Do not underestimate the difficulties of this trail or overestimate your abilities. Evan if lucky enough to have good weather the hike is long and strenuous. With weather at its worst even experienced hikers will encounter difficulties.

The steep climb from the Scales to the Summit of the pass is extremely intimidating. Exposure to wet, cold, and windy conditions combined with the exhausting climb to the Summit are major obstacles to all hikers. These extreme weather conditions may continue beyond the Pass as far as Happy Camp.

General location: Skagway, in Southeast Alaska and into Yukon Territory, Canada

Trail begins: 8.5 miles by the Dyea Road at the Taiya River Bridge, Skagway, Alaska

Trail ends: Bennett Lake, Yukon Territory, Canada

Maps: USGS Skagway B1, C1

Difficulty: Moderate to difficult.

Length: Thirty miles

Elevation: Fifty to 3,750 feet

Special attractions: Trekking the Chilkoot Trail takes hikers to an age when men were measured by their physical abilities, courage, native honesty, and open heart. This is a trail to test a hiker's mettle against those of men of history, the gold rush stampeders.

Best season: July and August

For more information: Superintendent, Klondike Gold Rush National Historical Park, P.O. Box 517, Skagway, Alaska 99840 (907) 983-2921

Finding the trailhead: Skagway Alaska is reached by State of Alaska Marine Highway Ferry, scheduled airline, chartered airplane, or the White Pass Rail system. Eight and one half miles from Skagway on Dyea Road near the bridge spanning Taiya River is a wooden sign marking the beginning of the trail.

The hike: Prior to 1897 Chilkoot Indians strictly controlled, what they called, the Dyea Trail. The route was used for trade and freighting to Atlin, the Mother River. When gold was discovered on Rabbit Creek the onslaught of gold seekers dissolved Chilkoot control. Today, just over 200 hardy hikers will make the trek during the hiking months of July and August. In February of 1889 over 4,000 prospectors crossed the summit into Canada. The trail is now named in honor of the Chilkoots.

During the gold rush, stampeders were required by the Canadian Government to show evidence of preparation prior to being allowed to cross the international boundary at the trail's summit. A Royal Mounted Police Customs Station was established and each miner was required to have a year's supply, 1,500 pounds, of food, and 400 pounds of other necessities before entering the Yukon. This rule required the miners to climb the steep trail with their goods or hire professional packers. Today's recreational hiker, with his thirty-pound, high-tech pack, may find it difficult to comprehend moving a ton of food and gear up the forty-degree slope and moving it over the thirty-mile trail from

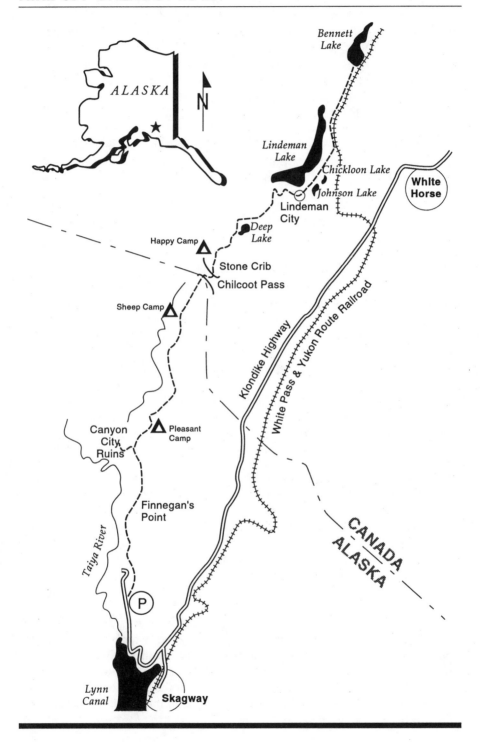

Skagway, Alaska to Bennett Lake, Yukon Territory.

Hikers are not required to carry a ton of gear but should be prepared for rapid weather changes. Good physical condition is a must to accomplish getting over the 3,750-foot pass. Weather may be a factor. Warm cloths and good quality gear is demanded. Just getting through the treacherous talus slope to the summit may take twelve hours. To comfortably enjoy the hike plan on two to three days to the pass and four to five days for the entire thirty-mile trek from tidewater in Alaska to Canada's Lake Bennett.

The sign at the trailhead gives distances to the more important points along the trail. White markers are set every half mile along the trail for the first sixteen miles. They start with Mile Post 0 and end at the half way point near the foot of the pass with Mile Post 16.

Mile Post 4.9 is Finnegan's Point, once the site of a corduroy bridge across the creek. A toll was extracted from miners by Finnegan and his two sons until hordes of gold seekers overwhelmed them. Evidence of the by-gone age survives at the natural camping site at the mouth of the Taiya River Canyon at Mile Post 7.8. Indian packers, early prospectors, and two freighting companies have used the area. Pleasant Camp, Mile Post 10.5, is where a toll bridge and restaurant were established for the stampeders. Buildings and equipment was washed out when the Taiya River changed its course.

Stampeders, ferrying to the pass, cached their goods at Sheep Camp at Mile Post 13). The Scales at Mile Post 16 got its name from freighters hauling to this point and weighing their goods and readjusting the fees. The climb up the forty-five-degree slope from the Scales to the Summit is over the "Golden Stairs" beginning at Mile Post 16.5. In winter stairs were chopped into the snow. In summer climbing the talus was treacherous

At the 3,00-foot level the climate changes from marine to sub-Arctic. Up to 200 inches of snowfall per year is reported in this Alpine Tundra Zone and winter temperatures may drop to minus fifty degrees. Plant life consists of mosses, lichen, dwarf shrubs, and low willows.

Once over the pass and descending into Canada, other climate changes occur resulting from the rain barrier of the Coast Range. Less dense forest consisting of alpine fir, pine, spruce, willow, and alder is found in the drier, boreal forest zone climate. Large areas are devoid of trees. Moose, black bear, and mountain goat may be seen along this area as well as wolves, porcupine, and squirrels. Grizzly bear and wolverine live here but are seldom seen.

At Stone Crib, Mile Post 17, near Crater Lake in the Yukon Territory hikers find the remains of the northern terminus of the Chilkoot Railroad and Transportation Company tramway. For seven cents a pound the tramway carried stampeders goods nine miles to Canyon City. The aerial tram consisted of forty-five miles of looping cable over towers and anchored by a stone crib.

The exact location of Happy Camp is unknown. It was located in the first trees after Sheep Camp. The Happy Camp designated camping area is at Mile Post 20.5. Lindenman Lake at Mile Post 26 was a tent city of 10,000 in the spring of 1898. During winter the stampeders rested and built boats to carry them the 600 miles to Dawson City. On a hill above the lake is the final resting place of eleven persons succumbing to the Trail of 98.

The trail ends at Bennett Lake where stampeders from both the White Pass and Chilkoot Trails gathered. When the ice went out on May 29, 1898 the tent city's 20,000 inhabitants launched their 7,000 boats, constructed during the winter, and headed down down river to Dawson City.

HIKE 88: THE CORRIDOR

General description: The Bureau of Land Management administers 2.7 million acres of public land in Northern Alaska, along the route of the Trans-Alaska-Pipeline. Known as the Utility Corridor, the parcel of land stretches 304 miles north from the Yukon River, and varies from six to twenty-four miles wide.
General location: The Dalton Highway is the north-south road paralleling the pipeline from Livengood to Prudhoe Bay. The trail follows, or is on the highway.
Trail begins: Yukon River
Trail ends: Disaster Creek
Maps: USGS Livengood, Tanana, Bettles, Wiseman, and Chandalar.
Difficulty: Easy walking-but lengthy. The Dalton Highway is a gravel road that can be very rough, dusty or slippery. Emergency help is available at the Yukon River Crossing trailhead, 139 miles from Fairbanks and at Coldfoot, 119 miles farther north. No other services are available to the public along the Dalton Highway.
Length: 155 miles
Elevation: 450 to 3,190 feet
Special attractions: Tundra vistas, birds, small animals, weather changes.
Best season: June through September
For more information: The Bureau of Land Management, Arctic District, 1150 University Avenue, Fairbanks, Alaska, 99709 (907)474-2250. Check with the Alaska Department of Transportation and Public Facilities at (907) 451-2249, for current highway and permit information.
Finding the trailhead: Drive north from Fairbanks to Yukon River via the Dalton Highway. The lower end of the bridge on the north shore of the Yukon River marks the southern boundary of the Utility Corridor and the trailhead.

The hike: The Dalton Highway's Yukon River bridge, at Mile 56, is 2,290 feet long and has a six-percent grade. The lower end on the north shore of the Yukon River marks the southern boundary of the Utility Corridor and the beginning of the trail. The Yukon River, fifth largest river in North America, headwaters near the border between Yukon Territory and British Columbia in Canada and flows 1,900 miles to the Bering Sea.

The Ray River, at Mile Post 70, is an old river system that shows crescent-shaped lakes called oxbows. Oxbows are formed when erosion of the outer banks gradually narrows the neck between successive meandering loops. Eventually the neck is breached and silt and sand are deposited at the ends of the loops and the river takes a new, straighter course. The isolated lake subsequently becomes a marsh and in time dries out.

At Mile Post 86, a side road to the west climbs to an abandoned gravel pit overlooking the highway and pipeline 500 feet below. To the northeast, there is an excellent view of granite tors, rock pinnacles left after less-resistant surrounding rock was eroded by weather. The Yukon Flats National wildlife Refuge is to the east, and Fort Hamlin Hills are to the southeast.

Finger Rock and surrounding tors, to the right of the highway at Mile Post 97.5, were used as landmarks by early aviators. For two miles beyond Finger Mountain summit, a panoramic view of the area and tors along the road will be seen.

The Arctic Circle sign at Mile Post 108 at Kanuti River is a sure stop for most hikers. Few can resist having their picture taken at north latitude sixty-six degrees thirty-three minutes. An undeveloped campsite provides hikers with good views to the south and the Kanuti National Wildlife Refuge to the west.

From the top of Gobbler's Knob at Mile Post 132 the South Fork Koyukuk River basin can be seen, flanked by the Jack White Range on the left and Pump Station number five is to the right. Peaks of the Brooks Range are on the horizon.

Jim River, at Mile Post 135.7, is an anadromous fisheries stream. Salmon caught within five miles of the Dalton Highway must be carefully released to protect the spawning fish. Grayling fishing is good near an undeveloped campsite next to the Jim River. The winter road to Bettles crosses the river here.

Grayling Lake, in a U-shaped trough at Mile Post 150.3 was scoured by a glacier of Sagavanirktok River age. It is much older than glacial valleys formed by the late Pleistocene ice advances in the Brooks Range.

Fishing and gold panning on the South Fork of the Koyukuk River at Mile Post 156 are available at the wayside east of highway. Panoramic views continue as scenic view of the river valley open to view. River access is on the west side of the highway.

At Mile Post 160 Chapman Lake may be viewed on the west side of highway and an old winter trail now used in the Coldfoot Classic Sled Dog Race is seen. Twelve Mile Mountain's 3,190-foot summit can be observed to the north with 3,000-foot-high Cathedral Mountain on the left, and the foothills of the Brooks Range on the right.

Coldfoot, at Mile Post 175, is the site of a historic mining camp at the mouth of Slate Creek on the east bank of the Middle Fork of the Koyukuk River. Its name changed from Slate Creek when early gold prospectors who traveled up the Koyukuk got cold feet as winter set in and left the country.

The written legend on the door jam of a maintenance shop at Coldfoot declared the occupants attitude on winter. As the outside temperature dropped, frost on the jam would creep up. The astute inhabitant marked the jam like a thermometer. He knew when the frost was a foot off the floor it was zero degrees outside. Here he had marked, "put on a coat." At the 10° below frost mark it was recorded, "wear a hat and keep hands in pockets." "Only go out for wood and creature necessities," was written at the frost mark at 20° below zero. At the 40° below mark the directive read, "use the pot behind the stove and only go out once a day to empty it." The shoulder high, 60° below zero frost mark on the door jam said, "the pot behind the stove froze, start packing." "Go home" was the final entry at the 70° degree below, eye level mark. It was summer when I was in Coldfoot, but I could read the handwriting on the wall. I got cold feet and left.

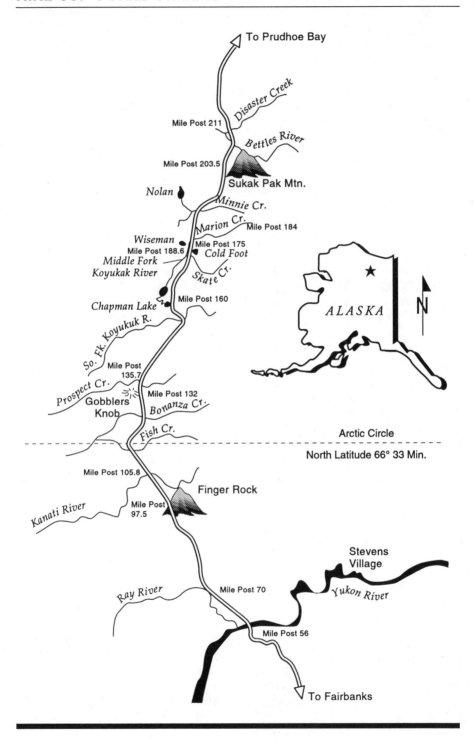

To Prudhoe Bay

Disaster Creek

Mile Post 211

Bettles River

Mile Post 203.5

Sukak Pak Mtn.

Nolan

Minnie Cr.

Marion Cr.

Mile Post 184

Wiseman

Mile Post 188.6

Mile Post 175

Cold Foot

Middle Fork
Koyukak River

Skate Cr.

Mile Post 160

Chapman Lake

So. Fk. Koyukuk R.

Mile Post
135.7

Prospect Cr.

Mile Post 132

Gobblers
Knob

Bonanza Cr.

Fish Cr.

Arctic Circle

North Latitude 66° 33 Min.

Mile Post 105.8

Finger Rock

Kanati River

Mile Post
97.5

Stevens
Village

Ray River

Mile Post 70

Yukon River

Mile Post 56

To Fairbanks

ALASKA

N

The Bureau of Land Management, National Park Service, and United States Fish and Wildlife Service operate a visitor information center at Coldfoot with displays and evening presentations. Food, gas, lodging, telephone and postal service are available.

A trail at Mile Post 184 leads to an undeveloped campsite on Marion Creek. At Mile Post 188.6 is the Middle Fork Bridge. It is a good place to fish for Dolly Varden, grayling, and whitefish. The road to the west leads to two historic mining communities: Wiseman and Nolan. Cross Gold Creek Bridge at Mile Post 197. The log cabin west of the highway was constructed in the early 1900's.

Ice-cored mounds dot the landscape at Mile Post 203.5. These form only in areas where there is a perennial discharge of water, permafrost, and long, cold winters. Water on the bedrock and upper slopes is trapped under the surface between the underlying perma-frost and thin seasonal frost layer. As water freezes, the ground heaves upward and mounds are elevated. Spectacular Sukakpak Mountain, elevation 4,459 feet, on the east side of highway contains limestone 275 million years old.

Disaster Creek at Mile Post 211 is the northernmost limit for general public travel. A road use permit from the Alaska Department of Transportation is required for travel beyond. Signs on both sides of the road indicate the turnaround point.

HIKE 89: *IDITAROD TRAIL*

General description: 1,049 miles from Seward to Nome across and through every known geography and climate zone in Alaska.
General location: Across Alaska from Seward to Nome
Trail begins: Mile 0 of Seward Highway in Seward
Trail ends: Nome
Difficulty: Easy in pieces—difficult in entirety
Length: 2,300 miles of hiking trails. For simplicity, only the 1,000 mile primary historic route is shown. Alternate routes and connecting trails not shown total an additional 1,300 miles.
Elevation: Sea level to 6,300 feet and back to sea level
Special attractions: Scenery, old townsites, people of the interior.
Best season: June through September. Best, run with dog team in winter.
For more information: For more information about specific portions of the trail, access points and user rules contact the following agencies: The Bureau of Land Management, Arctic District, 1150 University Avenue, Fairbanks, Alaska, 99709 (907)474-2250; Bureau of Land Management, Anchorage District Office, 222 West 7th Avenue #13, Anchorage, Alaska 99513 (907) 271-5555; Chugach National Forest, 201 East Ninth Avenue, Anchorage, Alaska 99501 (907) 271-2500; Fish and Wildlife Service, 1011 East Tudor Road, Anchorage, Alaska, 99503 (907) 786-3545; State of Alaska, Department of Parks and Outdoor Recreation, P.O. Box 107001, Anchorage, Alaska, 99510 (907) 762-2617; Chugach National Forest, Box 390, Seward, Alaska 99664 (907) 224-3374
Finding the trailhead: The southern terminus of the trail begins at Seward. Other

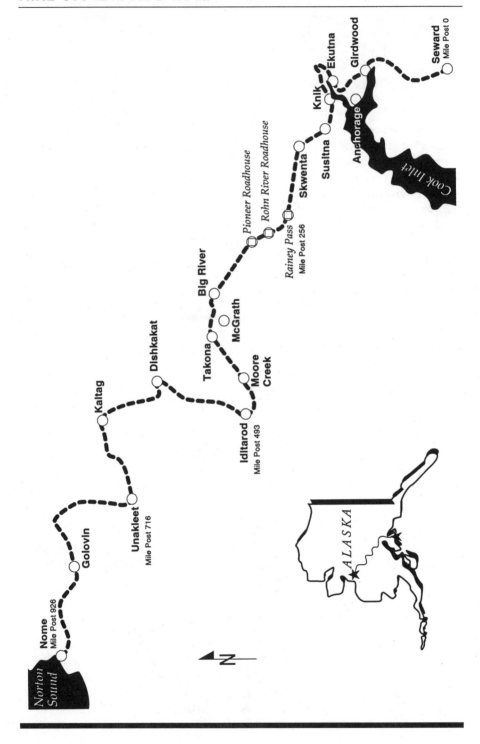

Above the Seward on Mt. Marathon. The Iditrod begins in Seward.

adventurers start their travels in Nome. The Iditarod is actually a network of more than 2,300 miles of trails now known as the Iditarod National Historic Trail

The hike: The Iditarod National Historic Trail, once used by ancient hunters, then by gold seekers, is actually a network of more than 2,300 miles of trails. When asked how much dirt in one day was moved to mine gold, it is reported that an old miner responded, "I did a rod." The trail name is actually taken from the name of an Athabascan Indian village on the Iditarod River near the site of a 1908 gold discovery. In 1910 a gold rush town flourished there and was the center of the Iditarod Mining District. The southern terminus of the trail begins at Seward. Settlers entering the Territory hiked, sledded, or snowshoed through heavily forested lands, now part of the Chugach National Forest. They would follow the route from Seward to Anchorage, around Knik Arm to the town of Knik, then across Rainy Pass to the mining districts. Other miners, arriving by boat, started their travels to the Iditarod country in Nome. As the two end portions of the trail developed they met at Iditarod. Surveyed by the U.S. Army's Alaska Road Commission in 1910, it was called the Seward to Nome Mail Trail and used as a major route until 1924 when the airplane came into use.

In 1925 a diphtheria epidemic threatened the town of Nome. Plans to send an airplane with a precious cargo of serum were thwarted by terrible weather. Instead, a relay of twenty dog teams were dispatched from the town of Nenanna. With courage and stamina they went down the Tanana and Yukon Rivers to the Iditarod Trail and on to Nome. The distance of 647 miles was covered in a little over 127 hours and the mushers became heroes as the era of the sled dog went out in a blaze of glory. President Coolidge sent medals to team members and Balto, the lead dog of the finishing team.

The Iditarod Trail was forgotten until 1967 when the first Iditarod race was staged between Knik and Big Lake on nine miles of the old Iditarod Trail. Another race was held in 1969 and in 1973 the race was run between Anchorage and Nome. The March Iditarod Trail Sled dog race, known as the Last Great Race, includes competitors from around the world.

Five institutional land managers and numerous private owners control the Iditarod in a complex trail system, stretching from Seward to Nome on the Bering Sea. It crosses lands owned by Native corporations, municipal governments, State of Alaska, and lands managed by the Bureau of Land Management, the U.S. Forest Service, the U. S. Fish and Wildlife Service and the Department of Defense.

Most of the Iditarod is in remote sections of Alaska. During summer most of the trail is covered with thick tundra vegetation and only part of the trail can be hiked. The Iditarod is a winter trail when tundra and rivers are frozen and easier to cross. Portions of the trail running through Chugach National Forest or Chugach State Park near Anchorage may be hiked during summer.

The Iditarod Trail is used for races of endurance and stamina. Dog races, cross country ski races, snow machine races, running, mountain bike races, and combination of these use sections of the Iditarod Trail in and around Knik, McGrath, Unalakleet, Nome, and other communities.

HIKE 90: MT. MCKINLEY

General description: Climbing the most challenging mountain in the United States. Not recommended unless thoroughly qualified.
General location: South of Fairbanks and North of Anchorage
Trail begins: Riley Creek Visitor Center
Trail ends: Riley Creek Visitor Center
Maps: USGS, Healy, Kantishna River, Mt Mckinley, Talkeetna; Special maps, USGS, Mount McKinley National Park, Bradford Washburn, "A Map of Mount McKinley, Alaska"
Difficulty: Most difficult.
Length: Length of the trail for Mt. McKinley is expressed in altitude of 20,320 feet
Elevation: 3,000 to 20,320 feet
Special attractions: Glacial travel, vistas, challenging weather and altitude, and reaching the summit of North America's highest mountain.
Best season: July or August
For more information: Mountaineering Ranger, Denali National Park and Preserve Headquarters, P.O. Box 588, Talkeetna, Alaska 99676 (907) 733-2231

The hike: Mt. McKinley is one of the coldest mountains in the world. The 20,320-foot peak is located further north than Everest and less than 200 miles south of the Arctic Circle. Temperatures on the mountain during the spring and summer climbing season may be as low as minus forty degrees and accompanied by winds of eighty to 100 miles-per-hour. The combined effect of cold, wind, and altitude may well present one of the most hostile climates on Earth.

The West Buttress, South Face, and Muldrow Glacier routes are the most frequently climbed routes on Mt. McKinley. Several other routes have seen only one ascent. Mt. McKinley is attempted by 600 to 850 climbers a year. Over 3/4 of these use the West Buttress route. An expedition on the West Buttress route might encounter 100 to 200 other climbers. Each route is a major expedition in an Arctic environment with climbing times commonly exceeding twenty-five days. Superior mountaineering skills, stamina, conditioning, equipment, and ability to survive in severe Arctic conditions are essential. Experience has shown that even these qualifications do not guarantee safety or success. Expeditions, even those planning alpine style ascents, should have supplies to wait out one to two weeks of bad weather.

Alaska glaciers are often heavily crevassed and glacier travel may be hazardous. Radio communication with outside monitors is extremely difficult from lower elevations. Each party must depend on its own resources for the duration of their climb.

There should be at least four members in a climbing party. A large party is better as it provides greater inherent strength and self-rescue capability. Each member of an expedition should be well experienced in glacier travel, extreme cold weather survival, and extended expeditionary mountaineering. The more difficult routes are technically very demanding, and all members attempting these routes should be highly skilled climbers. Experience has shown that a party composed primarily of individuals who have not climbed together tends to be a weak climbing group. Such mail-order expeditions are

Thousands of swans cross Alaska twice a year. Mt. McKinley is on their flyway.

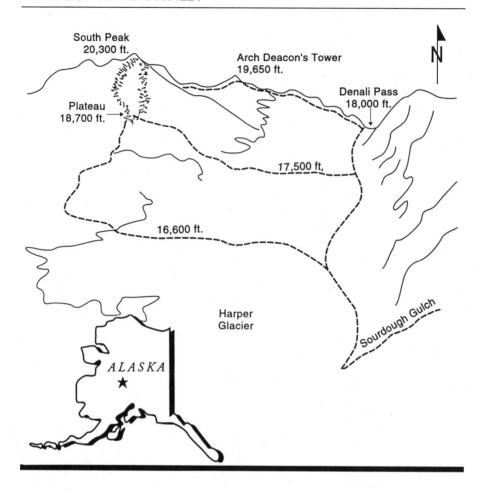

not recommended. The expedition leader must know the physical qualifications, physical conditions, and experience of each team member and should be able to verify claims made on each member's registration forms.

Snow conditions and weather for climbing is usually best from early May through early July. Colder minimum temperatures commonly occur in May. June and July are warmer but plagued by more unsettled weather. By August, travel on lower glaciers is made difficult by melting snow bridges over crevasses and by more inclement weather with heavier snowfall.

The National Park Service has reference materials on routes on Mt. McKinley and other peaks in the park. Specific questions on mountaineering in the Alaska Range can be answered. Valuable information often may be obtained from members of previous expeditions.

ALASKA PUBLIC LANDS:
AN ENDURING FRONTIER

Early people called it Alyeshka—The Great Land. Much of The Great Land's 375 million acres, will remain a permanent American frontier. Vast areas of special places in Alaska have been dedicated as public lands for the perpetual use by the family of man. Thirteen percent of Alaska, 51 million acres, is in public ownership as parks, preserves, wildlife refuges, monuments, and wild and scenic rivers. These lands and waterways comprise the finest parklands in the world, an immense collection of unadulterated wilderness where people can escape when responding to the call of the wild.

Alaska's parklands are inhabited by great herds of caribou, muskox, walrus, polar bear, grizzly bear, Dall sheep, moose, wolves, and wolverines. Expansive unblemished landscapes, creation-fresh rivers, legions of fish, numberless lakes, the continent's highest mountains, and the nation's most pristine valleys are Alaska's parkland treasures beyond any hiker's wildest expectations.

The size of land is staggering. The 49th State's land-mass constitutes an area one-fifth the size of continental United States. If you explored a thousand acres a day of just Wildlife Refuges, it would take over 1,000 years to see it all.

Alaska'a three million acres of state parkland comprise the largest state park system in United States. With more than 100 state park units, it holds nearly one third of America's state park acreage.

Alaska has the largest moose, the biggest bears, the tallest spruce, the greatest fishing rivers, scenery without match, hiking trails without number, and enormous nurseries for migratory birds. Alaska reminds us of a time of uncharted frontiers calling to our sense of adventure and hardiness.

All state and federal agencies just administer public lands have combined their information services in a central office in Anchorage. The general public may contact them either by telephone or writing. They will answer specific questions or disseminate generic information. Their service is free and they will send requested helpful information at no charge. Hikers may contact the Alaska Public Lands Information Center or the administrative agency direct.

For more information, contact: Alaska Public Lands Information Center, 605 West 4th Avenue, Anchorage, Alaska 99501, (907) 271-2737.

Alaska Peninsula Wildlife Refuge

Alaska Peninsula Refuge lies on the Pacific side of the Alaska Peninsula. The refuge's varied landscape includes active volcanoes, lakes, rivers, tundra and rugged coastline. Alaska Peninsula Refuge is dominated by the rugged Aleutian Range, part of a chain of volcanoes known as the "Ring of Fire" encircling the Pacific Ocean.

Plants composing the expanses of tundra are slow growing and small. The tundra, together with the influence of volcanos and Arctic seas, provide a showcase of how plants and animals adapt to an Arctic maritime environment.

Large mammals found on the refuge include, moose, caribou, wolves, brown bear, and wolverine. Brown bears are near productive salmon streams. Large populations of sea lions, seals, sea otter, and migratory whales inhabit shores and off stream waters. Populations of sea otter on the Pacific side of the peninsula numbers at least 30,000. In the 1880's they were nearly extinct. The entire refuge provides habitat for migratory birds: ducks, geese, and shore birds.

The Alaska Peninsula Refuge is renowned for big game hunting, especially caribou and brown bear. Fishing is outstanding for king and silver salmon, Arctic char, lake trout, northern pike, and grayling. The world record grayling was caught on the refuge.

For more information, contact: Refuge Manager, Alaska Peninsula Wildlife Refuge , P.O. Box 277, King Salmon, Alaska 99613, (907) 246-3339.

Aniakchak National Monument and Preserve

The central feature of Aniakchak National Monument and Preserve is the volcanic Aniakchak Caldera created by the collapse of the central part of a volcano. It covers thirty square miles and is six miles wide. This collapse took place sometime after the last glaciation. Later activity built a cone, Vent Mountain, inside the caldera. Aniakchak last erupted in 1931. The caldera's Surprise Lake, heated by hot springs, cascades through a 1,500 foot rift in the crater wall. Such volcanic features as lava flows, cinder cones, and explosion pits can be seen here, along with hardy pioneer plant communities inching life into a silent moonscape.

Wildlife includes occasional caribou, grizzly bear, and eagles. Sockeye salmon spawn up Aniakchak River which originates in Surprise Lake. Fish from this watershed are recognizable by their flavor of soda and iron characteristic of the caldera's mineral-laden outflow.

This is one of the most remote of Alaska's national park areas, and weather on Alaska Peninsula can be severe all seasons. Scheduled air service puts you within charter-flight distance via King Salmon or Port Heiden. Floatplanes can land on Surprise Lake.

For more information, contact:, Superintendent, Aniakchak National Monument and Preserve, P.O. Box 7, King Salmon, Alaska 99613, (907) 246-3305.

Arctic National Wildlife Refuge

Arctic is the most northern of the wildlife refuges. The refuge encompasses one of the world's most spectacular assemblages of Arctic plants, wildlife, and land forms. Designated to embrace the range of the great Porcupine Caribou Herd, Arctic National Wildlife Refuge is also home to free roaming herds of musk ox, Dall sheep, packs of wolves, and such solitary species as, wolverines, and polar and grizzly bear.

Winter on the refuge is long and severe; summer is brief and intense. Snow usually covers the ground at least nine months a year. Arctic-adapted plants survive even though perma-frost is within eighteen inches of the surface. Annual growth of trees and shrub is slight. It might take three hundred years for a white spruce at tree line to reach a diameter of five inches; small willow shrubs may be fifty to one hundred years old.

The Arctic offers a rich pageant of wildlife including 140 bird species. It protects a large portion of the migration route of the Porcupine Caribou Herd, 180 thousand animals, one of the two largest herds in Alaska. Caribou migrate from wintering grounds south of the Brooks Range to calving grounds on the northern coastal plains of the refuge and the Yukon Territory. The migration covers more than 1,000 miles. Arctic recreation use is increasing. Activities include, float trips, hiking, backpacking, hunting, fishing, and wildlife observation.

For more information, contact: Refuge Manager, Arctic National Wildlife Refuge, P.O. Box 20, Fairbanks, Alaska 99701, (907) 456-0253.

Becharof National Wildlife Refuge

Becharof lies between Katmai National Park and Preserve and Alaska Peninsula National Wildlife Refuge. The refuge is dominated by Becharof Lake, second largest lake in Alaska. The lake covers 1/4 of the refuge and is surrounded by low rolling hills tundra wetlands and volcanic peaks. Salmon spawning streams attract one of the largest concentrations of brown bear in Alaska. Some brown bear of Becharof have a unique habit of making dens on the islands of Becharof lake. Moose inhabit the refuge in moderate numbers and about 15,000 caribou seasonally migrate through, and winter in the refuge. Other mammals include wolves, wolverine, river otter, red fox, and beaver. In addition, thousands of sea mammals such as sea otters, sea lions, harbor seals, and migratory whales inhabit the seas along the shore.

Becharof Lake and its tributaries contribute over four million salmon annually to the Bristol Bay fishery. Salmon, Arctic char, and grayling flourish on the refuge. Waterfowl are common in the wetlands and coastal estuaries while nesting eagles, peregrine falcons, and thousands of sea birds inhabit sea cliffs and islands.

Becharof offers outstanding bear and caribou hunting. The refuge receives moderate sport fishing pressure for trophy-size Arctic char, grayling, and salmon. Commercial guide services are available for hunting and fishing.

For more information, contact: Refuge Manager, Becharof National Wildlife Refuge, P.O Box 277, King Salmon, Alaska 99613, (907) 246-3339.

Bering Land Bridge National Preserve

Bering Land Bridge National Preserve is a remnant of the land bridge connecting Asia with North America more than 13,000 years ago. The land bridge itself is now overlain by the Chukchi Sea and Bering Sea. During the glacial epoch this was part of a migration route for people, animals, and plants as ocean levels fell enough to expose the land bridge. Scientists find it one of the most likely regions where prehistoric Asian hunters entered the New World.

Today, Eskimos from neighboring villages pursue subsistence lifestyles and manage reindeer herds in and around the preserve, Some 112 migratory bird species may be seen here, along with occasional seals, Walrus, and whales. Grizzly bear, fox, wolf, and moose also inhabit the preserve. Other interesting features are rimless volcanos called Maar craters, Serpentine Hot Springs, and seabird colonies at Sullivan Bluffs.

Air service out of Nome and Kotzebue is the usual means of access to the quiet, isolated preserve's 2.5 million acres.

For more information, contact: Superintendent, Bering Land Bridge National Preserve, P.O. Box 220, Nome, Alaska 99762, (907) 443-2522.

Cape Krusenstern National Monument

The gravel beachscape of Cape Krusenstern National Monument chronologically records 5,000 years of marine mammal hunting by Eskimo peoples. These unrivaled archeological records are locked in 114 lateral beach ridges describing land growth into the Chukchi Sea. The beach ridges were formed by changing sea levels and the action of wind and waves. Artifacts from nearby creek bluffs date back 6,000 years and act as a benchmark for predating the cape's beach ridges.

Eskimos still hunt seals along the cape's outermost beach. With rifles instead of traditional harpoons, they hazard the dangerous spring ice floes to take the oogruk, or bearded seal. In shoreline camps, women trim and render the catch for the hides, meat, and seal oil still vital to their diet. As old sites became land bound by the shoreline's seaward advance, people abandoned their tents and sod houses to establish new camps nearer the sea. This process has continued ever since Eskimos of Arctic Alaska first turned to the sea.

For more information, contact: Superintendent, Cape Krusenstern National Monument, P.O. Box 1029, Kotzebue, Alaska 99752, (907) 442-3890.

Chilkat State Park

Chilkat State Park, south of Haines on the Chilkat Peninsula, offers spectacular views of glaciers across Chilkat Inlet. Visitors often spot whales, seals, and other wildlife from the coastline trail. There are campgrounds, picnic areas, and a boat ramp.

For more information, contact: Park Ranger, Chilkat State Park Headquarters, 400 Willoughby, Juneau, Alaska 99801, (907) 465-4563.

Wrangell St. Elias National Park is characterized by rugged mountains, remote valleys, wild rivers and extraordinary wildlife.

Chugach State Park

Development of Anchorage through the 20th century necessitated establishment of Chugach State Park. This area was set aside to assure an open, quality environment available to citizens now facing increasing pressures from urbanization.

Ranging from coastal forests and rushing streams to rugged, high-alpine cirques and glaciers, Chugach State Park provides a variety of recreational possibilities for young and old. The park opens doors to adventuresome experiences, rewards of health, personal satisfaction, and a renewed energy through freedom in the outdoors.

Foot travel is perhaps the best way to explore and experience the park. Hiking carries us at a pace governed by terrain and interests. Today, sections of Iditarod Tail and a historic settler's route, the old Johnson Trail, give hikers a glimpse into an intriguing era of Alaska history.

For more information, contact: Park Ranger, Chugach State Park Headquarters, HC 52 Box 8999, Indian, Alaska 99540, (907) 345-5014.

Denali National Park and Preserve

Mount McKinley, at 20,320 feet, is North America's highest mountain. The Athabascan Indians called it Denali, "The High One," and in 1980 McKinley National Park's name was changed to Denali.

Mount McKinley is a massive mountain—measured from base to summit, it is the world's highest—the towering centerpiece of the glacier-strewn Alaska Range. Under its shadow in Denali National Park and Preserve are barren-ground caribou, grizzly bear, wolves, moose, Dall sheep, and other wildlife. Meandering, glacier-born rivers laden with silt, or rock flour, create natural dams and periodically change course across their wide flat valleys.

The area is accessible by car, railroad, and scheduled air service. To protect wildlife and to preserve opportunities to see it, private vehicle use is restricted on the park road. Shuttle bus service operates from the entrance to Wonder Lake along the eighty-five mile wilderness road. The shuttle bus will drop you off, or pick you up wherever you like, and at no cost.

For more information, contact: Superintendent, Denali National Park and Preserve, P.O. Box 9, Denali Park, Alaska 99755, (907) 683-2294.

Denali State Park

Denali State Park is an integral part of one of North America's most spectacularly beautiful regions. The park's 324,240 acres, almost one-half the size of Rhode Island, provide visitors with a great variety of recreational opportunities ranging from roadside camping to wilderness explorations.

The park is about 100 air miles north of Anchorage and is divided roughly in half by the George Parks Highway, the major link between Anchorage and Fairbanks. Situated between Talkeetna Mountains to the east, and Alaska Range to the west, the landscape varies from meandering lowland streams to alpine tundra. Dominating this diverse terrain are Curry and Kesugi Ridges, a thirty-five-mile-long north-south alpine ridge, the backbone of the eastern half of the park.

Denali State Park's western boundary is shared with its much larger neighbor, Denali National Park and Preserve. The Tanana Indian word "Denali," means "The High One." Denali is the original name for Mt. McKinley. At 20,306 feet, Mckinley is North America's highest peak. It literally and figuratively towers over south-central Alaska from its base in Denali National Park.

The great mountain, and its companion peaks are accented by spectacular valley-glaciers and steep ice-carved gorges and a year-round mantle of snow and ice above 8,000 feet. Glaciers, such as Ruth, Buckskin, and Eldridge, are from fourteen to thirty-eight miles long and up to four miles wide. They flow from the high peaks and melt into the broad U-shaped Chulitna Valley, giving Chulitna River a milky-colored water and braided channels typical of glacial streams. Though only thirty-five miles from the summit of McKinley, the Chulitna floodplain is but 550 feet in elevation.

Denali State Park has superb vantage points for viewing the breathtaking heart of the Alaska Range. Perhaps the best roadside view anywhere of the Alaska Range is at mile 135.2, Parks Highway. An interpretive bulletin board at this site names the mountains and other terrain features. Other excellent views of Mt. McKinley along the highway are at mile 147.1, 158.1, and 162.3. Day hikers on Kesugi Ridge, or backpackers in the Peter Hills in the western end of the park, have an unencumbered view of the Denali massif that is almost overwhelming in grandeur.

From the alpine tundra of Curry Ridge to the river bottoms of the meandering Tokositna River, the park's varied landscape is home to a diverse exhibit of wildlife. Moose, grizzly and black bears are found throughout the park. Though seldom seen, wolves frequent much of the park, and caribou occasionally reach the park's northern end. Smaller, elusive residents include lynx, coyote, red fox, snowshoe hare, land otter, flying and red squirrel. The weasel family is well represented by ermine, marten, mink and wolverine. Wet areas are habitat for muskrat and beaver, while pika squirrel and marmot may be found in rocky areas above timberline.

Tapestry of habitats in the park yield an especially rich bird community. More than 130 species use the park for breeding or stop during migration. The champion marathoner of the bird world, the Arctic tern, flies 12,000 miles to breed in Denali, repeating the journey to winter in Antarctica. The lesser gold plover nests on alpine tundra after wintering in faraway Polynesia.

For more information, contact: Park Ranger, Denali State Park Headquarters, HC 32 Box 6706, Wasilla, Alaska 99654, (907) 745-3975.

Gates of the Arctic National Park and Preserve

Gates of the Arctic National Park and Preserve lies entirely north of the Arctic Circle. It includes the scenic heartland of the Brooks Range, northernmost extension of the Rocky Mountains. The park and preserve combined, are four times the size of Yellowstone National Park. The area's austere beauty and grandeur defy description. This is ultimate wilderness capturing the heart and imagination of Arctic explorer Robert Marshall in the 1930's.

Barren-ground caribou and grizzly bear range the area's spacious and fragile tundra, gathering a living from the thin veneer of Arctic soils. The park

Long days and short nights allow hikers in Penali National Park many hiking hours in each day.

straddles the crest of the Brooks Ranges, its southern flank sampling of boreal forest in Alaska's interior and its north slope at the edge of a polar desert with precipitation comparable to the Earth's driest regions. Two distinct cultures are represented here: Athabascan peoples of the spruce-taig forests, and Nunamiut Eskimos, who hunt caribou in the high valleys. Both cultures continue to follow traditional subsistence patterns of life in the park and preserve. Scheduled flights from Fairbanks serve Bettles, Evansville, and Anaktuvuk Pass.

For more information, contact: Superintendent, Gates of the Arctic National Park and Preserve, P.O. Box 74680, Fairbanks, Alaska 99707, (907) 456-0281.

Glacier Bay National Park and Preserve

Glacier Bay National Park and Preserve contains the world's most impressive examples of tidewater glaciers. The bay has experienced at least four major advances and four major retreats of glaciers and thus serves as an outdoor laboratory for contemporary research. Mountains rise in the preserve almost three vertical miles from tidewater. The dramatic variety of plant communities range from terrain just recovering from glacial retreat to lush temperate rain forest. Nowhere is the story of plant succession more richly told than at Glacier Bay.

The park and preserve harbors brown and black bears, whales, seals, plus eagles, and more than 200 hundred species of birds. Mount Fairweather is the highest peak in Southeast Alaska.

Glacier Bay is accessible by commercial cruise ship, charter boat, aircraft, or by scheduled air and boat service from Juneau and other Southeast Alaska communities.

For more information, contact: Superintendent, Glacier Bay National Park and Preserve, Box 140, Gustavus, Alaska 99826, (907) 697-2232.

Innoko National Wildlife Refuge

Innoko is about 300 miles northwest of Anchorage in the central Yukon River Valley. The refuge comprises most of Innoko River Basin and is composed of two separate sections totaling 4.25 million acres. About eighty percent of the refuge is wetlands providing nesting habitat for at least 250,000 waterfowl. Innoko provides habitat for wolf, black bear, grizzly bear, caribou in winter, and fur bearers. It is renowned for its beaver population. In some years forty percent of all beaver trapped in Alaska originate on the refuge. The annual beaver harvest is about 20,000 pelts. Other fur bearers include muskrat, weasel, wolverine, lynx, marten, and red fox.

The abundant moose on Innoko has meant a food supply for early residents, explorers, trappers, gold seekers, and river boat crews as well as today's residents. The success of the moose population is attributed to flooding along streams enhancing the growth of willows, the major winter food for moose.

A float trip on Innoko River provides an excellent opportunity to view wildlife. Fishing is excellent for northern pike. Sport hunting for moose and black bear is popular.

For more information, contact: Refuge Manager, Innoko National Wildlife Refuge, P.O. Box 69, McGrath, Alaska 99627, (907) 524-3251.

Izembek National Wildlife Refuge

Izembek faces the Bering Sea on the tip of the Alaska Peninsula. The landscape includes volcanos with glacier caps, valleys, and tundra uplands that slope into lagoons adjoining the Bering Sea. Izembek Lagoon contains a valuable eelgrass bed, one of the largest in the world. The beds are part of a large estuary providing a haven for migratory birds. The world's population of black brant, thousands of Canada and emperor geese, and other waterfowl congregate on the lagoon. They feed on eelgrass before they fly south. Most waterfowl arrive on the refuge in late August or early September. By early November a second wave of northern waterfowl, primarily sea ducks, arrive to winter on Izembek. The colorful Steller's eider, that nests on the Arctic coast of Alaska and Siberia, is the most common wintering duck in the lagoon. In addition, thousands of shore birds feed on invertebrates of the bay at low tide. At high tide they gather in such large flocks that, in flight, they appear as smoke clouds. Other wildlife includes brown bear, caribou, ptarmigan, and fur bearers. Izembek has outstanding waterfowl hunting. Ptarmigan are often hunted in conjunction with waterfowl. Caribou hunting is good. There are some roads and trails to the refuge from Cold Bay but most of the refuge is accessible only by boat or foot.

For more information, contact: Refuge Manager, Izembek National Wild Life Refuge, Box 127, Cold Bay, Alaska 99571 , (907) 532-2445.

Kachemak Bay State Park

Kachemak Bay State Park is 250,000 acres of ocean, mountains, glaciers, forests, and wildlife. The waters of Kachemak Bay are some of the most productive in the world and are inhabited by whales, sea otters, seals, and many species of fish. The bay's twisted rock formations are evidence of the powerful forces of the movement of the earth's crust and are highlighted by constantly changing weather patterns.

Park visitors will find opportunities for hiking, boating, fishing, and beach-combing. Intertidal zones offer natural settings for marine studies. Many species of birds inhabit the bay, include puffins, gyrfalcons, and bald eagles, making it a popular area for bird watching. Hiking and camping along the shoreline and in the surrounding forests and mountains are excellent, and once above timberline, hikers and climbers will find glaciers and snowfields stretching for miles.

Special attractions in the park include Grewingk Glacier, Poot Peak, China Poot Bay, Halibut Cove Lagoon, Humpy Creek, China Poot Lake, and the Tuka Lagoon Hatchery.

For more information, contact: Park Ranger, Kachemak Bay State Park Headquarters, P.O. Box 1247, Soldotna, Alaska 99669, (907) 262-5581.

Katmai National Park and Preserve

In 1912 a tremendous volcano erupted in the unexplored wilderness that today is Katmai National Park and Preserve. The blast, in which Mount Katmai collapsed, was one of the most violent ever recorded. Afterward, in what would become known as Valley of Ten Thousand Smokes, fumaroles by the thousands issued steam hot enough to melt zinc. Only a few active vents remain today and the Katmai crater holds a lake.

Katmai's scenery boasts lakes, rivers, glaciers, waterfalls, and a coastline of plunging cliffs and islets. This is the home of huge brown bear—Earth's largest terrestrial carnivore—which in summer fishes the park and preserve's streams to feast on migrating salmon. Scientists regard this area as critical for the brown bear's survival on the Alaska Peninsula. It also boasts some of Southwest Alaska's best trophy sportfishing.

Scheduled jets from Anchorage serve King Salmon on the park's west side. From June through Labor Day, daily commercial flights operate between King Salmon and Brooks Lodge. Air charters from King Salmon or Iliamna are available from May though October.

For more information, contact: Superintendent, Katmai National Park and Preserve, P.O. Box 7, King Salmon, Alaska 99613, (907) 246-3305.

Kanuti National Wildlife Refuge

Kanuti straddles the Arctic Circle approximately 150 miles northwest of Fairbanks. It is composed of Kanuti Flats, an interior basin characterized by the rolling plains of Kanuti and Koyukuk rivers. The basin is interspersed with lakes, ponds, and marshes. The refuge provides nesting habitat for waterfowl, primarily Canada and whitefronted geese and ducks. Kanuti's contribution to waterfowl increases when the prairies of south-central Canada and northern midwestern United States lie baked and dry. In times of drought, birds displaced from traditional breeding areas fly northward to stable waters. Additional loss of prairie wetlands from draining and filling, will further increase importance of northern wetland such as Kanuti.

The refuge supports sixteen species of fish including whitefish, northern pike, grayling and salmon. Other wildlife includes moose, black bear, grizzly bear, wolf and wolverine.

Few people visit Kanuti and those who do, primarily hunt, fish and view wildlife. Fishing for northern pike and grayling is excellent. Because it is remote, the adventurous will find Kanuti Refuge a true wilderness experience.

For more information, contact: Refuge Manager, Kanuti National Wildlife Refuge, P.O. Box 11, Fairbanks, Alaska 99701, (907) 456-0329 .

Kenai Fjords National Park

Kenai Fjords National Park features the seaward interface for Harding Ice Field, one of four major ice caps in the United State. This may be a remnant of Pleistocene ice masses once covering half of Alaska. Along the coastline are the scenic Kenai Fjords, whose shoreline was carved by glaciers. Sea stacks, islets, and jagged shoreline are remnants of mountains that today inch imperceptibly into the sea under the geological force of the North Pacific tectonic plate. Exit Glacier, the most accessible area of the park, can be reached by car and a short walk.

Moose and large populations of mountain goats inhabit the land. Steller sea lions haul out on rocky islands at the entrance to the fjords. Harbor seals rest on icebergs. Killer whales, porpoises, sea otters, and several whale species also are found here. Thousands of sea birds—horned and tufted puffins, common murres, and black-legged kittiwakes—rear their young on steep cliffs.

Seward, 130 miles south of Anchorage via the Seward highway, is gateway to Kenai Fjords. Served by scheduled bus and commuter flights, it offers charter boats and aircraft services. The park Visitor Center is next to the Harbor master's office in Seward's small boat harbor.

For more information, contact: Superintendent Kenai Fjords National Park, P.O. Box 1727, Seward, Alaska 99664, (907) 224-3874.

Kenai National Wildlife Refuge

The Kenai Refuge consists of the western slopes of the Kenai Mountains and forested lowlands bordering Cook Inlet. The low lands are composed of spruce and birch forests intermingled with hundreds of lakes. The Kenai Mountains, with their glaciers, rise to more than 6,000 feet, presenting a barrier on the southeastern boundary of the refuge. The refuge is a miniature Alaska, containing examples of all its habitat types: tundra, mountains, wetlands, and forests. Kenai Refuge was established to preserve and maintain a large population of moose on the Kenai Peninsula. In addition, the refuge is host to Dall sheep, mountain goat, caribou, coyote, wolf, grizzly bear, black bear, lynx, wolverine, beaver, small mammals and birds. Kenai Refuge provides undisturbed spawning for many Cook Inlet salmon.

The refuge is accessible from the Sterling highway. Travelers are treated to a panoramic view along the 110 mile drive from Anchorage to Kenai's mideastern boundary. Fishing is excellent. There are over 200 miles of established trails and routes including the Swanson River Canoe Trail. Visitors can fly to remote lakes, hike or take horse pack trips into roadless areas, or float a whitewater river. Developed facilities are available year-round for day and overnight camping.

For more information, contact: Refuge Manager, Kenai National Wildlife Refuge, 2139 Ski Hill Road, Soldotna, Alaska 99669, (907)262-7021.

Kodiak National Wildlife Refuge

Kodiak is composed of mountains, forests, bays, inlets, and wetlands. The refuge comprises about two-thirds of Kodiak Island. In addition, the refuge encompasses a portion of Afognak Island, north of Kodiak Island. Kodiak Island has an irregular coastline of bays, inlets, and rugged mountains covered with alpine vegetation. Spruce forests dominate the northern part of Kodiak Island and all Afognak Island portion of the refuge.

The interior of the refuge is covered with lush, dense vegetation. Southwestern Kodiak is covered with hummocks of grass. No place on the 100 x 40 mile island is more than fifteen miles from the sea. Kodiak was established to protect the habitat of brown bear. Besides brown bear there are only five other änative land mammals on Kodiak: red fox, river otter, short-tailed weasel, little brown bat, and tundra vole.

Black-tailed deer, beaver, and several other species of mammals have been successfully introduced to the island. Bald eagles reside year-round on the refuge in such numbers they are in view continuously. An estimated two million sea birds inhabit the bays, inlets, and shores. Kodiak is known worldwide for brown bear hunting. Fishing is excellent for all five species of Pacific salmon. Wildlife observation, hiking, photography, rafting, and camping are popular activities. The island is served by commercial flights and the Alaska State Ferry system. A limited number of cabins are available.

For more information, contact: Refuge Manager, Kodiak National Wildlife Refuge, 1390 Buskin River Road, Kodiak, Alaska 99615, (907) 487-2600.

Kodiak state parks

Kodiak Island has a uniqueness and beauty all its own. The warm Japanese current creates a mile maritime climate and plenty of rain. It is an island of rough, glacier scarred terrain—mountains rise from the sea, rocky coasts and tide pools beckon the coastal explorer. Forested areas occur infrequently. The majority of the island is blanketed in grasses, willow and alder thickets, and profusion of wildflowers.

There are four state parks within the Kodiak Archipelago. Except for Shuyak Island State Park, all are accessible on the Kodiak Island road system. These parks welcome visitors with scenery, wildlife, history, and relaxation. Visitors find a variety of opportunities for recreation and education. Over 200 species of birds have been recorded in the Kodiak Archipelago, and bird watching is a main attraction. The parks are laced with trails through lush rain forest in a tranquil setting.

Fort Abercrombie State Historic Park provides a variety of recreational opportunities. Visitors will find quiet forests for tent camping and hiking, tide pools to be explored, and a stunning view from Miller Point. During early summer, gray, humpback, and minke whales can be spotted as they migrate through nearby Whale Passage. August brings ripening salmon berries, which can be picked in any part of the park. Guided and self guided historical walking tours are available.

Shuyak Island State Park, a 11,000-acre coastal wilderness fifty-four air miles north of Kodiak, contains virgin Sitka spruce forests, rugged coastline, beaches, and protected waterways. The area supports sea birds in infinite numbers as well as sea otters, whales, harbor seals, sea lions, Sitka blacktailed deer, and a small population of Kodiak brown bear. Popular with hunters and anglers, it is also a rewarding sport for bird and wildlife watchers.

For more information, contact: Park Ranger, Kodiak State Parks Headquarters, SR Box 3800, Kodiak, Alaska 99615, (907) 486-6339.

Koyukuk National Wildlife Refuge

Rivers are the heart of Koyukuk country, its living pulse, and historic past. Fourteen rivers and hundreds of creeks meander throughout the refuge providing habitat for salmon, beaver and waterfowl. There also over 15,000 lakes. The topography is relatively gentle featuring an extensive floodplain surrounded by hills with boreal forests.

The landscape includes the Nogahabara Dunes, a 10,000-acre active dune field. The field was formed from wind-blown deposits about 10,000 years ago. It is one of two active dune fields in Alaska. Spring flood waters of the Koyukuk River carry away signs of the past season and recharge the lowlands.

The floodplain provides ideal nesting habitat for ducks, geese, and other water-adapted birds. By September more than 4,000,000 ducks and geese migrate from the refuge to southern wintering grounds. Black bear are abundant in forests and grizzly bear inhabit the open tundra. Fur bearers on Koyukuk include otter, lynx, beaver, marten, muskrats, and mink. Wolves and moose are common. Other large mammals on the refuge include caribou from the Western Arctic Herd that often winter on portions of the refuge. Koyukuk has excellent moose hunting and fishing for northern pike and Arctic grayling.

For more information, contact: Refuge Manager, Koyukuk National Wildlife Refuge,, P.O. Box 287, Galena, Alaska 99741, (907) 656-1231.

Klondike Gold Rush National Historical Park

When an 1897 issue of the Seattle Post-Intelligence reported a steamer from Alaska putting in at Seattle with a ton of gold aboard, it set off the last great gold rush. At the height of the rush John Muir called Skagway "a nest of ants taken into a strange country and stirred up by a stick." Klondike Gold Rush National Historical Park preserves historic buildings from this period in Skagway, Alaska, and portions of the Chilkoot and White Pass trails into the Klondike.

The park offers a variety of experiences, from small town to wilderness. A lively nightlife thrives in Skagway, a regular port of call for cruise ships. The Trail of 98 Museum is housed in Alaska's first granite building. Backpacking over the passes has become popular. Access is by ferry, cruise ship, commuter airline, air taxi, or by car.

For more information, contact: Superintendent, Klondike Gold Rush National Historical Park, P.O. Box 517, Skagway, Alaska 99840, (907) 983-2921.

Kobuk Valley National Park

Today's dry, cold climate of the Kobuk Valley still approximates that of late Pleistocene times, supporting a remnant flora once marking the vast Arctic steppe tundra bridging Alaska and Asia. Great herds of caribou still cross the Kobuk Ricer at Onion Portage, and are hunted by today's Eskimo peoples. These herds once fed Woodland Eskimo peoples of 1250 AD. Human occupation at the portage dates back to 12,500 years ago, forming a benchmark by which all other Arctic sites are measured. The valley remains an important area for traditional subsistence harvest of moose, bear, caribou, fish, waterfowl, and many edible and medicinal plants.

The great Kobuk Sand Dunes—twenty-five square miles of shifting dunes where summer temperatures can exceed 100 degrees—is the largest active dune field in Arctic latitudes. Both the Kobuk and Salmon Rivers offer easy canoeing and kayaking.

Daily jet service is available from Anchorage and Fairbanks to Kotzebue. Scheduled air service is available to nearby villages and local air and boat charter is available by advance arrangement.

For more information, contact: Superintendent, Kobuk Valley National Park, P.O. Box 1029, Kotzebue, Alaska 99752, (907) 442-3890.

Lake Clark National Park and Preserve

Lake Clark National Park and Preserve has been described as the Alaska Alps, for here Alaska and Aleutian ranges meet. Set in the heart of Chigmit Mountains along Cook Inlet's western shore, the park boasts great geologic diversity. Its jagged peaks, granite spires, glaciers, two active volcanoes, and fifty-mile-long Lake Clark provide a dazzling array of scenery. The lake, fed by hundreds of waterfalls throughout its rimming mountains, is part of an important red salmon spawning ground. These features combine to create a maze of natural river-running and hiking routes providing spectacular wilderness experiences.

Brown and black bear, caribou, moose, Dall sheep, salmon, and trout inhabit these scenic environs. Within the park and preserve are coastal lowlands of spruce and marshes, alpine meadows, and tundra plains backed by ever-changing mountain scenes.

Air charters are available from Anchorage, Kenai, or Iliamna. Lodging, from primitive to modern, is available from private operators within the park and preserve.

For more information, contact: Superintendent, Lake Clark National Park and Preserve, 4230 University Drive, Suite 311, Anchorage, Alaska 99508, (907) 271-3751.

Maritime National Wildlife Refuge

Alaska Maritime consists of more than 2,400 islands, headlands, rocks, islets, spires, and reefs off the Alaska coast. The refuge stretches from Cape Lisburne on the Chukchi Sea to the tip of the Aleutians and eastward to Forrester Island on the border of British Columbia. The 4.5 million acre refuge is a spectacular blend of tundra, rain forest, cliffs, volcanos, beaches, lakes, and streams. Most of the refuge 2.64 million acres is wilderness.

View of Liberty Falls

Alaska Maritime is synonymous with sea birds—millions of them. About seventy-five percent of Alaska's marine birds, 15 to 30 million birds among fifty-five species, use the refuge. They congregate in "bird cities" or colonies along the coast. Each species has a specialized nesting site—rock, ledge, crevice, boulder, rubble, pinnacle, or borrow—an adaptation allowing many birds to use a small area of land. The refuge has the most diverse wildlife species of all refuges in Alaska including thousands of sea lions, seals, walrus, and sea otters.

Visitor activities include wildlife observations, backpacking and photography. Bird watching is popular on Attu Island in the Aleutians where Asian birds stop on their migrations. Some islands have restricted access in order to protect wildlife Military clearance is required to visit Adak, Shemya, Amchitka, and Attu Islands of the Aleutian Chain.

For more information, contact: Refuge manager, Alaska Maritime National Wildlife Refuge, 202 Pioneer Avenue, Homer, Alaska 99603, (907) 235-6546.

National Wild and Scenic Rivers

Wild free-flowing rivers born in cold mountain lakes or nurtured by runoff from remote highlands provide transportation corridors through some of Alaska's most spectacular geography. Crags and peaks, narrow canyons, rolling tundra-cloaked hills, or forested slopes present themselves in a constantly changing panorama during a float trip.

Congress established the National Wild and Scenic Rivers System to preserve a free-flowing condition for rivers of remarkable scenic, recreational, geologic, fish and wildlife, historic, cultural, or other similar value. All or part of twenty-five such rivers in Alaska are designated wild and scenic. The National Park Service administers thirteen of these, all designated "wild." With one exception, the designated sections lie within the boundaries of parks, monuments, or preserves. Because of their classifications, only minimal development will be allowed along the banks of these rivers. Included are the following rivers: John, Kobuk, Noatak, Alagnak, Alatna, Charley, Koyukuk, Mulchatna, Tilkakila, Tinayguk, Aniakchak, Chilikdrotna, and Salmon North Fork.

For more information, contact:, Alaska State Office, Bureau of Land Management, 222 West 7th Avenue # 13, Anchorage, Alaska 99513, (907) 271-5477.

Noatak National Preserve

Noatak National Preserve protects the largest untouched river basin in the Unites States. Above the Arctic Circle the Noatak River runs from glacial melt atop Mount Igikpak in the Brooks Range out to Kotzebue Sound. Along its 425-mile course it has carved out the Grand Canyon of the Noatak. This striking, scenic canyon serves as a migration route for plants and animals between sub-Arctic and Arctic environment. In recognition of this fine and vast wilderness, UNESCO has made the Noatak River Basin an International Biosphere Reserve.

The Noatak serves as a natural highway not only for plants and animals, but also for wilderness travelers. The preserve is especially popular for canoeing and kayaking, because the river is slow moving and gentle along most of its course. Only in the headwaters is the Noatak rough water. Backpacking in the foothills is an attractive recreational activity. The preserve offers outstanding wildlife watching opportunities. Among its large mammals are grizzly and black bear, caribou, wolves, lynx, and Dall sheep in abundance. Bird life abounds, too, as summer brings migratory birds to Noatak Basin from Asia and tip of South America. The river itself supports Arctic char, white fish, grayling and salmon.

Charter flights out of Kotzebue and Bettles/Evansville, which are served by air from Fairbanks or Anchorage.

For more information, contact: Superintendent, Noatak National Preserve, P.O. Box 1029, Kotzebue, Alaska 99752, (907) 442-3890.

Nowitna National Wildlife Refuge

Nowitna is approximately 200 miles west of Fairbanks in the central Yukon Valley. The refuge encompasses forested lowlands, hills, lakes, marshes, ponds, and streams. The dominant feature on Nowitna is the Nowitna River, a nationally designated Wild River. The magnificent river provides spawning grounds for northern pike and sheefish. However, the primary reason the refuge was established was to protect waterfowl and their habitat.

Nowitna is one of our refuges, Nowitna, Innoko, Kanuti, and Koyukuk refuges, encompassed by a solar basin. A solar basin is characterized by encircling hills, light winds, low rainfall, severe winters, and short warm summers. The summer sun encircles these refuges without setting. The refuge's mix of habitats supports varied wildlife. Black bear and moose are common throughout Nowitna. Marten, mink, wolverine, beaver, and muskrat are important fur bearers and provide income, food, and recreations for local residents.

The Nowitna River is an outstanding river for floating. Moose and bear hunting are a major activity. Fishing for northern pike and sheefish is excellent.

For more information, contact: Refuge Manager, Nowitna National Wildlife Refuge, P.O. Box 287, Galena, Alaska, 99741, (907) 656-1231.

Point Bridget State Park

Point Bridget State Park, a beautiful 2,850-acre park, is located forty miles north of Juneau. It offers meadows of wildflowers, forested mountains, cliffs, spectacular views, rocky beaches, and the sea. In the winter the meadows and open forest allow excellent skiing and snowshoeing opportunities. Long before white men arrived, the Auks, a group of Tlingit Natives, had summer homes here and harvested the area's rich natural resources. Point Bridget was named in 1794 by Captain Vancouver, probably for his mother, Bridget Berners. Cowee Creek was named after the Auk Chief who was credited with guiding Joe Juneau and Dick Harris to the gold in Silver Bow Basin in 1880. This led to the founding of Juneau. Gold was found north of Berners Bay and east of Point Bridget but there is no record of a discovery within the park.

For more information, contact: Park Ranger, Point Bridget State Park Headquarters, 400 Willoughby Avenue, Juneau, Alaska 99801, (907) 465-4563.

Prince William Sound State Marine Parks

Prince William Sound State Marine Parks, about sixty miles east of Anchorage, are undeveloped parks on the shores of Prince William Sound. The sound offers views of tidewater and upland glaciers, forested islands, and fjords surrounded by mountains rising to 13,000 feet. Scenery and wildlife, include brown and black bears, whales, sea otters, eagles, salmon, and many species of marine birds. It is a favorite area for boating, hiking, and photos.

For more information, contact: Park Ranger, Prince William Sound State Marine Parks Headquarters, P.O. Box 1247, Soldotna, Alaska 99669, (907) 262-5581.

Selawik National Wildlife Refuge

Selawik straddles the Arctic Circle in northwestern Alaska about 360 miles northwest of Fairbanks. The refuge is composed of estuaries, lakes, river deltas, and tundra slopes. The most prominent feature is the extensive system of tundra wetlands nestled between Waring Mountains and Selawik Hills. Selawik is located where the Bering Land Bridge once existed. Plants, animals, and humans migrated freely across this land mass connecting Asia and North America many years ago. The refuge retains evidence of these migrations.

Selawik is a breeding and resting area for a multitude of migratory water birds returning from North and South America, Asia, Africa, and Australia. Nesting ducks number in the hundreds of thousands. Thousands of caribou winter on the refuge as they feed on lichen-covered foothills. Other common mammals include moose, grizzly bear, and fur bearers. Sheefish, whitefish, grayling, and northern pike inhabit lakes, ponds, streams, and rivers. Sheefish weighing forty to fifty pounds are not uncommon.

Portions of Selawik River are nationally designated as a Wild River. The river provides good river rafting and sportfishing. A limited commercial guides service is available.

For more information, contact: Refuge Manager, Selawik National Wildlife Refuge, P.O. Box 270, Kotzebue, Alaska 99752 , (907) 442-3799.

Sitka National Historical Park

Sitka is one of Alaska's most scenic and historic cities. Sitka National Historical Park and Preserves is the site of the 1804 battle marking the last major resistance of the Tlingit Indians to Russian colonization. This was Alaska's economic and cultural capital for half a century, serving as the center of Russian-American Company's fur and trading operations. The park displays a collection of totems and its visitor center explains Pacific Northwest Coast Indian art.

The Tlingit long ago followed salmon streams southward to settle here at Shee Atika, as they called Sitka, on this island-dotted coast. They enjoyed a rich culture, aesthetically and spiritually, in a world of natural abundance. This was interrupted by the Russian-American Company under determined leadership of Alexander Baranov. The 1804 Battle of Sitka ended when the Tlingit ran out of ammunition and withdrew. Baranov burned their fort and built a new town he named New Archangel.

Sitka is reached by state-operated ferries, commercial cruise ships, and daily jet service.

For more information, contact: Superintendent, Sitka National Historical Park, P.O. Box 738, Sitka, Alaska 99835, (907) 474-6281.

Tetlin National Wildlife Refuge

Tetlin is a showcase of geologic and ecological features found throughout Interior Alaska. Here in a broad valley, the Chisana and Nabesna rivers join near the center of the refuge to form Tanana River. Nearly everywhere the work of wildfires, permafrost, and fluctuating river channels have created a diversity of habitats. For example, extensive stands of birch, aspen, and willow are testimony to positive effects of wildfire.

In these woodlands, moose, black bear, grizzly bear, ptarmigan, grouse, wolf, coyote, and red fox find food and shelter. Thousands of refuge lakes and ponds are interspersed with rolling hills, boreal forests, and snowcapped mountains. Tetlin Refuge supports a high density of nesting waterfowl on its wetlands. Shallow marshes of the refuge thaw early, providing a needed rest stop for birds migrating to nesting grounds throughout the state. The refuge provides habitat for 143 species of nesting birds and seven migrant species. Sandhill cranes move through the refuge each fall and spring in a spectacular event. Other notable birds include Arctic and common loon, osprey, bald eagle, trumpeter swan, and three species of ptarmigan.

Hunting, trapping, hiking, fishing, and photography are common activities. Moose and waterfowl hunting are especially popular. Common fish species include: northern pike, grayling, and burbot (fresh-water ling cod).

Tetlin is one of two road-accessible refuges in Alaska. The Alaska Highway borders the refuge for nearly seventy miles. Interpretive information is available along the Alaska Highway and at the Interagency Visitor Center in Tok.

For more information, contact: Refuge Manager, Tetlin National Wildlife Refuge, P.O. Box 155, Tok, Alaska 99780, (907) 883-5312.

Togiak National Wildlife Refuge

Togiak is between Kuskokwim and Bristol bays in southwestern Alaska. Topography includes mountain crags, fast-flowing rivers, deep lakes, marshy lowlands, ponds, estuaries, coastal lagoons, and sea cliffs. The broad glacial valleys of the Ahklun Mountain range cut the tundra uplands and opens onto a coastal plain. Ahklun Mountains encompass eighty percent of the refuge. Togiak is a breeding and resting area for waterfowl and shore birds returning from wintering areas in Russia, Japan, Mexico, South America, New Zealand, and the South Pacific. During summer, numerous sea birds inhabit off-shore waters and cliffs near Capes Newenham and Pierce.

Spotted seals, walrus and seven species of whales use the off-shore waters. The refuge provides more than 1,500 miles of streams and rivers of spawning habitat for salmon. The finest salmon and trout sport fishing waters in Alaska are on Togiak River. Coastal portion of the refuge provides excellent opportunities for photography and wildlife observation. River rafting is popular on several refuge rivers. Commercial guides are available for sport fishing, brown bear hunting, and river rafting.

For more information, contact: Refuge Manager, Togiak National Wildlife Refuge, P.O. Box 270, Dillingham, Alaska 99576 , (907) 842-1063.

Tongass National Forest

Over ninety percent of Southeast Alaska is in the largest National Forest in the United States. Tongass covers 16.7 million acres, a land of glaciers, mountains waterways, and thousands of islands, separated by straits, narrows, and channels. Tongass has over 11,000 miles of coastline, about half that of the entire country. The land is heavily forested with Sitka spruce, hemlock and cedar. It is home to both black and brown bear, Sitka black-tailed deer, mountain goats, and numerous small animals such as beaver, lynx, wolf, wolverine, red fox, and weasel.

The Forest Service maintains more than 150 recreational cabins at remote lakes, rivers, streams, or on beaches. Cabins are usually placed near good fishing or hunting spots, terrific scenery, hiking areas, or frequently, a combination of all three. The cabins can be reserved at a cost of $15 per night. Most of the cabins are remote and accessible only by boat or aircraft. Getting there can be the main expense.

For more information, contact: Forest Supervisor, Tongass National Forest Headquarters, Federal Building, Ketchikan, Alaska 99901, (907) 225-3101.

Wrangell St. Elias National Park and Preserve

Wrangell St. Elias National Park and Preserve abuts Canada's Kluane National Park across the border in Yukon territory. Together they have been placed on the internationally recognized World Heritage List for outstanding natural areas. This is North America's "Mountain Kingdom." Here the Wrangell-St Elias, and Chugach mountain ranges converge. The park and preserve contains North American continent's largest assemblage of glaciers and its greatest collection of peaks over 16,000 feet elevation. One glacier, the Malaspina, is larger than the State of Rhode Island. Mount St. Elias, at 18,008 feet, is the second highest peak in United States.

The park and preserve is characterized by rugged mountains, remote valleys, wild rivers, and exemplary populations of wildlife. It also embraces coastal beaches on the Gulf of Alaska. The area abounds in opportunities for wilderness backpacking, lake fishing, car camping, river running, cross country skiing, and mountain climbing. In both stature and numbers, Dall sheep populations of the Wrangells are considered the world's finest.

Access is by road from Chitna to McCarthy, generally passable in summer, by road from Slana on the Tok cutoff to Nabesna, and by air from Glennallen, which is 200 miles by paved highway from Anchorage or Yakutat or Gulkana,

For more information, contact: Superintendent, Wrangell-St. Elias National Park and Preserve, P.O. Box 29, Glennallen, Alaska 99588, (907) 822-5234.

Yukon Delta National Wildlife Refuge

Yukon Delta and Kuskokwim Rivers dominate the landscape of the Yukon Delta. The rivers form a treeless, wetland plain noted for wildlife variety and abundance. An intricate maze of lakes, ponds, and meandering streams provide nesting and feeding habitat for over 750,000 swans and geese, 2,000,000 ducks, and 100,000,000 shore and water birds. Moose, caribou, grizzly bear, black bear, and wolves inhabit the northern hills and eastern mountains.

The 1.1 million acre Nunivak Island portion of the refuge supports an introduced herd of muskox and reindeer. Muskox vanished from Alaska in 1865. The introduced herd of muskox on Nunivak island has been prolific. The herd is used as breeding stock to establish herds elsewhere in Alaska and Soviet Union. The reindeer herd is a major source of food and income for island residents.

Over the centuries the abundance of wildlife has made the Yukon Delta the heart of Yupik Eskimo culture. The refuge encompasses forty-two Eskimo villages whose residents depend on the wildlife resources. The legislation establishing Yukon Delta enables rural residents to continue a life style allowing them to live off the land.

Fishing, hunting, and back country recreation may be excellent, although aircraft transportation is needed. The Andreafsky is a nationally designated wild river. Visitors may view wildlife resources and obtain complete information at refuge headquarters visitor center.

For more information, contact: Refuge Manager, Yukon Delta National Wildlife Refuge, P.O. Box 346, Bethel, Alaska 99559, (907) 543-3151.

Yukon Flats National Wildlife Refuge

Yukon Flats is about 100 miles north of Fairbanks, the most northerly point reached by the Yukon River. Here the river breaks free from canyon walls and spreads unconfined for 200 miles through a vast flood plain. In spring, millions of migrating birds converge on the flats before ice moves from the river. The migrating birds come from four continents to raise their young. The refuge has one of the highest nesting densities of waterfowl in North America. By August the surfaces of over 40,000 lakes and ponds ripple with scurrying ducklings and molting adults. Yukon Flats contributes more than two million ducks and geese to the flyways of North America.

Birds are not the only migratory wildlife dependent on wetlands of the flats. Salmon from Bering Sea ascend the Yukon River to spawn in fresh water streams of their birth. Some salmon travel nearly 2,000 miles into Canada. Runs of king, coho, and chum salmon pass through and spawn in the flats each summer—the longest salmon run in United States.

Mammals on the refuge include moose, caribou, wolves, black and grizzly bears. Most summer use of Yukon Flats is confined to major waterways. Several rivers are floated by canoe, kayak, and rafts. Fishing for northern pike can be excellent.

For more information, contact: Refuge manager, Yukon Flats National Refuge, P.O. Box 14, Fairbanks, Alaska 99701, (907) 456-0440.

Yukon-Charley Rivers National Preserve

The Yukon-Charley Rivers National Preserve contains 115 miles of historic Yukon River and the entire eighty-eight-mile Charley River Basin. Old cabins and relics recall the Yukon's importance in the Gold Rush era. Archaeological and paleontological sites in the preserve provide knowledge of both thousands and million of years in the past.

The two rivers are quite different: the broad and swift Yukon flows with glacial silt while the smaller Charley flows crystal clear. Charley is considered one of Alaska's finest recreational streams. The rivers merge between the early-day boom towns of Eagle and Circle. Cliffs and bluffs along the two rivers provide nesting habitat for peregrine and gyrfalcons. Beyond the riverbanks grizzly bear, Dall sheep, and moose may be seen. Floating the Yukon, whether by raft, canoe, or powerboat, is a popular way to see wildlife and scenic resources. The Charley River demands more advanced river skills.

Access is by Taylor Highway to Eagle or Steese Highway from Fairbanks to Circle. Scheduled flights serve both towns from Fairbanks.

For more Information write: Superintendent, Yukon-Charley Rivers National Preserve, P.O. Box 167, Eagle, Alaska 99738, (907) 547-2233

Wood-Tikchik State Park

Wood-Tikchik State Park, bounded by rugged mountains to the west and open tundra to the east, is Alaska most remote state park, and the largest state park in the United States. Visitors are attracted by superb fishing, boating, and hiking in Tikchik Lakes and Wood River Lakes areas. Private lodges offer visitor services and sport fishing packages by advance reservations only. The park is 300 air miles west of Anchorage and is accessible by charter flight from Dillingham.

For more information, contact: Park Ranger, Wood-Tikchik State Park Headquarters, General Delivery, Dillingham, Alaska 99576, (907) 842-2375 Summer, (907) 762-2614 Winter.

FALCONGUIDES	★ *Starred titles are new in the* **FALCON**GUIDES *series.*	
★ Angler's Guide to Alaska		$ 9.95
Angler's Guide to Montana *revised*		$10.95
★ Arizona Scenic Drives		$11.95
Back Country Byways		$ 9.95
Beartooth Fishing Guide		$ 7.95
Floater's Guide to Colorado		$11.95
★ Floater's Guide to Missouri		$ 9.95
Floater's Guide to Montana		$ 8.95
★ Hiker's Guide to Alaska		$ 9.95
★ Hiker's Guide to Alberta		$ 9.95
Hiker's Guide to Arizona *revised*		$ 9.95
Hiker's Guide to California *revised*		$11.95
Hiker's Guide to Colorado *revised*		$11.95
Hiker's Guide to Hot Springs		$ 9.95
Hiker's Guide to Idaho *revised*		$11.95
Hiker's Guide to Montana *revised*		$ 9.95
Hiker's Guide to Montana's Continental Divide Trail		$ 9.95
Hiker's Guide to Nevada		$ 9.95
Hiker's Guide to New Mexico		$ 9.95
★ Hiker's Guide to Oregon		$ 9.95
★ Hiker's Guide to Texas		$ 9.95
Hiker's Guide to Utah *revised*		$11.95
★ Hiker's Guide to Virginia		$ 9.95
Hiker's Guide to Washington		$11.95
★ Hiker's Guide to Wyoming		$ 9.95
Hunter's Guide to Montana		$ 9.95
Recreation Guide to California National Forests		$ 9.95
Rockhound's Guide to Montana *revised*		$ 9.95
Scenic Byways		$ 9.95
★ Scenic Byways II		$11.95
★ Trail of the Great Bear		$ 9.95

Falcon Press Publishing Co. · Call toll-free 1-800-582-2665